BREAKING
THROUGH THE
STATUS
QUO

The innovative authors of this book are members of the exclusive **NextGeneration Benefits Network**.

These NextGeneration Benefits Advisers are leaders of a true **Benefits Revolution** that is breaking through the Status Quo in both benefits and healthcare.

This revolution is redefining both the role of the benefits adviser and the relationship between the adviser and the employer.

Working with business owners and C-Suite executives NextGeneration Advisers are helping employers take control and lower the cost of health care, making it affordable and sustainable for employers and their employees.

If you are a benefits broker or adviser...

...get a complimentary copy of the **"NextGeneration Benefits" infographic** and discover how you can become a disruptive NextGeneration firm or practice.

And receive a complimentary customized **"NextGeneration Growth Quotient Report"** on your firm or practice to see how close you are & the steps to take to reach NextGeneration status.

Take the 2-minute online benchmarking assessment at...

NBNAdviser.com

and grab your "NextGeneration Benefits" infographic!

Welcome to the Benefits Revolution!

BREAKING
THROUGH THE
STATUS
QUO

How Innovative Companies Are
CHANGING THE BENEFITS GAME
To Help Their Employees
AND Boost Their Bottom Line

Proven Strategies from Leading Business Consultants
& NextGeneration Benefits Advisers

ASSOCIATION
FOR INSURANCE
LEADERSHIP

AIL
PRESS

Published by AIL Press
Part of the Association for Insurance Leadership
A division of Bottom Line Solutions, Inc.
101 Creekside Crossing
Suite 1700 – Box 304
Brentwood, TN 370276
(615) 369-0618

Association for Insurance Leadership
    Breaking Through The Status Quo: How Innovative Companies Are Changing The Benefits Game To Help Their Employees AND Boost Their Bottom Line / Various
        p.cm.
    1. Business. 1. Title
    ISBN 978-0-9882823-3-9

Author portrait photography by Basel Almisshal of StudioBasel, Philadelphia.
www.baselalmisshal.com

Printed and bound in the United States of America

Dedication

This book is dedicated to those business leaders who are open and willing to embrace fresh, new approaches to create more positive and sustainable results for their organizations and their employees.

TABLE OF CONTENTS

FOREWORD

To any Chief Financial Officer or other C-level executive, *Breaking Through The Status Quo* is a MUST read. I can't be any more emphatic. If you want to understand why your benefits spend is both sky-high and seemingly out of control, you *must* read this book. If you want to know how you can seize control of your benefits spend, you *must* read this book. And if you want to begin to control the cost drivers to reduce your benefits spend without reducing the quality of your benefits, you *must* read this book.

As a CFO myself, I know the frustration and sense of powerlessness as year after year the HR department brings annual increases (often double digit) in the benefits budget, accompanied by earnest assurances that "This really is the best we could do" or "We're fortunate that our increase is below national trend!" Inquire deeper of your broker or consultant and you're told, "There's not much we can do. You're at the mercy of medical trend" or "We have influence with the insurance carrier but, in the end, it's up to the actuaries." So we've learned to settle—and be grateful—for a "less bad" renewal increase.

Read this book and you'll finally discover for yourself the exciting and empowering truth I recently discovered from my own benefits adviser, a NextGeneration Benefits Adviser who is one of the authors of this book.

I learned that I CAN control my benefits spend; that I DO have the power to reduce the cost of my employees' healthcare; and that I CAN offer affordable, sustainable benefits without shifting cost to my employees or cutting their benefits.

I also realized—and you will, too, if you read this book—that status quo brokers, which is most of them, have treated CFOs and CEOs like mushrooms…they've kept us in the dark and fed us a steady diet of manure. These status quo brokers are not bad people; they just have misaligned incentives that keep them from exploring alternatives to the status quo…because, frankly, the status quo works for them. It just doesn't work for me or other business leaders who offer employee benefits.

I should point out that my interest in the strategies in this book derives from more than just my professional responsibilities as a CFO. I'm also the founder of The CFO Solution, an organization whose mission is to help you, the private company CFO, by conveying proven best practices that solve problems for your company and introducing you to proven, better partners to execute these best practices.

With the CFO Solution, I'm committed to identifying proven and cutting-edge solutions to the big problems facing the C-Suite today. And few problems rise to the level of the typical corporate benefits budget, whose unchecked but unpredictable growth is choking off employee pay raises and creating huge uncertainty in the business planning process.

Breaking Through The Status Quo is almost a one-stop shop for proven solutions for employee benefits and the benefits spend. And, frankly, it's not rocket science. My adviser and this book make plain that the real problem with employee benefits is that we in the C-Suite simply have not treated our benefits like we do every other key part of our business.

Fiduciary oversight? Yes, of every business unit in the company…
except benefits. Executive management? Yes, of every business unit in
the company…except benefits. Supply chain management? Of course,
for every single business unit in the company…except benefits.

My adviser and the other authors of this book are bringing these
essential business practices to our benefits budget and our employees'
healthcare spend. They are working with the CFO to ensure fiduciary oversight, shifting the strategic decision-making on the benefits
budget from HR to the C-Suite to engage executive management,
and providing supply chain management to the employees' healthcare to promote appropriate utilization of medical services and plan
resources.

As a CFO, this just makes perfect sense to me. So, in a way, what's
been missing from my benefits process—and what my NextGeneration
Benefits Adviser is working to get into the process is—me, as CFO.
What's missing from your benefits process, then, is you, as the CFO
or CEO of your company.

And, just as I don't do supply chain management for my other
business units, I don't have to with benefits. That's what my benefits
adviser does. And does well.

My adviser has helped me lower my costs dramatically AND has
improved our benefits. We recently had him as our guest speaker at a
CFO Solution forum and the attendees, both the CFOs and their HR
teams, were impressed and anxious to engage!

My adviser has found EBITDA trapped in my benefits budget
and he's helping me get it out and back on my bottom line where it
belongs, which he's done for other of his clients. That's a terrific result
that I'm quite excited about.

If the idea of converting part of your benefits spend into EBITDA
appeals to you, if the idea of taking control of your benefits spend

appeals to you, if the idea of reducing healthcare costs while improving your benefits appeals to you…you'll love the strategies in this book. So, like I said, you MUST read this book.

—**Gary Bender,** CFO
SISD, Inc.
Founder, The CFO Solution
www.thecfosolution.org

PREFACE

The mission of the Association of Insurance Leadership (AIL) is to elevate the employee benefits industry, in part by providing and promoting collaboration and thought leadership.

What better way to fulfill the AIL mission than by publishing this remarkable collection of strategic insights, innovative strategies, and effective techniques to improve the quality of employees' healthcare while reducing the cost of that healthcare for both the employee and the employer. This information is willingly shared by the authors, who are leading business consultants and NextGeneration Benefits Advisers who daily are using the information between these covers to improve the benefits and the finances of their employer clients across the U.S.

The authors are members of the NextGeneration Benefits Network, an elite group of employee benefits firms from across the nation that are innovating to challenge the status quo in the employee benefits industry and in healthcare. These NextGeneration Benefits Firms are in the vanguard of the industry, setting the standard for both quality of the benefits offered employees and the cost-effectiveness and sustainability of the benefits plan for employers.

The intended audience for this book are the organizational leaders who are responsible for both the benefits on which their employees depend and the large and ever-increasing benefit budget that, for most companies, ranks in the top two or three line items on the P&L statement. The strategic insights and innovative strategies are intended for the C-level executives with the strategic and fiduciary responsibility for the benefits program. The proven techniques are intended for the benefits professionals in HR with the operational responsibility to implement and execute the benefits program.

Every day, the authors of this disruptive book are elevating the industry by providing better benefits at lower cost to employers and their employees. They are elevating the industry by raising the bar for other benefits firms in their market. This is the progressive, forward-thinking leadership that will move the employee benefits industry squarely into the 21st Century.

The Association for Insurance Leadership is delighted and honored to present these NextGeneration Benefits strategies and techniques to the men and women responsible for benefits at their company.

INTRODUCTION

The status quo in employee benefits continues to deliver rising costs for employers and reductions in benefits for the employees that depend on them. Employers that accept that status quo and do the same thing year after year receive, not surprisingly, the same bad results year after year. The status quo is failing employers and employees.

The bad news is that most benefit brokers continue bringing you strategies and best practices that reinforce the status quo…because they're status quo brokers. They don't know any better.

So how about some good, no, some *great*, news?! If you believe that the status quo in employee benefits and healthcare is broken and unsustainable, relief is within reach. With the proven solutions you are holding in your hands, you finally can begin to take control of your healthcare budget and, despite the prevailing wisdom, actually *improve* your employee benefits while *controlling and reducing* the costs of your employees' healthcare.

The visionary NextGeneration Benefits Advisers who have authored this book have committed to breaking through the status quo in both benefits and healthcare and are helping employers across the country provide better benefits AND reduce the cost of those benefits.

These benefits agency leaders, all members of the elite **NextGeneration Benefits Network**, are among the most innovative, forward-thinking, and effective advisers in the country. They are setting the standard for the industry with their "next practices" that are improving employees' benefits, engaging and educating employees on those benefits, and containing and reducing healthcare costs to ensure that these benefits are affordable and sustainable for their employer clients.

These pace-setting advisers are also among the most collaborative in the industry, meeting quarterly to share and improve their "next practices" and learn and innovate other strategies and techniques. So it was a natural next step to bring them together to author a collaborative book with their best ideas and strategies to break through the benefits status quo.

These are real-world strategies and ideas straight from the trenches, not the half-baked product of ivory-tower thinking and conjecture. Using the information in this book and working with the authors, employers across the U.S. are improving their benefits offering while cutting costs…something status quo brokers will tell you is impossible. But the authors are doing it every day for their clients.

Mindset and toolset

This book gives the C-level executive and the HR professional both the mindset and the toolset needed to break through the status quo and take control of their benefits spend.

The authors reveal:

- how NextGeneration Benefits Advisers are shattering the status quo in both benefits and healthcare (Chapters 1 & 2);
- the NextGeneration Benefits mindset that will allow you to break through your own benefits status quo (Chapters 4, 10, 13 & 16);

- why it's *critical* (and how) to ensure your benefits adviser's incentives are aligned with yours (Chapter 3)
- how "best practices" in benefits and healthcare are failing you and your benefits budget (Chapter 12);
- strategies to take control of your benefits plan and budget to reduce costs (Chapters 4, 5, 10, 11, 14 & 15); and
- how to identify and select a NextGeneration Benefits Adviser (Chapter 19).

In other chapters, the authors provide specific, proven strategies for cost containment, alternative funding, employee financial wellness, leveraging data, technology, and employee engagement communication. These are the innovative and effective nuts and bolts of their work with clients to break through the status quo and enhance their benefits while reducing costs.

It's no wonder the information in this book is so innovative and impactful that the status quo doesn't stand a chance. The authors are not just another broker.

The industry's elite

This book's authors include some of the industry's most distinguished and acclaimed benefits advisers, the recipients of many industry accolades. Three of them—*Will Glaros* (2014), *Tim Olson* (2015) and *Mick Rodgers* (2017)—have been honored as **Employee Benefit Adviser of the Year** by *Employee Benefit Adviser* (*EBA*) magazine. As a finalist for 2017 **Broker of the Year**, *Felipe Barganier* was recognized by *BenefitsPRO* magazine as one of the top benefits advisers in the country.

Eric Silverman was named 2017 **Voluntary Adviser of the Year** by *EBA* magazine for his work with Enhanced (formerly "voluntary") Benefits, designing effective strategies to improve benefits for employees and reduce costs for employers using these valuable, supplemental life & health benefits.

Two others—***Dawn Sheue*** and ***Karin Rettger***—were named by *EBA* magazine to their list of **Most Influential Women in Benefit Advising**. Additionally, Karin was recognized as one of the **Top Women Advisers** by the influential National Association of Plan Advisers.

Craig Lack was called "**the most effective consultant you've never heard of**" by *Inc.* magazine.

Brian Tolbert, *Randy Hansen*, and *Rudy Garcia* have been recognized by the Association for Insurance Leadership for creating a **NextGeneration Benefits Firm** that "provides a superior and more cost-effective benefits plan for employers and enhanced benefits for employees."

Gary Becker, *Craig Lack*, and *Pete Scruggs* are each a recipient of the prestigious **"Innovation Award"** from the Association for Insurance Leadership for their "contribution to the advancement of innovation in the employee benefits industry."

Dawn Sheue, *Eric Silverman*, and *Trey Taylor* have been elected to the exclusive **Advisory Board** of the Workplace Benefits Association.

And many of them—including ***Will Glaros***, ***John Sbrocco***, ***Bob Gearhart Jr.***, ***Kim Eckelbarger***, ***Andy Neary***, ***Brian Tolbert***, ***Dan Thompson,*** and ***Derek Rine***—have been featured in top industry publications including *EBA*, *BenefitsPRO*, *Business Insurance*, and *Rough Notes*.

These achievements and honors reflect directly on the vast expertise and deep experience of the authors. These smart and accomplished NextGeneration Benefits Advisers have shared willingly with the CFOs, CEOs, and HR professionals who read this book their knowledge, strategies, and techniques.

This is game-changing information. The authors want you to use it to break through your own benefits status quo to help your employees AND boost your bottom line.

—Nelson L. Griswold

Author, *DOING MORE WITH LESS: No-Cost Strategies for HR* and *DO OR DIE: Reinventing Your Benefits Agency for Post-Reform Success*
Chairman, Association for Insurance Leadership
Managing Director, NextGeneration Benefits Network

CHAPTER 1

BREAKING THROUGH THE STATUS QUO

Nelson L. Griswold

Although the U.S. healthcare system is highly complex, there is a very straightforward reason that controlling healthcare costs is seemingly impossible: misaligned incentives. Employee benefits, specifically, employer-sponsored health insurance and certainly the healthcare system that it funds are rife with misaligned incentives. Under the current status quo system, the *only* active* stakeholder in the health care equation that is incentivized to contain and lower healthcare costs is the payor...the employer that sponsors the plan,

---

* In a self-funded account, the stop-loss carrier also benefits from controlling healthcare costs but it plays a passive role, with no ability to influence the frequency and severity of claims.

has fiduciary responsibility, and pays the majority of the bills. No other stakeholder—insurance carrier, ASO, TPA, PBM, hospitals, physicians, drug companies, plan members, benefits brokers/consultants—is incentivized to reduce healthcare costs. In fact, all but the ASO and TPA are incentivized to *increase* healthcare costs.

If the U.S. is to solve the healthcare cost problem, we must break the status quo in these key areas:

- Employer strategy for purchasing & managing healthcare
- The benefits broker's role & relationship with the employer client
- Healthcare delivery & pricing

If the status quo is broken in all three of these in enough companies, the U.S.—and certainly the companies themselves—can begin to control and reduce the cost of healthcare.

Let's start with the employer, since all the power in this complex dance—*and* the means to solve the healthcare cost problem—really lies with the payor. In fact, the only leverage, which currently is almost never exercised, is the payor's power of the purse. So how do employers break the status quo in how healthcare is bought and managed?

Breaking the employer status quo

There are a number of changes necessary for an employer to break the status quo in their healthcare purchase and management, all occurring at the C-Suite level involving the Chief Financial Officer (CFO) and/or the Chief Executive Officer (CEO) or President:

- Active engagement in the benefits spend at the strategic level
- Aggressive fiduciary oversight of the healthcare spend

- Intensive supply chain management of the employees' healthcare
- A shift from viewing the benefit spend as a variable OpEx buried in the SG&A to a manageable CapEx that produces ROI
- Requiring that their benefits broker/adviser align incentives with the organization's goals

The first and most essential change required to break the status quo is for company and organizational executives in the C-Suite (CEO, CFO, President) to actively engage in strategic discussions and decisions about the employee benefits, particularly, health insurance. While the Human Resource leadership will retain operational control of the benefits and certainly should be a part of the high-level strategy conversations, the CFO and/or CEO need to play a central role in the strategy for what is, for most companies, a top-three P&L expense.

Given the sheer number of dollars being spent, the CFO/CEO should *want* to be involved in the strategic decisions on the benefits spend. By law, however, the CFO and/or CEO actually are *required* to be engaged so that they can fulfill their responsibilities as plan fiduciaries. Under ERISA, the U.S. Department of Labor considers executive leadership to be fiduciaries for the health plan and, thus, responsible for "paying only reasonable plan expenses" and "acting solely in the interest of plan participants and their beneficiaries and with the exclusive purpose of providing benefits to them."** So, it's not just imperative that the executives participate in strategic decision-making and oversight of the healthcare spend, it's the law.

** Employee Benefits Security Administration (2015). *Understanding your fiduciary responsibilities under a group health plan.* Washington, D.C.: U.S. Department of Labor, pp. 2-3.

Another shift in executive thinking necessary to break the status quo is from viewing the benefits spend as as an operating expense (OpEx) to a capital expense (CapEx) that is expected to generate a return on investment (ROI). As a CapEx, the benefits spend, properly managed, should increase employee morale, boost retention, decrease absenteeism/presenteeism, and increase productivity—all of which will produce a positive ROI.

But the exciting news for C-Suite executives is that, contrary to what their status quo broker/consultant tells them, they actually do have the opportunity and ability to control their benefits spend by reducing healthcare costs. What most CFOs/CEOs don't realize is that, unlike every other part of their business, their healthcare has almost no supply chain management. That is, there is no rigorous oversight of the supply of healthcare products and services to ensure that it is as effective, efficient, and economical as possible. Put another way, in most companies no real effort is made either to maximize the quality of the healthcare purchased by the company for employees or to make sure the cost of that healthcare is "reasonable and customary." Supply chain management is what allows the CFO/CEO to control and reduce healthcare costs.

But—and, in many ways, this is a highly critical point—no CFO, CEO, or anyone on their staff knows how to manage the healthcare supply chain. Certainly, the operational staff in HR has no under-standing of healthcare supply chain management. So, as responsible fiduciaries, the C-Suite must rely on outside counsel in the person of the benefits broker/adviser to ensure that the healthcare purchased is "effective, efficient, and economical." And the best brokers/advisers know how to put in place the management components that will ef-fectively manage the supply chain. But to make sure that their broker/ adviser is working diligently and effectively on the company's behalf

and in its best interests, the C-Suite must require that the broker/
adviser's incentives are aligned with the company's goals.

To ensure this alignment, the broker/adviser must not take any
commissions from the insurance company on the medical insurance,
instead being compensated by fees paid by the employer. Additionally,
the broker/adviser must have some meaningful percentage (33% to
100%) of this fee compensation at risk contingent on the performance of the health plan. Only when the broker/adviser's success is
contingent on the employer's success can the C-Suite be sure that the
broker/adviser is working in the company's best interests.

Not until the CFO/CEO is focused on the strategic decision-making and fiduciary oversight of the healthcare spend can healthcare costs
be controlled and reduced. But, as noted, the C-Suite needs the help
of a properly incentivized benefits broker/adviser that also has broken
his or her own status quo.

Breaking the benefits broker status quo

We've established the need for the broker/adviser to be compensated with fees for strategically and tactically managing the healthcare
supply chain. And for a substantial percentage of those fees to be on
the risk based on the performance of key metrics around the employer's health plan.

(Frankly, for a broker to operate at the high performance level
required to meet the needs of an engaged C-Suite, he or she — and his
or her firm — will have moved from the transactional broker role to a
consultative advisory role, serving as a strategic adviser to the client.
So the term "adviser" will be used from here instead of the status quo
"broker.")

For the status quo broker to break out of the status quo and become a NextGeneration Benefits Firm® that can provide the employer with the strategic guidance needed to take control of the benefits spend and reduce healthcare costs, a number of changes must occur:

- Fee & performance-based compensation paid by the employer (when allowed by state law/regs)
- A move from a transactional to a consultative role
- Elevation from working primarily with HR to serving as a strategic consultant to the C-Suite
- Unless otherwise indicated, a move to self-funding to take control of the health plan
- An active embrace of innovation for cost-containment & employee engagement
- A move from administration by insurance carrier or ASO to an unbundled TPA
- Aggressive management of the employer's healthcare supply chain

Even before moving to fee and performance compensation, the adviser will have moved from a passive transactional role in managing the renewal of the healthcare insurance to an active consultative role in managing the healthcare supply chain. This adviser can provide the C-Suite with high-level, strategic guidance and insights and is focused on the reduction of healthcare costs, not the reduction of an often-capricious premium increase. This consultative adviser will leverage the power of claims data and employee health data and predictive analytics to more effectively manage the plan.

While the status quo adviser works exclusively with HR, the NextGen adviser has moved beyond the HR department to work with the C-Suite on strategy. In fact, the necessary engagement of the

C-Suite with the benefits spend is most likely a result of a NextGen adviser awakening the CFO/CEO to the opportunity and necessity of his or her active participation in benefits strategy. Once the adviser elevates to the C-Suite to work with the CFO/CEO, serious innovations and aggressive supply chain management have a good chance of being approved and implemented.

Working as a consultant to the CFO/CEO, the adviser must now look at the feasibility of moving the client out of a fully insured health plan, which allows little to no access to claims data and no control for supply chain management. When it makes actuarial and economic sense, the employer can get unfettered access to claims data and the all-important control to implement cost-containment strategies by moving to some form of alternative funding (level-funded, partially self-funded, coalition, fully self-funded). This is a necessary change that the adviser must drive to be able to manage the supply chain.

Once the employer has reclaimed control of the health plan, the adviser must bring innovative strategies and resources to implement the supply chain management that will ensure that their employees' healthcare is "effective, efficient, and economical." This requires a proactive search for and embrace of innovation of all sorts…technological, operational, administrative, etc. As the final section of this chapter notes, the status quo of the healthcare system must be disrupted and it is innovation that will do most of the disruption.

One final break from the broker status quo necessary for success in reducing healthcare costs is a move away from using insurance carriers and their ASO (Administrative Services Only) units for administering the health plan and to TPAs (Third-Party Adminstrator). It's important, however, that the TPA be transparent in its pricing and be "unbundled," meaning that the adviser can use any cost-containment or other vender in lieu of the TPA's usual vendor for PBM (Pharmacy

Benefit Manager), medical management, etc.

Once a status quo broker has transformed into a NextGeneration Benefits Firm, it can partner with a company's C-Suite to begin to break the healthcare status quo with the only leverage that the providers and other stakeholders in healthcare recognize and respond to: **money**, the healthcare dollars being spent by the employer as the payor.

Breaking the healthcare status quo

Since breaking the healthcare status quo to reduce healthcare costs is the bailiwick and area of expertise of the NextGeneration Benefits Firm, this final section will be fairly succinct.

Once again, the problem with the healthcare providers as with all the other stakeholders is misaligned incentives. Since structural reform of the healthcare system, including incentives, is beyond the reach of benefits advisers and even employers in their role as payor, the challenge is to implement strategies and tools that address the biggest drivers of healthcare spending. These include employee misuse of healthcare (e.g., unnecessary use of the Emergency Room, poor choice of providers), misdiagnosis, unneeded medical care (defensive medicine), overcharges (especially by hospitals), opaque billing (bundled bills instead of itemized bills), and provider networks and the carriers' misleading network discounts.

The high healthcare costs due to these cost drivers can be mitigated and often eliminated with effective strategies and resources, many of which you will find in the other chapters of this book. Here's a quick look at some of the strategies and tools and the cost drivers they address.

- **Misusage by Employees:**
  - Employee engagement & education
  - Medical management
  - Financial incentives
  - Direct Primary Care (DPC)

- **Misdiagnosis**
  - Medical management
  - Mandatory second opinions
  - DPC
  - Bidding services for surgery

- **Overcharges & Exorbitant Pricing**
  - Direct contracting with preferred provider(s)
  - Bidding services for surgery
  - Providers offering transparent, bundled pricing
  - Healthcare Abroad (medical travel)
  - Reference-based reimbursement or pricing (RBR or RBP)
  - Transparent, fiduciary PBMs
  - Pharmacy cost-mitigation programs

- **Opaque Pricing & Billing**
  - Medical management claims review
  - RBR or RBP

- **Provider Networks/Network "Discounts"**
  - RBR or RBP
  - DPC

One other category not mentioned and technically not a healthcare problem but certainly a cost driver are those employees that are high utilizers due to serious or chronic conditions. Such programs as the SIHRA (Spousal Incentive HRA) can provide a zero out-of-pocket health plan for some qualifying employees and their entire family while dramatically reducing the budget impact for the employer.

The status quo in employee benefits and healthcare is simply unsustainable and is destroying America's middle class as rising healthcare costs cannibalize wage increases. In this system of misaligned incentives, only the payor—the employer—has the power to control and reduce the otherwise out-of-control healthcare costs. Only an engaged CFO and/or CEO can provide the strategic leadership and fiduciary oversight required to ensure effective supply chain management of its employees' healthcare. Only a NextGeneration Benefits Firm is equipped and properly incentivized to counsel, guide and support the C-Suite in taking control of and reducing the cost of the company's healthcare spend.

This desirable sequence of events occurs only when an employer has broken its status quo approach to purchasing & managing its employees' healthcare to partner with a broker that has broken its own status quo model to become a NextGeneration Benefits Firm. Together, this employer/adviser partnership can leverage the payor's economic power to effectively work around the healthcare status quo to control and reduce healthcare costs. When this happens enough times in the marketplace, a critical tipping point can be reached where other companies refuse to be victims of a perverse healthcare system and force structural reform to the healthcare system.

In the meantime, any company now has the opportunity, ability, and **power** to control and reduce its own healthcare costs with the help of a NextGeneration Benefits Firm.

Nelson L. Griswold

Chairman
Association for Insurance Leadership
Nashville, TN

Nelson Griswold is recognized as one the industry's leading authorities on how the changes brought by the ACA are creating an unprecedented opportunity for employers finally to take control of their benefits spend while improving both their benefits and the healthcare outcomes for their employees. He is co-author of the book, *Doing More with Less: Innovative Strategies for HR*, a handbook for HR and benefits professionals.

One of the premier thought leaders in the benefits industry, Nelson also is the author of the industry bestseller, *DO OR DIE: Reinventing Your Benefits Agency for Post-Reform Success*, a blueprint for agency leaders to re-engineer their firm to align their interests to match their clients' interests, bring innovative business solutions, and drive actual results. A respected consultant to employee benefits firms across the country, his clients include Aon Hewitt, HUB, and top independent agencies.

He is a leading strategic consultant on employee engagement and next-generation enrollment strategies to insurance companies including Aetna, Trustmark, Aflac, Humana, Allstate, Principal Financial, Anthem, RBC Insurance of Canada, and Assurant. He also advises a number of companies using technology and other innovative strategies to change and improve the benefits landscape.

A monthly columnist for *Employee Benefit Adviser* magazine, Nelson also writes for *Employee Benefit News, BenefitsPro, HealthCare Consumerism Solutions*, and other leading industry publications. An in-demand keynote speaker and presenter at industry conferences, he serves on the boards of the Voluntary Benefits Association and the Workplace Benefits Association.

www.AIL-assn.org
nelson@insurancebottomline.com
615-369-0618

CHAPTER 2

BEYOND BENEFITS & BROKERS

*The Three Essential Steps to Break
Through the Status Quo*

Scott Cantrell

Objects at rest tend to stay at rest.
– Sir Isaac Newton

As Sir Isaac Newton discovered with his law of inertia, getting something to move requires an external force. This concept also often
applies to life and business, as well. Let's face it, the status quo is a
stubborn thing. While resistance to change is not unusual in most
situations, it is especially pervasive when there is chaos, uncertainty,
and challenging problems to solve. Thus, when it comes to healthcare
and health insurance (two very different issues), change and moving

beyond the status quo is often ignored, dismissed, or pushed away.

However, as with all things in life and industry, change is inevitable. The question is will you and your organization embrace it to your productive and profitable advantage or will you resist it even to the detriment of your employees' well-being and your company's bottom line?

The fiscal and human costs of the current system of healthcare and health insurance are simply too great to merely ignore, dismiss, or push away any longer. Change is demanded, and the opportunity to create a more positive, productive, and profitable workforce and company has never been greater.

There are three essential steps that must be acknowledged and then acted upon in order to move beyond today's status quo. Ever-increasing premiums combined with a largely confused and concerned employee population are not sustainable, much less enjoyable, for any organizational leaders whether they be HR directors or C-level executives.

It's time to embrace meaningful change, to do things differently and BETTER. It's time to break through the status quo, to move beyond benefits and brokers.

Step 1 — Realization

You do not have to (and should NOT) settle for the status quo.

Because objects tend to remain in their current state unless acted on by another force, it stands to reason that the default processes and beliefs of the marketplace related to employee benefits and health insurance purchasing will be the same ones that have been widely used and accepted for decades. The point is, the status quo that company leaders face is a very stubborn one.

Thus, the first step to ensure you do not continue to accept ever-increasing premiums along with confusion, uncertainty, and an unhealthy employee population is to realize that **you do not have to accept the status quo**. In fact, you SHOULD NOT; almost certainly, it's not in your organization's best interest nor does it best serve those people you depend on most—your employees.

Naturally, on the flipside, it's naïve to think there is a silver bullet or little blue pill that will immediately cure all of a company's ills around skyrocketing healthcare and insurance costs. But there are powerful, meaningful, and measurable methods that can be leveraged to achieve far superior results than the status quo annual renewal process provides. Many of those strategies are presented elsewhere in this book, so do not think that your options are limited to a tiny few.

With the vast number of strategies, tactics, tools, and services that you can leverage, it's not a lack of solutions that will prevent you from breaking free of the current antiquated process. Instead, for most organizations and leaders, the resistance to meaningful change will be found in one or more of the following:

- **Lack of knowledge**—As you hold this book in your hands, this should no longer be an issue for you or your organization. Obviously, you are willing and able to gather new knowledge and, let's assume, implement it for the betterment of your company and employees. Still, far too many leaders (HR and C-level, alike) have far too little knowledge on why and how to break through the status quo. Honestly, that is not their fault; they've be held captive to those who want to maintain the status quo as long as possible to serve their own needs (i.e., insurance carriers, brokers, providers, etc.). Please don't misunderstand, there are many fine individuals and companies within each of those categories who do good work. That said, there has been and continues to be both a pervasive ignorance as well as a "self-censoring" of sorts related to many valuable methods and approaches that would provide better healthcare, better patient experience, and better outcomes…all for a better price. Continue to educate yourself with books like this one, staying updated on what's available and how you and your company can perform at a higher level in these areas.

- **Lack of belief**—In large part due to "lack of knowledge," HR and C-level executives simply don't believe that there are meaningful answers and solutions to the problems and challenges organizations face around healthcare and health insurance. When a broker, or an HR leader, or a CFO/CEO doesn't really believe that a given strategy will work, then it's virtually impossible to implement that approach in the right way. Because the status quo has been around for so long, even the smartest leaders begin to believe there must not be any other way. They begin to forget (or not pay attention to) the fact that change really is possible to produce better results. In other words, if someone believes a problem has no answer, then it will not be long before the problem stops being perceived as a "problem" and starts to be seen as "just the way it is." Too many leaders have been and are saying, "It is what it is."

- **Lack of capability**—Finally, even when company leaders and decision makers do have the knowledge and belief, they may not be properly empowered and able to execute the key strategies needed to produce the results. Often, this comes down to either a lack of willingness or ability on the part of their strategic adviser on benefits—who often is neither strategic nor a true adviser. (See Step 2 below). Secondarily, lack of capability may come from a lack of investment to be able to effectively implement the desired changes. To move beyond the status quo will require investment of time, effort, and yes, financial resources. The key lies in understanding the value of investing (and expecting a return) as opposed to merely expending.

If you realize that the status quo no longer serves your company or your employees in the best way; if you realize your current situation (consistent annual premium increases) is simply not sustainable; if you realize that your employees need a better, simpler, more guided health insurance and healthcare experience; then you can move beyond the traditional benefits and brokering approach to a new model that is much more efficient, effective, and valuable for your organization and its employees.

Step 2—Partnership

Do NOT work with a benefits "broker" ever again.

The health insurance status quo is quickly going extinct and it's taking another breed along with it, that of the "broker."

Before I go any further, let me be exceedingly clear—an organization absolutely must work with a strategic adviser and consultant to enact the type of changes necessary to a more efficient, effective, productive, and profitable result around its benefits spend and plan.

When referring to a "broker," I'm talking about the transactional person who shows up only once a year to talk about your renewal increase, shops your health plan, and then, brings you the quotes to choose from. If that's all they do, this individual is a "keeper of the status quo"; they are not focused on improving the condition of your organization—the definition of a true business consultant or adviser.

This book is filled with a myriad of thoughtful, strategic, and innovative contributions from consultative, strategic advisers and consultants from all over the U.S. They are not "brokers" even though they may use the word "broker" from time to time. True strategists and advisers are focused on producing results, not just activity. They have the objective of producing positive results and outcomes for the clients they choose to serve.

Traditional "brokers" are generally the bringers of bad news in the form of higher premium renewals and most of them are not too upset with those higher renewals because that means a bigger commission check for them. In short, the broker's incentives are not aligned with yours.

So, what are the key differences between a "broker" and a strategic consultant? Below are a few of the key ones to remember and look for when choosing who you should work with.

- **Strategic As Well As Tactical**—A real adviser has the expertise, network, and resources to provide insightful strategic guidance to help you and your organization plan not just for this year, but for years to come. Strategic advisers are interested the positive long-term transformation of your company, not just in managing an annual transaction. For instance, standard practice for most of the contributors of this book is to provide their clients with a 3-5 year strategic plan they can follow to ensure the company is acting in a positive and proactive manner as opposed to merely reacting to the latest renewal hike or regulation. Consider what questions your adviser asks you — are they strategic or just tactical? Of course, strategic consultants are still more than capable of delivering the tactical and operational services as well, but now those actions are based on a cohesive and comprehensive approach.

- **Business Not Just Benefits** — The type of consultant you want to work with should have a comprehensive, global view of your business rather than only paying attention to employee benefits and ignoring everything else. The reality is, benefits affect (directly or indirectly) virtually every other area of an organization. Consider the health, presence, and productivity of your workforce; without them, there is effectively no business. You should find a partner who understands how seemingly separate parts of the company affect one another and speaks to those issues in a knowledgeable and strategic way.

- **Outcomes Not Just Activity** — Ultimately, you need to engage a partner who has his/her incentives aligned with yours; one who is focused on the results produced and not only on the activities and services rendered. Too many brokers for far too long have held up their so-called "capabilities binders" to unsuspecting prospects, seducing them with all the "stuff" and "services" they bring. While there may certainly be value in some (or even most) of those capabilities, smart organizations understand that "more

capabilities" is often just a smoke screen for "less results."
Your strategic partner should be talking about actual,
meaningful, and measurable *outcomes* they can help you
produce for the company and its employees. If they deflect
an "outcomes" conversation, then you need to move on and
find a new, truly consultative and strategic adviser.

Perhaps the fastest and easiest way to break through the status quo
is partnering with a thoughtful, intentional, and innovative adviser
prepared to help you break your status quo. By the way, that's likely
not a family member, or a close friend from college; in other words,
this challenge is too important to depend merely upon a personal
relationship. You must identify a partner with the expertise and willingness to strategically help you navigate beyond the status quo.

Step 3 — Commitment

Stay the course even when it's hard.

One of the most common challenges leaders have when trying
to break the status quo is not being committed enough to stay the
course. When challenges arise, the "gravitational pull" of the status
quo increases, pulling them back to where they were. This is true in
any aspect of our lives; it's hard to make change stick. It's especially
true when we're talking about a business with employees combined
with a confusing and challenging industry like healthcare and health
insurance.

Nevertheless, for change to be meaningful to an individual or an
organization, that change has to be committed to. We cannot expect
that all of the problems, challenges, issues, etc. that the system has

created in the last decades will be corrected overnight, but we can expect them to be dealt with in turn, and strategically, over time. This is why **Step 1: Realization** and **Step 2: Partnership** are so critical; they are vital to ensuring your company will truly commit to moving beyond the status quo and fulfilling the promises of lower health-care costs & lower health insurance premiums and creating healthier, happier, more productive employees—all translating to a more positive bottom line.

By committing to make important changes in how you fund, purchase, and deliver healthcare to your employees, you can have massive impact on so many other areas of the organization. However, a lack of commitment will only create more challenges and problems as the organization moves down one path only to then go backwards. By no means will this change be a perfectly smooth transition or transformation, but it is absolutely worth it. There are countless success stories that have been written by the companies my co-authors serve; you'll read about many of them elsewhere in the book. Companies that have saved millions of dollars, companies that have saved the lives of their employees and their family members, companies that have boosted their EBITDA substantially—all because they realized they didn't need to settle for the status quo, and so partnered with a strategic adviser and committed to making the changes that produced phenomenal outcomes.

In Closing...

Of course, the process of breaking through the status quo will not be easy.

It will require a real desire to at least improve if not reinvent your approach to purchasing and managing employee benefits. It will require a shift in the leadership's mindset and approach to employee benefits and healthcare—one of a company's most expensive (yet valuable) investments. It will require a true benefits adviser partner with the expertise, strategic approach, and capability to provide a customized solution set for your organization. It will require a broader scope of analysis to strategically plan how the seemingly disparate pieces related to benefits, healthcare, turnover, productivity, employee health, etc. all directly affect one another and the company's bottom line.

As challenging as this change may seem on the surface, it is absolutely achievable for your organization. Do not let the fear or anxiety of "doing things differently" keep you from the vast returns and rewards that await you, your organization, and your employees just outside your comfort zone. Ultimately, the status quo is unsustainable and, thus, change is inevitable. The sooner you take control and manage that change productively, the easier and more positive it will be.

I challenge you to move beyond benefits and brokers; it's time to break through the status quo!

Scott Cantrell

Partner
Bottom Line Solutions, Inc.
Nashville, TN

Scott Cantrell is a partner in Bottom Line Solutions and is one of the insurance industry's leading marketing strategists and practice management consultants. A top expert in direct marketing strategies for insurance, he provides clients with high-ROI marketing strategies that can be held accountable for results.

He's the co-author of *Doing More with Less: Innovative Strategies for HR*, a handbook for HR and benefits professionals

As Director of the Agency Growth Mastermind Partnership, he helps guide the programming & development of this national executive peer-exchange program for leaders of benefits firms that has produced two national Benefit Advisers of the Year, two of *EBA* magazine's "25 Most Influential Women in Benefit Advising," and "the most effective consultant you've never heard of" according to *Inc.* magazine.

Scott's work has been featured in *Employee Benefit Adviser*, *Producers eSource*, *Canadian Insurance Top Broker*, and other leading industry publications. He speaks frequently at industry events. He is an Associate Board Member of the Workplace Benefits Association.

CHAPTER 3

THERE IS A MOVEMENT HAPPENING IN EMPLOYEE BENEFITS

Michael "Mick" Rodgers

Healthcare benefits program design is a complex process; as with many complicated processes, it requires tremendous expertise enabled by advanced technology to fully understand and navigate the many industry variables. Advances and changes in medical technology, regulations and controls, new prescription drug mandates, and evolving healthcare coding requirements are all factors that are moving at a very rapid pace. All of these have had dramatic effects on the increasing cost of an employer to offer comprehensive healthcare to their employees. In addition, employee benefits are a big part of employee satisfaction and retention, which both correlate to organizational productivity and profitability. Therefore, there is an added element of pressure to find the perfect balance of benefits that meet employee expectations and financial requirements.

From an industry progression perspective, the first significant milestone in the transition to a new healthcare benefits purchasing model began with data-driven analyses by buyers in pockets throughout the U.S. in the early 2000s. At that time, the complexity of healthcare coding had surpassed the capabilities of standard evaluation methodologies, making it extremely difficult and inefficient to fully understand benefits usage. Advisers, and subsequently, purchasers, were at a disadvantage as they were faced with buying benefits based on projected population-based usage and not actual usage for their employee population. This resulted in expensive plans and diminished confidence in coverage.

The introduction of direct usage-based benefits allowed organizations to leverage the healthcare data of their employee population to optimize plans based on the benefits they used and not what they didn't. This model gave more control to the buyers' community and initiated a power shift that became a catalyst for change across the industry. As it became more widely adopted, so did the mentality for transformation.

As organizations realized what was possible, they also realized the reality of what they had been doing, which was buying products that, perhaps, weren't what they seemed. Or rather, that they were buying benefits packages based only on what providers offered them; and that the choices they seemingly had, presented by their Advisers, were not representative of what was truly available. However, what organizations didn't know was that the insurance community wasn't purposefully holding back information or advanced processes to take advantage of companies. It simply hadn't yet figured out how to use the new technology-based methodologies. Nonetheless, and understandably so, insurance companies became villains and Advisers weren't to be trusted.

This mentality continued to foster increased skepticism and cast more doubt on the industry as a whole, which was then predominantly fed by a commission-based compensation model. With continued pressure to lower cost while improving coverage; increasing complexity of reimbursement processes; changing federal regulations; and an atmosphere of distrust, the entire healthcare benefits ecosystem had reached a level of toxicity that demanded change.

The Employee Benefits Transformation Movement (what we like to call our *Movement*) — was born to solve a primary challenge — end employer and Adviser frustration from an underperforming healthcare system and the associated damages it yielded. To break the status quo, Our Movement's mission is to continually advance employee benefits design and delivery practices, and foster trust through collaboration, ingenuity, precision, and results. Its goal is to improve the entire system from within to make it better, not only for our employer clients, but their employees as well.

There are three main areas of focus and commitment that are critical to achieving the mission that are discussed in more detail below:

1. Adviser collaboration;
2. Maximizing purchasing power for customers; and
3. Adviser compensation model reform and transparency.

However, at the core of our Movement — what has helped it gain traction and become accepted in the industry; and what ensures its success is sustainable, is an Adviser community that is dedicated to ensuring past frustrations are not part of future endeavors, understands the true value of this new way of working, and believes in continuous improvement; and a Buyer community that recognizes the significant advantages and immense potential the Employee Benefits Transformation Movement makes possible.

Collaboration seems like common sense. Sharing best practices within the Adviser community is a logical way to advance processes, methodologies, implementation strategies and execution. However, when a best practice is a key point of differentiation in a highly competitive market, the instinct is often to protect it as an asset and cultivate it through one's individual practice. This way of thinking was the primary reason direct usage-based benefits took almost 10 years to become a standard practice. It had become a barrier to growth across the industry. The launch of our Movement has been integral to breaking that barrier and creating an atmosphere of open dialogue and sharing. As some independent Advisers began to join together, the opportunity for improvement began to flourish, including enhanced operations, optimized processes and a growth environment that was catapulted even further by great results. One Advisers' competitive advantage was the solution to another's issue, which in turn, fueled the betterment of the original idea. It is a cycle of change that everyone can believe in and wants to be a part of. A living, breathing entity that's bigger than any one component or company. This teamwork approach was and remains integral to advancing the industry and the bottom-line for all stakeholders — Sellers, Advisers, and Employers.

Maximizing purchase power for employers through bulk purchasing is fundamental to achieving significant cost savings. Everyone understands that buying in bulk, works for almost all purchasing applications. It is why a lot of consumers shop at Costco or Walmart, so they can access the best price per unit. Advisers and Employers also understand that the largest companies in the U.S. purchase healthcare differently and at a lower cost than their small and mid-size counterparts. The reason is that their size allows them to buy bulk or access the insurance markets more efficiently than others. In healthcare purchasing specifically, there are other important attributes that become available with higher volume as well, including increased stability and predictability in the larger risk environment. As an example, if you look at any national studies, small and midsize employers purchasing fully insured plans continue to pay upwards of 15-20% more than larger employers. The challenge smaller companies have is something they can't overcome on their own; their size.

A Healthcare Purchasing Coalition (HPC) is a group of like-minded companies that purchase health insurance together. This process is facilitated by an Adviser that understands how to make 10 independent 100 employee companies, purchase 10 independent programs, and act like a single 1000 employee company, for purposes of the insurance protection purchase. It gives buyers more power and simplifies decision-making using advanced data and analytics. By joining an HPC, organizations have access to the same benefits larger companies do, but without the high premiums they would normally be subject to, because of their smaller size. Each company is underwritten and priced independently, and the employer is responsible for their own "risk" with monthly and annual caps. Once the upper limits are met, the remaining balances are shared between the HPC pool that has been created and/or traditional reinsurance.

From a cost perspective, if a fully insured plan costs a small-to-midsize employer $1.00, an integrated plan through group purchasing via an HPC should costs an employer on average $0.73. The math works. As important as cost is, however, improving stability and predictability are equally as imperative for companies looking to mitigate risk and stabilize their benefits model over time. HPCs are able to aggregate many employers together to access that bulk process, and have been proven to consistently drive down, and in many instances, return a large portion of unused premiums to the member companies; something that is unheard of in a traditional insurance arrangement for companies in this size range.

Since the aggregation process happens in the background, it's important to understand that an HPC does not necessarily dictate the actual benefits employees have and touch. The 10 companies from the previous example may have 10 different levels of benefits and still act as a single large employer for an underwriter. It's not a slash and burn or lower the benefits level technique. It also does not dictate that all members use a single carrier network. The HPC is a purchasing method for an employer to access without necessarily changing or lowering the current level of benefits, carriers or networks they offer employees. The reduced volatility and cost savings achieved, makes becoming a part of an HPC a smart way to align a company's specific benefits needs with, with employee expectations and financial requirements. Joining an HPC requires selection of the purchasing group that makes the most sense for the specific business, and then initiating the migration process.

Selection of an HPC is very simple. In instances where the company is part of an industry vertical that already has a designated HPC, such as staffing, healthcare, manufacturing, biotech, tech, or accounting, it likely makes sense to leverage the existing group. For organizations that are early adopters of the HPC model and their industry do not have a mature HPC, or they wish to align with members in a different way, an Incubator or holding HPC may be the best option. An Incubator HPC provides the flexibility to access the same techniques without being part of a common industry. An employer may remain in the incubator until a vertical HPC is established, or remain there forever. Vertical and Incubator HPCs provide the exact same advantages, with the only difference being the member mix.

The standard method for joining an HPC is a process called progression. Progression moves employers across a spectrum from Fully Insured to HPC in a way that make the transition easy to manage, and mitigates risk.

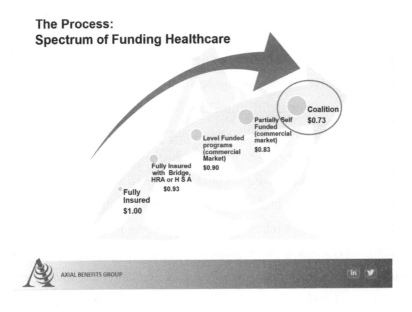

The Process:
Spectrum of Funding Healthcare

Coalition $0.73

Partially Self Funded (commercial market) $0.83

Level Funded programs (commercial Market) $0.90

Fully Insured with Bridge, HRA or H S A $0.93

Fully Insured $1.00

AXIAL BENEFITS GROUP

As organizations meet milestones, and Advisers start to understand their specific underwriting risk factors, costs begin to come down, and they seamlessly shift into the next phase as new techniques are layered on. Generally, the migration process takes about one to two renewal cycles, but financial results are seen and measurable within the first year of the process. When employers reach the final stage — the HPC — all of the techniques come together, and the foundation is set for long-term success.

The coalition model provides reliability and structure for continued success maximizing purchasing power, achieving results within a stable, predictable benefits environment.

Adviser compensation model needs to reform, and complete transparency is critical in strengthening Adviser/Employer relationships and trust from clients. With the traditional commission-based compensation model, Advisers are paid a percentage of the cost of benefits programs they facilitate. This presents a fundamental issue with the way benefits have historically been purchased or even "sold," as some still may consider it. Advisers are paid more when their clients, Employers, renewals are higher. In that dynamic and at a very basic level, Advisers are incented to have clients pay more or, in the least, are not aligned with the client's outcomes. From an Employer perspective, it becomes difficult to completely trust that what they are buying is 100% in their best interest. Shifting to a fee-for-performance based Adviser compensation model removes that cloud of uncertainty and makes a meaningful difference. In the new fee-for-performance employee benefits purchasing structure, Advisers are paid more when an Employer's programs perform better. Not only does this help build trust, it also motivates Advisers to continually improve program options and seek new ways to optimize performance. Additionally, some Advisers have moved from a commission based model to a fee-for-service model, but it's not enough. Fee-for performance puts our best work forward and produces results for the employers. Fee-for-performance will need to be the standard for advisers going forward to separate the professionals from those "just selling benefits services."

The layered approach enables better solutions for lowering employer costs and building trust. The HPC can be an excellent example of this compensation process at work. When companies were initially asked to participate in coalitions or consider any of the cutting edge techniques in this book, many were hesitant to join and break away from the traditional approach to benefits, even though they were frustrated. On paper, HPCs looked too good to be true, and the numbers seemed impossible to achieve. However, when Advisers were willing to put their compensation at risk, it suddenly became real, and Employers were willing to take a chance.

Fee-for-performance compensation has helped Advisers and Employers come together in a different way than before, to design mutually beneficial processes and programs. It is a proven technique that has been imperative to achieving, perhaps, the loftiest goal of our Movement; complete transparency.

Companies rely on their Advisers to educate them throughout the process and identify the best options for their business and employees. While it may not be necessary for an employer to understand every detail behind every detail, it is critical that they have visibility into the underlying methodologies and tactics used to build and form benefits programs, so they can be confident in the decisions they are making. Transparency into all aspects of the process—compensation, planning, and implementation—alleviates any potential ambiguity and ensures authenticity and trust at every step.

Collaboration, purchasing coalitions and fee-for-performance compensation, combined with a series of other EBTM techniques in our movement and in this book, may work together to create a healthcare benefits ecosystem that not only works for Advisers and Employers, but helps both businesses grow in a predictable, sustainable way. Equal stake in success, means equal responsibility and accountability. Everyone plays an important role in fostering a benefits ecosystem of excellence by driving collaboration and remaining open-minded to new ideas. The Employee Benefits Transformation Movement is one we all share.

Michael "Mick" Rodgers

Principal and Managing Partner
Axial Benefits Group
Burlington, MA

Mick Rodgers is principal and managing partner of Axial Benefits Group (ABG). An engineer by training, Rodgers founded ABG in 2004 with the belief that deconstructing traditional employee healthcare benefits programs, using data to op-timize the parts and rebuilding them in a way that yielded better benefits at lower costs could transform an industry struggling to keep pace and give employers, employees and their families access to the best healthcare possible.

As the creator of Healthcare Purchasing Coalitions, Rodgers is regarded as an industry innovator and the pioneering architect of a benefits purchasing model that enables midmarket companies to access the same "bulk buying" advantages of larger companies with increased predictability and stability. A fierce advocate of total transparency in compensation, Rodgers was the first benefits adviser to offer a fee-for-performance model, tying his compensation directly to the success of his customers.

Under Rodgers' leadership, ABG has built four successful Healthcare Purchasing Coalitions, including The Staffing Exchange, which is the largest coalition of its kind. ABG has been named a Massachusetts top 25 Benefits Adviser three years in a row. In 2017, ABG returned an unprecedented $3.2 million in unused premiums to its coalition members.

Rodgers was named *Employee Benefit Adviser* magazine's 2017 Employee Benefit Adviser of the Year.

www.axialbg.com
mrodgers@axialbg.com
781-273-1400

CHAPTER 4

AN INNOVATIVE MINDSET

*The Competitive Advantage of a
Blue Ocean Benefits Strategy*

John Clay

We are at a unique point in history. *Shark Tank* is not just a hit television series. It's become a reimagining of the American dream. More people than ever are striking out to build their own businesses, tackling problems and opportunities with unrivaled creativity. These entrepreneurs are at every level of business, not just start-ups and side-hustles. Major corporations are hiring visionaries specifically to behave like entrepreneurs—sometimes calling them "intrepreneurs"—from inside of their established cultures. And longtime family businesses are being taken over by the next generation of business leaders who have a different view of what the world can be and how even the oldest businesses can run and function differently.

In all cases, these entrepreneurs are looking at a wide-open canvas of opportunities with little to no competition. They are looking for open water, the blue ocean. They are not satisfied with the status quo. They want to blaze new trails and tap into new opportunities, both in terms of making a meaningful difference in the world and in terms of growing their businesses.

The entrepreneurial mindset is incredibly powerful, but too often, we see it applied to only part of a business. Growth is great, yet leaving the rest of the business to chug along permits the same mistakes and missing out on the same opportunities as everyone else.

I challenge you to approach all aspects of your business with an entrepreneurial mindset to build a competitive advantage at every point, from your products to your employee benefits. When you think like this, you become the kind of business owner who top experts want to collaborate with.

The blue ocean under your roof

Kentucky has a variety of state parks, and some include beautiful lakes. On weekends and holidays, lakes can fill up with a 'navy' from out of town. It gets crowded with choppy water and watercraft everywhere. Weekdays though, you'll find a beautiful, clear glass lake. Some business owners indulge in a go-fast boat. Speeding across the water at 90 miles per hour (or more) is exhilarating, and it takes skill to do so safely, reading the water, avoiding obstacles and calculating turns. Boaters, however, often forget to think about how the water inside of the boat affects their travel, worrying only about what traffic is in front of them.

Boats of all sizes depend on an auto-bailer, which is a device that forces water from the inside of a boat to the outside. As a normal part of boating, taking on water is expected, and an auto-bailer helps to eliminate this excess. Therefore, to truly maximize performance and keep your craft in peak condition, the auto-bailer needs to work to eliminate drag. At the end of a trip, the captain may come in to some situational awareness: The auto-bailer has not kept up with the rate of incoming water. As a result, the boat has burned far more fuel than anticipated.

To passengers on the boat, everything looks fine—after all, the boat arrived at its destination. However, a sharp boater will quickly realize that some fuel was wasted that could have been put toward the next trip. In business, the exact calculations to determine the amount of waste and how to fix the auto-bailer would be handled by others, but it should still be a chief concern to the boat's captain.

Usually, an entrepreneur does not want to get bogged down in the unsexy parts of the business. He or she has a vision for what the business can accomplish, and takes an aggressive approach to establishing competitive advantages for the business. They're at the captain's wheel, hand on the throttle, pushing their boat to go as far and as fast as it can. The comparison between boaters and entrepreneurs is similar. Both have a strong passion for rising far, far above their competitors and feel the need to find 'open water.' However, both require a moment to evaluate the inner workings of their business, so that they may discover what adjustments need to be made to their craft.

When you view employee benefits with a blue ocean mindset, you can transform a pivotal part of your business. What would you do with an extra $50,000 in capital? $100,000? What if you could better serve and therefore retain your top talent? What if you could do this year over year while your competitors, again and again, miss the opportunities that you seize?

Turning your entrepreneurial mindset inward, and applying that lens to a facet of your business, like how you handle and administer benefits, unlocks a wealth of opportunities for you to get more miles per gallon. When you grow, you're going to take on new employees and therefore need to provide benefits, much in the same way that a boat speeding across a lake will inevitably take on water. When your auto-bailer—your employee benefits program—is strategically aligned with your business goals, you can still go as fast as you want, but get more for every dollar in your budget.

An injection of capital from within: Two brief case studies

When you take any off-the-shelf benefits plan, you are wasting valuable capital. In these cases, you are buying a plan that has been built backwards. The focus is on the rule makers—insurance companies—not the members' experiences in the healthcare system; which means the house will always win. Recently, we worked with a construction company with about 30 employees. They were using a packaged benefits plan provided by a construction association—which is typical for the industry—and thought they were making the smart move because of the prestige they associated with Blue Cross Blue Shield. They felt they were doing right by their employees, and therefore, right by their business.

The problem with this status quo, beyond its inflexibility, is that a rate increase year over year is standard. Traditionally, and this has been an unshakeable industry trend, that increase in premiums also comes with a reduction in benefits. It's like spinning a roulette wheel to see what the increase is each year.

By switching to a self-insured, level-funded plan, this company was not only able to provide a better benefits experience for their employees—like a 24/7 benefits concierge with telehealth access to a physician, tools to help find more affordable prescriptions, electronic enrollment, and a mobile app custom-tailored to their plan—they also improved the benefits with an enhanced voluntary strategy all based on a 3 to 5 year plan. For this 30-person group, the business saved $40,000 by moving away from a fully funded plan, and they were able to roll an excess $32,000 into an employee 401(k) program instead of leaving that money in benefits limbo.

From the business owner's perspective, these solutions provide a destination with measurable milestones and are delivering, first year, $40,000 extra in profit or in workable capital. That money could be used to reward leadership in the company or reinvested in any aspect of the business, such as marketing, hiring extra help, product development, research, or infrastructure.

From the employee's perspective, this improved benefits experience is a major boost in employer loyalty. The positive experience with using the custom benefits—from the cost to the convenience—combined with the boost in the 401(k) fund, makes the most talented employees more likely to stay. They are being treated well, and they see their leadership reinvesting in them.

Later in this chapter, we will walk through a benefits checklist to help you identify whether you are spending your benefits dollars inefficiently, but for now, the simple strategic lesson is this: you need to reevaluate your benefits if you are using a fully funded plan. You are likely wasting thousands of dollars that could be better spent elsewhere in your business. More good news: you can correct this misstep without hurting your people.

Before we go through the checklist, let's explore a case study for the alternative: fearing the unknown of a self-funded or level funded plan and deciding to keep a fully funded plan instead.

This company had nominal competition in their industry and about 70 employees for a total of approximately $560,000 in annualized premiums. New managers in the human resources department saw the perceived complexity of a self-funded or level funded plan as unnecessary—an unfair assessment if you have an expert adviser guiding you through the process, but I digress—they remained with a standard off-the-shelf fully funded plan. In three short years, they added about 30 employees. Spread-sheeted carrier changes and inattentive management allowed annualized premiums to jump to over $1.1 million.

That story may sound extreme, but it happens. Contrasted with the small case, these examples demonstrate how powerful a mission-driven, blue ocean approach to your benefits can be. The potential return can increase exponentially as your business grows. If your competitors don't have the foresight to evaluate their benefits plans like you do, your sheer capital advantage may be significant even after a single year.

The first example, the story where the business owners boosted their bottom-line with a strategic benefits plan, is what happens when you take on the behaviors of a new innovative mindset. This business owner is critical of every aspect of their work and is willing to ask challenging questions of the benefits advisers courting them for business. When you engage potential advisers in a strategic business discussion, you quickly weed-out the advisers who simply do not have the expertise or insights to build the plan your business needs.

All hands on deck

Few businesses today, even ambitious start-ups, have a single sole decision maker. Entrepreneurs long ago recognized that one of the keys to success is surrounding yourself with smart, driven people, so even a small business of seven or nine employees will discuss major changes in strategy rather than relying on the instincts of any one person.

Managing multiple, simultaneous risks across an organization requires a strategy outline on how to execute and eliminate risk. By the time the business has the need for a dedicated chief financial officer (CFO) or a human resources director, each has a different job description, and turf wars may develop. A leader should be able to outline the mission and develop a collaborative environment to pull the best insights from multiple perspectives. The problem, however, is that without a mission or strategy, there is a tendency to create silos. Each specialist does their work in isolation, communicating with the other experts in the business only in limited capacities.

Granted, I understand having a benefits adviser talk to you about the dangers of corporate silos and the value of opening channels of communication across your organization can seem out of place at first. I mean, you expect your benefits adviser to talk to you about benefits, right?

If you want an adviser to come into your business and hock their line of benefits products, you can call up any insurance company. Those advisers are everywhere, big agencies with large blocks of fully insured business. If you want your business to rise above the status quo, you should find an adviser who rises above the status quo in his or her own work.

For my part, after a few decades in the industry, I have had the opportunity to work inside of hundreds of businesses from a wide range of industries. Through collaboration, study, and experience, I have developed solutions for and worked with businesses like yours and businesses much different from yours to attack many problems and challenges. This means you can get the advantages of cross-sectional insights from one source, applying the culmination of countless individual experiences to making your business more effective and more profitable.

You probably think about your key hires in this way as well. You may want experts that understand your industry, yes, but you also want individuals with varied experiences, so that they can think differently from your competitors, uncovering opportunities that people entrenched in the dogma of "how it's always been done" will not see. So, you go out of your way to hire the best and brightest for your business—internally as full-time employees and externally as consultants or advisers—and then what happens next? They don't ever talk to each other.

When it comes to employee benefits, the circumstances usually play out like this: the human resources director picks the most straightforward option on the table, usually from the adviser whom he or she likes the most. This is not a knock on the director. Human resources directors have a lot on their plates, and they often err on the side of a benefits plan that (they perceive) are easiest to implement. Human resources directors do not own the profit & loss statements, and they certainly are not thinking that a benefits plan can dramatically elevate the overall performance of a business. That's not their specific objective.

The CFO, however, does care about the profit & loss statement, but the CFO will rarely talk to the human resources director about the strategy behind a benefits plan. The line item keeps going up, but the CFO does not have the human resources knowledge to recognize that there is an opportunity there. As a result, benefits spend all too often becomes another operational expense. And the business owner, the entrepreneur steering the ship, well, he or she is racing toward the opportunity on the horizon and planning for a future, five or ten years away.

This is the status quo scenario. An average business-owner prospect won't even be involved in the benefits sales conversation. A generic adviser will ring up the HR department, talk nice, and woo his or her way into a close.

Adopt an innovative mindset. Find your blue ocean. Fix your auto-bailer. Stop spinning the 'wheel of misfortune' in employee benefits. Break down the silos. Get your decision makers and team leaders in a room with a knowledgeable adviser and have a frank conversation about what a benefits plan can mean for your business. There is simply too much money and opportunity on the table for your experts to work in isolation.

How to see benefits opportunities

You do not need to become a benefits adviser to see a benefits plan opportunity. Learning the ins and outs of a rapidly changing health-care landscape is a full-time job in itself, and you do not need to step away from the vision for your business to seize the advantages I have outlined. Bringing in an adviser is a lot like bringing in an engineer: you don't need to be an engineer to see a problem that could benefit from an engineered solution.

Here is a quick checklist that can help you identify a benefits opportunity in your business:

- Are you using self-funded or level funded plan?

- Is your plan different from your competitor's plans?
- Was your plan heavily customized to fit your unique needs?
- Does your benefits plan actively save you capital and help you retain key employees?
- Are you actively bucking the national trend of rising premiums and reduced coverage?
- When you implemented your benefits plan, did you incorporate the insights of multiple experts (CFO, HR, etc.)?
- Are your enrollment logistics using an electronic benefits platform with direct feeds that integrate with payroll and benefits (making enrollment changes near-instantaneous)?
- Does your benefits plan take an aggressive approach to prescription drugs?
- Does your benefits plan take an aggressive approach towards value based pricing for physicians and specialists?
- Does your benefits plan include a 24/7 concierge service?
- Does your benefits plan take advantage of a mobile app to deliver benefits information and service?

If you answered "no" to any of these questions, there is likely an opportunity in your business to transform how you handle and deliver employee benefits. These questions are accessible by design. You do not need to be an expert to recognize when you need one, and this simple checklist will give you a starting point for engaging benefits advisers. If your adviser cannot elaborate on how these questions might impact your bottom-line (and starts to steer you back toward the rocks of a classic benefits plan; the kind that every one of your boring, unimaginative competitors uses), bring in another adviser, one who can keep pace with your drive for breaking the status quo.

Short-sighted advisers and some mid-level managers will push a one-size-fits-all product because that's what's easiest for them, and the business-owner prospects who haven't committed to being better than the average will buy that generic product. An adviser who thinks like an entrepreneur will work with you to build a strategy for short-term *and* long-term wins that will truly make the difference in how you run your business. Find an adviser who can talk to you as a peer, someone who understands your goals as an entrepreneur, and can help you make smarter, strategic decisions.

Time to set sail

The intention of this chapter, from the very beginning, was to focus on the strategic opportunity hidden within your business. The nuances of an effective employee benefits plan are significant, but your role as an entrepreneur does not mandate that you become an expert in every aspect of your business. It's simply impossible. Any adviser can rattle off dozens of products features and benefits or push a benefits package across the table for you to sign. Product knowledge matters, but that's not what will deliver the business-changing solution we explored here.

A real solution comes from an adviser who is as passionate as you are about finding the open water, the blue ocean of opportunity. So, gather your team, reevaluate your benefits plan, and then start looking for an adviser who can help you put more of your capital back onto the table while delivering the kind of benefits experience that attracts and retains employees. That's what an innovative mindset can provide.

John Clay

President
BetterSource Benefits
Somerset, KY

John Clay is a business and insurance consultant with over 25 years of experience. John creates a unique strategic approach for each of his clients so they can achieve their business goals to drive more revenue to the bottom line while also giving them a meaningful competitive advantage. He has built BetterSource Benefits to deliver valuable solutions that solve critical business and HR problems.

John is a member of National Association of Health Underwriters (NAHU) as well as a former regional vice president of National Association of Insurance and Financial Advisors (NAIFA-Kentucky). He is also a Charter Member of the Association for Insurance Leadership and a member of University of Kentucky Alumni Association.

www.bettersourcebenefits.com
j.clay@bettersourcebenefits.com
606-678-0583

CHAPTER 5

SELF-FUNDING STRATEGIES & THE NEED FOR AN EXPERIENCED CONSULTANT

Paula Beersdorf

How many times have you as the CEO or CFO, sat down with your broker and insurance carrier representative and been delivered an unsustainable premium increase with the *only options suggested* being to either fund the unaffordable increase, strip benefits away from your employees and their families, or a combination of both? How many times has your broker told you your high claims are driving the premium increase, and the only remedy is for you to pay more in premium? When will your broker become your advocate and the insurance carrier become your partner and not your second or third highest paid vendor?

My firm, Sun Risk Management, has been advising clients in the self-funded arena for over 30 years. As many of the provisions of the Affordable Care Act (ACA) has made self-funding more attractive, there are more brokers advising their clients about self-funding, who have NO experience whatsoever—buyers beware! Even the large national consulting houses are less inclined to explore self-funding with clients.

There is a self-funding strategy for EVERY employer, as there are many different vehicles that may be used within the "alternate funding" world. The most important thing to keep in mind when you the employer, are making decisions is to be 100% confident that you have the most experienced and ethical CONSULTANT available, who has YOUR best interest in mind, and not theirs or anyone else's. Following is an outline of self-funding strategies we have used with our clients, with much success.

Design an employer-sponsored health reimbursement arrangement (HRA) under Internal Revenue code Section 105 plans

A simple self-funding strategy which can be used by employers of any size, what we like to call "self-funding on training wheels," is an employer sponsored Health Reimbursement Account (HRA). The requirements of an HRA are the plan must be funded solely by the employer and reimbursements must be for qualified medical expenses defined by IRS Code Section 213(d). There is no restriction (minimum or maximum) on the amount of money an employer can contribute, and the amount contributed is tax-deductible to the employer and non-taxable to the employee. Typically, an employer will fund an account with a specified dollar amount annually, and will allow the employee to access the funds to cover deductibles, coinsurance, co-payments and other expenses allowable by the IRS, but not necessarily covered by the fully insured health plan. The employer hires a third party to assist with administrative duties, such as plan documents, account balances, provide debit cards, and perform substantiation of claims made by members.

What most consultants do not advise their clients, is how much control an employer has when designing their HRA—you as the employer may restrict which medical plan expenses may be reimbursed under the plan, as a set dollar contribution is not required. An experienced consultant will present their client with an array of options, should that client not be in a position to partially self-fund their entire benefit program. For example, when an employer is fully insured—traditional arrangement where insurance company assumes all risk and employer pays a fixed premium—very few options are available at renewal time.

- **Option 1:** Remain with your current carrier with an increased premium.

- **Option 2:** Remain with current carrier and reduce benefits to members in exchange for lower premiums.

- **Option 3:** Choose a different carrier; pay less premium, with reduced benefits.

Option 4: None of the above—fight the status quo!!

Following is an excellent example of how my firm designed an HRA to assist a client with an unaffordable renewal—several years ago, a municipality client of ours with an extremely rich benefit plan due to its police and fire personnel's collective bargaining contracts ($0 deductible, very low out of pocket costs to members) was presented with a sizable premium increase.

One of the options to reduce costs presented by the insurance carrier was to impose a separate $250 copayment for radiology services such as MRI's and PET Scans—and the overall premium would be reduced by 5% or $45,000 annually. We advised the City to set up an HRA plan with the sole benefit being to reimburse covered employees, and their family members for the cost of the radiology copayment, if incurred.

Basically, the City was "self-insuring" the cost of this copayment, instead of paying a fixed premium to the insurance company *regardless of whether or not a member had an MRI*. The City saved $45,000 in premium, and paid out less than $4,000 in claims that first year, using this simplified HRA strategy—a win-win for everyone!

Another great use of the HRA plan design is to fund the higher deductible...

Level-funding or level-premium arrangements

Level-Funding is a form of self-insuring a benefit plan, but has the predictability of a fully insured plan, as these arrangements allow employers to pay a fixed dollar amount monthly. This method of self-insuring has become increasingly popular over the past several years, and is mainly available through national insurance carriers or Third Party

Administrators (TPA's).

Level-Funding is an excellent introduction of self-funding concepts and processes to employers who are looking to cut costs, but are not quite ready to go full steam into a partially self-funded plan. Employers pay a fixed monthly premium cost which is made up of essentially three components - administrative fee to carrier or TPA who will process the claims and provide access to a provider network, cost of reinsurance or stop loss which is made up of an individual deductible and aggregate coverage to insure the plan against catastrophic claims, and a pre-determined claims cost developed after the group has been underwritten.

The administrative fees and the cost of the reinsurance or stop loss, are known as the "Fixed Costs" and are not recoverable by the employer. The portion of the premium identified as the claims cost is the amount of money funding the claims as they are incurred and paid out on a monthly basis. At the end of the year, the overall experience of the plan is evaluated. If the group performed well—meaning there were less claims paid out than expected -the employer gets all or a portion of those dollars back, depending upon the agreement with the administrator. If the experience of the plan was not good, the excess claims were paid for by the reinsurance carrier and the employer should expect an increase in the fixed costs and projected claims costs for the following year.

The benefit of entering into a Level-Funded arrangement is that now, the employer has access to its claims and utilization data. Detailed reporting highlighting where members are spending healthcare dollars, and sometimes, more importantly, where they are under spending their dollars, i.e., preventive care or maintenance medications. With this kind of information now available, employers can fully customize their benefit plans to the needs of their members, and work to understand which cost containment efforts are viable and which are not.

It is very important for employers to choose an experienced consultant when evaluating Level-funded partners, in order to limit their financial exposure. Each insurance carrier and TPA offering this type of contract may work with several different stop loss carriers who offer differing contractual terms. The contractual terms on when and how the stop loss will reimburse the employer are VERY IMPORTANT, as this is the mechanism protecting the employer's cash flow and exposure.

You need to be completely confident that the stop loss deductible applied to each individual under the contract is affordable, should a catastrophic claim arise—because they will! You also need to make sure the stop loss carrier is financially sound, and we would recommend they have an A.M. Best rating of A or higher.

In addition, some carrier or TPA contracts may require that they retain a share of the claims fund in a good year, which cuts into the employer's savings. Many TPA or carriers expect to share in the claims surplus at rates of 30% or more—so be sure you understand what the contract or carrier requires. If you have a good claims year, you should retain ALL of the surpluses.

Lastly, should the employer decide the level-funding option is not the right fit for them, or they want to change to a different TPA or insurance carrier, it is essential they are aware of the termination provisions. A few questions to ask—Does the surplus get returned if the contract is not renewed? How long is the "run-out" provision? Meaning if a loss is presented a year or two later, which occurred when the plan was operating—are you protected under your stop loss contract? This can happen, especially in the case of Medicare secondary payer rules, and one of our clients has experienced it, but they were protected because they had an experienced consultant who had the right contract in place.

Group employee benefit captives

A captive insurer is generally defined as an insurance company that is wholly owned and controlled by its insured; its primary purpose is to insure the risks of its owners, and its insured's benefit from the captive insurer's underwriting profits. Captives have been used broadly and for many years within the property and casualty insurance arena to manage predictable property and liability risks, such as worker's compensation or malpractice. Due to rising health insurance costs, employee benefit captives have become increasingly popular within the last few years.

The main function of the employee benefit captive is to insure a layer of risk by ceding premium into the first risk layer, for example, on claims between $25,000 and $250,000. By retaining the premiums that would have been paid to a traditional carrier, and the risk associated with those premium — the employers have a potential to retain any profits should the losses be less than the ceded premium. Any losses over $250,000 would be paid through traditional stop loss coverage.

There are several reasons a mid-size employer (50 employees or more) might consider joining an employee benefit group captive. A group captive enables an employer who would otherwise remain fully insured, the opportunity to consider a partially self-funded plan, as they would be sharing a portion of risk with other like-minded employers. Since the captive assumes the risk of a larger and more diverse group, made up of several employers, the risk becomes more predictable than if that 50 employee size group were on their own.

In most cases, each employer has control over their own health plan, may choose their own third party administrator, and may set their internal stop-loss deductible levels. In addition, what we have found is that employers within a captive must collaborate with each other to manage the captive, and that collaboration breeds best in class cost containment and risk management practices.

Partially self-funded health plan

A "partially" self-funded plan means there is some form of insurance covering a specified risk — a policy that stops your losses. The employer assumes the direct risk for claims incurred and purchases reinsurance, also known as stop-loss insurance, to protect against unpredictable losses or high-dollar claims for diseases like cancer. A major difference between conventional fully insured plans and partially self-funded plans is that the stop loss insures the employer — not the member.

There are essentially two types of stop loss insurance — specific and aggregate.

Specific deductible stop-loss provides protection for the employer against a high dollar claim <u>per individual</u> covered under the plan. This protects the employer from catastrophic claims like cancer or multiple sclerosis for a single member, and the insurance carrier reimburses the employer throughout the contract year, once a member exceeds the deductible level.

Aggregate stop-loss provides an overall maximum claims liability or ceiling, on the amount of claims the employer is responsible for, within the entire contract year. The carrier will reimburse the employer after the end of the contract period for claims that exceeded the ceiling. As described above — contract terms in a stop-loss arrangement are very important as is the stability and experience of the stop-loss carrier. There are various contract term lengths and provisions you must understand — or for which you will need an EXPERIENCED consultant — to navigate in the stop-loss world.

There are many benefits — financial and otherwise — when comparing self-insuring a health plan to being fully insured with a large insurance carrier:

- Employers may design their benefit offerings to meet the needs of their members as opposed to purchasing a plan offered by the insurance carrier.
- Employers are not subject to state health regulations or benefit mandates, as self-insured plans are regulated under federal law (ERISA). This is especially beneficial to employers who have members across multiple states.
- Employers are not subject to state premium taxes, which can be as high as 2 to 3% of your overall fully insured premium.
- Employers maintain control over cash flow, only funding claims, as they are incurred, allowing for the accumulation of reserves, which can be invested or earning interest.
- Employers have the ability to choose who they work with — vendors for claims administration, pharmacy benefit managers, medical providers, etc., and may change those arrangements, as their needs or workforce changes.

In summary, partially self-funding a health plan provides employers with TRANSPARENCY in all aspects of managing their plan. Self-funding provides the employer with complete control over the way their health care dollars are spent. They may be proactive when they understand how their population is utilizing their benefit plan, and can react almost immediately when they see the need for improvement. Employers who partially self-fund their benefit plans no longer dread the delivery of the renewal of their fully insured plan—and their plans are experiencing below trend increases, or in some cases, decrease in spending.

Paula J. Beersdorf

President
Sun Risk Management, Inc.
St. Petersburg, FL

Paula J. Beersdorf is the President of Sun Risk Management, Inc.—a strategic business and employee benefits consultancy. Her mission is to provide meaningful guidance and assistance to help employers achieve their benefits and business goals.

Having worked with Millard G. Gamble for 25 years, Paula has developed a rich expertise in helping clients maintain control through self-funding strategies. As a member of the exclusive Agency Growth Mastermind Partnership, Paula stays on the forefront of the latest trends, technology, tools, and tactics for her clients.

www.sunriskinc.com
paulab@sunriskinc.com
727-367-3231

CHAPTER 6

DIRECT CONTRACTING WITH VALUE-DRIVEN HOSPITALS

Jeffrey D. Fox

Direct contracting with providers is an idea that is well overdue in the benefits world. The Preferred Provider Organization (PPO) networks are a shell of the original concept, which has been bastardized by a series of developments over the years and the result is a sham.

PPOs once were a good idea. The concept that an employer will steer their member's medical services to a particular provider(s) in exchange for greater discounts is sound. Successful "preferred seller" arrangements exist in many forms in our economy, but not in healthcare.

Why don't they exist in healthcare? Employees exert pressure on their Human Resource managers to make certain a particular provider is included. The term "Disruption Analysis" became a common term and eventually a PPO was measured on *how many* providers were included. As providers realized that their market traffic wasn't going to increase, the negotiated "discounts" were soon watered down.

The result? Employers do not benefit by *participating* in a network. Instead, they are penalized by NOT being in a network. The employer's net cost actually increased. The "discounts" are hyped percentages off a billed charge arising from the hospital's "chargemaster," which bears little relationship to the procedures performed, services rendered, or cost of service. On top of that, the employer was charged an access fee to the PPO. A terrible way to conduct business.

I entered the Direct Contracting business by virtue of my working relationship / friendship with Gary Everling, Executive Director, Business Development at Hendricks Regional Health (HRH), in Hendricks County, Indiana. Several years ago, when Gary was at a larger hospital system, we put together a direct contract for a local school system. We received best in class discounts in exchange for steerage to that provider. Nothing too fancy yet it served my client well.

After Gary transferred to Hendricks Regional Health, on the outskirts of Indianapolis, we met for lunch. We asked each other why we couldn't take our experience with direct contracting and apply it to some of my local clients in the Hendricks County area. Specifically, we targeted Hendricks County Government and the Town of Plainfield.

HRH has always been considered progressive, the services are well regarded by residents, and the facility is modern. Generally, it's well respected, an easy sell to patients, employees and employers.

We compared charges from the Centers for Medicare & Medicaid Services (CMS) for a selection of standard procedures from several providers in the Indianapolis area. These are the providers from which a Hendricks County claimant likely would choose for their medical care. We then compared each provider's total for all procedures against the average for all providers.

Hendricks Regional Health's cost was 35% below average while many of their competitor's charges were up to 30% higher than average. Shown to the public, it's an easy sell. If you are paying for a C-Section, would you prefer your member utilize HRH, or the hospital at 30% above average? Now integrate this into a medical plan design, and the savings will begin.

In addition to the natural savings element we urged HRH to implement Reference Based Reimbursement (RBP) into this network. Employers dislike the idea of basing their reimbursement on a discount off an unknown value, which only will be revealed weeks after the procedure has been performed. A common-sense person knows the cost of a service BEFORE it is performed. To ask a buyer to do otherwise is ludicrous. Right? Well, it happens in healthcare every day.

While RBP is a fairly new concept in healthcare, we felt it would resonate with employers opting for this network. It wasn't a matter of bankrupting the hospital, but rather showing good faith in their reimbursement program. RBP utilizes recognized industry sources, such as Medicare reimbursement rates, as the reference benchmark. Set the reimbursement at a percentage above Medicare, at a level that meets the provider's income needs, but do so in a system that was transparent like RBP.

We felt that a governmental entity would not be willing to mandate this network to their employees. So instead we made it an optional choice for employees at enrollment. Hendricks County Government offers a Traditional and High Deductible Health Plan/ HSA plan to their employees. We continued both offerings within the HRH Network and the Open Access Network. So now employees had four options:

1. Open Access Network — Traditional Plan
2. Open Access Network — HDHP/HSA
3. HRH Network — Traditional Plan
4. HRH Network — HDHP/HSA

Both Traditional and both HDHP/HSA plans were identical regardless of which network option was chosen. The difference was in the employee contribution levels. Looking at the options above, the plans became progressively less expensive from 1 to 4. In our initial year, we increased the Open Access Rates slightly while significantly reducing the contributions below current in the HRH Network options.

We implemented the program in 2015. It was a win-win-win proposition. The Provider's traffic increased. The Employer's cost decreased. The Employee's take-home pay increased.

The enrollment results were as follows:

	2014	2015		2016		2017	
		HRH	Open	HRH	Open	HRH	Open
EE	130	85	42	103	41	124	46
EC	93	55	36	67	26	109	32
ES	83	65	20	63	20	49	13
FAM	89	74	19	76	17	37	7
Total	395	279	117	309	104	319	98
% of TTL		70%	30%	75%	25%	76%	24%

The enrollment meeting went well and the HRH Network was well accepted. HRH was already the provider of choice within Hendricks County so the transition would be easier for them. For others, the cost savings was enough to warrant a change in providers. Others weren't willing or were unable to alter their current level of care through their Non-HRH provider so they opted for the Open Access Option.

We fully explained that for those opting for the HRH Network would need to utilize HRH or suffer Out-of-Network benefits. This applied to any procedure that was available through HRH.

We allowed a transition period for employees who were in the middle of treatment. This was available for a limited time and for those who couldn't accept this, we suggested they remain in the Open Access Network.

For services unavailable at HRH, it is mandatory the patient contact the Referral Advocate at HRH. Self-referrals did not take the place of the Advocate and would result in Out-of-Network benefits. Certain procedures can't and aren't provided at HRH. For those acute situations, the Advocate will assist in the referral to the appropriate facility.

We since learned the importance of the advocate. HRH employed an RN for just this purpose and it has generated goodwill beyond our original expectations. The Advocate assists patients on a variety of services and can soft-transfer the patient to the Third Party Administrator (TPA) if there are benefit questions or issues to resolve. Patients love the service.

Hendricks County Government's medical claims have significantly reduced as a result of the HRH network. Comparing the three years prior to HRH Network implementation to the 2 ½ years post implementation shows significant results:

	2012	2013	2014	2015	2016	2017 (through July)
Medical claims	$4,289,421	$4,344,947	$5,471,753	$3,778,507	$4,125,572	$2,089,948
EE Count	399	395	394	398	406	415
PEPM	$895.87	$916.66	$1,157.31	$791.14	$846.79	$719.43

Average 2012-2014	Average 2015-2017
$989.94	$785.79

% Reduction
20.6%

A 20+% reduction!!!

Hendricks Regional Health is pleased with the result. From a community relations standpoint, it has achieved their goal. In addition, the traffic to HRH has increased.

The two-year average (2013 & 2014) prior to implementation of the HRH Network, Hendricks County Government plan members used HRH facilities 37.2% relative to other providers. In 2015 they utilized HRH facilities 56.1% when considering both network options. The HRH Network members utilized HRH Facilities 75.9%. In 2016 the total HRH utilization was 61.1% while the HRH Network members averaged 71.3%.

A huge success: Enrollment in the HRH Network plan increasing each year, leading to greater usage of HRH Facilities, leading to lower relative costs for the Hendricks County Plan.

A year later, on January 1, 2016 we implemented the HRH Network Option at the Town of Plainfield, located in Hendricks County. 63% of the employees chose the HRH Network option. When considering the lag in health care expenses, we have less than a year's experience to view. Compared to the average of the three years prior to implementation (2013, 2014 & 2015), our claims per employee per month is down 1.7%.

HRH administrators began spreading the word throughout the Hendricks County area. An official for one of the business coalitions asked if this network could be made available to other smaller businesses within Hendricks County. Beth Cisco, Business Development and Strategic Marketing at HRH, approached me about the possibility.

Beth and I went to work. We approached Unified Group Services (UGS) the TPA with whom I've partnered on most of my benefit plans.

Through this partnership, we bring a partially self-funded offering that utilizes the HRH Network and the inherent savings.

It's an easy story to tell. Even before the program was officially introduced to the community, I was approached by Washington Township in Avon, Indiana. With 67 employees on their plan, they had been notified that their fully insured plan would no longer be offered. As a result, they had to move a month earlier than their original renewal date.

We showed them the Hospital Cost comparison that was mentioned earlier and told them, forget "insurance." Where would you want a C-Section done? At Hendricks Regional for 35% *below* average cost, or at one of the inner-city hospitals for up to 30% *above* average?

Washington Township was already in discussions with HRH regarding a near-site medical clinic. HRH currently provides clinic management to Hendricks County Government. Washington Township, with only 67 employees, is too small to fund a clinic on their own.

As a part of the HRH Network, employers will be given access to the HRH clinics. Currently HRH manages six clinics for specific employers. They hope to merge all clinics and allow members from any of the employers on the plan access to all of the clinic locations.

Washington Township, on September 1, 2017, was officially our first client aboard the **HRH Network Partnership**. While we offered the HRH Network as an "option" at Hendricks County and Town of Plainfield, we are offering only the HRH Network to these smaller employers. Drawing a 30-mile radius from the employer's location, any employee outside the 30-mile radius will be allowed to use a non-HRH provider and still enjoy in-network benefits.

We are in the planning stages of hosting a breakfast meeting for about 20 Hendricks County employers where we will introduce the program. We believe we'll have a great turnout and significant interest.

Hendricks Regional Health is a truly remarkable group of people. They are ahead of their time in planning for the future. I've had many conversations with associates in the benefits community who have tried unsuccessfully to partner with other hospital providers in offering such a program.

Many hospital administrators get bogged down in the process and overthink the program. I also believe they've grown so accustomed to the "just build it and they will come" mentality that they can't visualize the marketing end of this product.

A direct-contract network is a product that is desired by employers. Assembling a network comprised of providers that provide great value as opposed to one just containing every provider, regardless of value equation, will be a welcomed sight. One whose time is now.

Obviously, not every hospital system is the right candidate for such a program. Those with exorbitant costs are not good value. While these providers may be necessary for acute situations, the normal, everyday procedures can be provided at a much better value elsewhere. These procedures can be provided at Hendricks Regional Health at a far lower cost, successfully, and therefore are a much greater value.

I've already started the conversation with another hospital, very similar to Hendricks Regional Health. In the spirit of cooperation, Gary Everling of HRH accompanied me on one of my visits with them. He told of the success he's witnessed in Hendricks County.

Working with another client, we've approached one of the larger facilities within Indianapolis with the hope of designing a single direct contract with them.

The time for this concept is near. While not a concept that every employer will welcome, it's a concept that many employers will take notice of and will implement.

Does a direct-contract program inconvenience an employer's plan members? Yes. Consider, though, how many of us drive 30 minutes or more to shop, to dine at a restaurant, to visit friends, to attend a sporting event, etc. While we haven't wrapped our minds around traveling this same distance for medical care, we often do.

Why can't we wrap our minds around a network that causes us to drive 30 minutes or more for a procedure? Employers will force the issue as their costs continue to increase. Employers will force the issue when they are approached by a provider who can deliver 20% cost savings on an expense that adds $10,000 to $18,000 per employee per year to their bottom line.

Employers may not be ready to force a 30-minute or more drive yet, but many are ready to incentivize care within their smaller communities to providers that offer greater value. The time for this is **NOW**.

The natural evolution to the 30-minute or more medical commute will be soon. Sooner than many providers understand or want to admit.

Jeffrey D. Fox

Principal & Benefits Practice Leader
HJ Spier
Indianapolis, IN

Jeff Fox has been in benefit consulting for over 30 years. For the majority of his career, he has been in sales/consulting with three different prominent Third Party Administrators. Because he has dedicated himself to the TPA marketplace, he has a keen understanding of self-funding and the inherent ability to manage plan assets. In 2003, Jeff joined HJ Spier Co., Inc. as their lead employee benefits consultant and since has become a principal in the firm.

Jeff enjoys a very loyal customer base, due in large part to his personal attention to their needs. Through Jeff, his clients are presented with fresh and creative ways to manage their plan costs. He is aware of the ever-changing marketplace and will not hesitate to introduce new concepts and ideas that enable his clients to offer a competitive, yet affordable benefits package.

Jeff creates a partnership with his clients and strives to become a trusted member of their benefits team. He hopes to create an environment of trust and respect, where his clients have his counsel on a regular basis to help them reach their goals.

www.hjspier.com
jfox@hjspier.com
317-815-2812

CHAPTER 7

THE BEST DEFENSE
IS A GOOD OFFENSE

*Proactive Strategies & Solutions
to Serve Your Employees
& Organization*

Felipe Barganier

One of the most important things that most employers could do to drive down cost is to have a consultant that takes a proactive approach to their employee benefits plan. Too often, I have met with prospects that have benefits plans that aren't reflective of the demographics or future demographics of their employee base. This could save many companies tens of thousands and in many instances, millions of dollars annually, in not only health insurance costs but also in decreased employee absenteeism, increased employee retention, and in attracting quality employees. The following pages will focus on what I call "future proofing" your employee benefits program.

Every year, there are more and more companies touting the next great thing for employees and employers, and it is my responsibility to my clients and their employees to stay on top of industry trends and the latest products that can benefit my clients. Our firm believes that, in order for us to do what is best for our clients, we must always think about what our clients' short term, mid-term, and long-term goals are. In taking this approach, we are able to analyze the various products and services that are available. When a client puts the current and future needs of its employees as a priority, it will always have a workforce with high morale and low turnover.

Let's examine the impact of a company implementing a health wellness program over time. A properly implemented wellness program cannot only help lower catastrophic claims, but it also can help increase the productivity and longevity of its workforce. I have a 14-year client with 12,000 employees. When I first began working with them, the rage was wellness attached to voluntary benefits plans. These products were your cancer, accident, critical illness plans, etc. that had benefits that would pay the employee anywhere from $25.00 to $125.00 per year for having various tests done as part of their normal physicals. This program gave the employee a financial incentive to get annual checkups that they may have otherwise skipped. These were great benefits when the employer allowed the employees to receive regular communication regarding them.

When we begin offering these plans to this particular client's employees, we were heavy on educating the employees on the true value of the wellness benefit to employees' overall health. Having personally lost a loved one to stage 4-lung cancer, I know how precious and important early detection is, as it relates to cancer survival. We had employees that typically wouldn't buy a cancer plan who were now buying the plan because they saw the immediate value in its annual wellness payments, but had no idea how it would end up helping them years later. One employee, in particular, had begrudgingly purchased a family cancer plan with wellness when we first started offering them, and a few years later her spouse was diagnosed with cancer at stage 1 during his annual wellness checkup. His wife told one of our counselors that had it not been for the $100.00 he received for the test, he probably would have never gone to get the checkup.

Now, initially, you may realize that this wellness incentive helped save his life, but if you dive deeper, you will realize it did much more. One, it potentially saved the employer tens of thousands, if not hundreds of thousands of dollars in cancer treatment costs, because the cost to treat it early is much less than at stage 4. Numerous studies have been conducted regarding various cancers and the drastic difference in costs from stage 0 to stage 4. The primary driver being the cost of chemotherapy and non-cancer treatments at the various stages.

Secondly, the employee was able to miss less time from work because the cancer was detected early enough that the treatments didn't cost either her or her spouse a significant amount of time from work. Thirdly, the employee now views the benefit as being tied to her employer, which in turn, created a sense of gratitude for her employer allowing her to have access to a benefit that potentially saved her husband's life. As you can see, just offering this one benefit with wellness to their employees allowed our client to save several hundred thousand dollars over the last decade. Additionally, the employee tells the story to everyone; what do you think that does to employee perception about the company's benefits program?! Finally, this program has likely saved the client several million dollars over the last decade in health and various costs. These benefits have now morphed into standalone offerings that go much deeper into the employees' lives and are more impactful to their overall physical, mental, and emotional well-being.

The emergence of wellness plans that now reward employees for healthy eating, utilizing health clubs, starting active, etc. has the potential to lower the overall costs of healthcare for many employers. We have a number of clients that have experienced significant savings on their renewals by simply having a robust active wellness program. One of our clients, in particular, was experiencing a surge in employees on maintenance drugs and treatments for diabetes, high blood pressure, etc. and was desperate to find a way to reduce the cost of the drugs that the employees were using. We suggested that in addition to carving out the prescription drug program, that they also implement a wellness program centered around reducing obesity and promoting healthy lifestyles. The client implemented Wellness Wednesdays centered around healthy eating, and Fitness Fridays which consisted of employees using the stairs instead of elevators, and weekly weigh ins utilizing a team accountability approach. After 18 months, the employer realized a 10% reduction in its overall health care costs, decreased absenteeism, and a more upbeat office. The company realized that a properly implemented wellness program pays off in more ways than expected.

In addition to wellness, there a number of other solutions that can create meaningful intangible results. One has been the introduction of prepaid legal services as an employee benefit. This particular product initially didn't seem like one that would yield a significant result on the overall mental health of employees. However, once you realize that everything that bothers an employee at home can impede productivity at work, it's easy to understand you why this solution is in high demand for many employees. From bankruptcies to divorces to traffic citations, these products allow your employees to have legal representation and advice for a fraction of what it would cost to retain an attorney otherwise.

As part of our overall wellness strategy, we look at the socioeconomic backgrounds of the workforce and craft a 3 to 5-year plan that will result in a better, more productive workforce and lower overall health costs.

Another underutilized service that can help decrease employee absenteeism and decrease health plan abuse is telemedicine. In my opinion, every employer should offer telemedicine as an employer paid benefit. When properly communicated to an employee population, this product will produce significant savings to the employee and employer by eliminating unnecessary emergency room visits and the costs incurred. Besides direct costs, telemedicine can save the employee time missed from work and increase productivity due to the employee being able to get prescriptions filled without having to go to their primary care physician. The employers that have experienced the most success seen success have placed dedicated phones in their offices to encourage employee participation.

Last, but not least, the most important thing an employer can do to protect their employees' future for their family is to offer life insurance. It is estimated that a whopping 38% of Americans don't have life insurance and that as many as 70% don't have adequate coverage. You may ask how is this a part of a discussion regarding being offensive and not defensive. Well, in many cases, employers are offering plans that are only good while the employee is employed up to a certain age, and then the benefit decreases.

Numerous times employees have told me they would never have

purchased life insurance had it not been for their employer offering it via payroll deduction. People hate to think about death, but that is the most certain thing in life. In addition to that, employees typically don't think about the need for life insurance until they are older, which is also when they are at an increased risk of having health issues. Employees should always have access to some sort of permanent insurance solution that has a guaranteed issue provision in it. Without this protection, they often would find themselves having to purchase inferior and expensive solutions on the individual market. The employer is able to help an employee leave a legacy that they probably wouldn't have been able to, and guess what the employee's family remembers: that their loved one's employer offered excellent benefits that allowed them to leave a meaningful legacy

As you can see from the aforementioned examples, there are a lot of things that typically would not be thought of when considering benefits, unless addressed by your adviser. Our firm works in an advisory capacity with our clients and their employees, to make sure that the benefits that our clients offer their employees are in line with what their competitors are offering. However, we also implement programs that most of their competitors aren't even aware of, for various reasons, often making our clients the "employer of choice" in a certain industry.

Employees entering the marketplace today are driven by technology and apps. Just as important as the plan you offer is how the employee is able to interact with the plan and utilize it. There's a plethora of technology solutions available to allow the employee a better open enrollment and ongoing experience, but only a few are what I would consider game-changing. Just like the internet and other technological advances have changed the way people shop and interact with each other, the same can be said for employee benefits. Your benefits plan and the way it is administered should be reflective of the 21st-century world in which we live.

In today's job market, it is vitally important that you offer a benefits package that is reflective of the talent you have, and effectively attracts the talent you want. Failure to understand the current and future needs of your employees can cause you to lose a valued employee over the lack of something that your competitor down the street offers. You should always view the benefits you offer as a part of the employees' overall compensation package. Thus, it's imperative that the comprehensive benefits program you create not merely be developed defensively, but rather designed and implemented proactively to best serve your employees and your organization.

Felipe Barganier

CEO
GAB International LLC
Atlanta, GA

Felipe Barganier is the founder of Atlanta-based GAB International LLC. After 15 years in the financial services and insurance industry, he started the firm as a direct result of seeing that there was a need in the insurance industry to not just sell insurance to groups and individuals but to help employers and employees make more informed decisions and help them contain cost.

GAB International is rapidly expanding and is a fast-growing brand in the large group market and currently is expanding nationally as its reputation for excellence and value within Georgia has garnered Felipe national recognition.

Felipe was recognized recently as one of the top five employee benefit advisers in the country as a finalist for 2017 Broker of the Year in *BenefitsPro* magazine. He was also honored as a 2016 award recipient for GMBA Insurance Industry of the Year for the state of Georgia and in 2017 was featured in *Who's Who in Atlanta*.

www.gabint.com
fbarganier@gabint.com
404-965-3538

CHAPTER 8

OPEN ENROLLMENT IS YOUR ALLY

Allison De Paoli

As an employer, you work incredibly hard to deliver a great benefits package at an appropriate cost. Your employees want the same for themselves and their families—great benefits at an appropriate cost. Let's talk about how you can help them understand and appreciate the value of what you offer.

This year (2017), the Society for Human Resources Professionals top concern is recruiting top notch employees and keeping them.

Why is it important?

There is a significant amount of research that illustrates how employees understand (or don't understand) their benefits, how employers feel about communicating them and the effects of this dynamic.

- Only 7% of employees understood each of the following basic concepts: healthcare premium, health plan deductible, out of pocket maximum, co-insurance (United Healthcare's 2016 Consumer Health Study)
- Most employees (65%) can't afford an unexpected $1,000 expense according to multiple studies, including The 2017 Aflac Workforces Report.
- 73% of employees agree that Employers have a responsibility for the health and well-being of their employees. Likewise, 82% of employers agree (Met Life's 15th Annual US Employee Benefits Trends Study).

Met Life's study goes on to illustrate that *employers are increasingly aware that a rich benefits package increases employee satisfaction, productivity, loyalty and helps attract employees.*

Offering a robust open enrollment—and full year communication strategy—allows you to:

- Educate your employees on how to use their plan most effectively—helping you save plan resources and reduce out of pocket costs for them.
- Demonstrate to your employees what non-insurance resources are available—helping you save plan resources.
- Show your employees that you value them—helping you reduce turnover and foster positive employee morale.

What to do?

Open enrollment doesn't happen in a vacuum. Most employers don't plan the enrollment process; it is simply something that gets done in some form before the renewal date. Employee Benefit Adviser (EBA) magazine's latest study shows that benefits enrollment preparations are at a standstill, even for employers who are renewing their plans in the 2nd and 3rd quarters of the year! This is the time to begin data analysis of claims/benefits usage to look for new trends, reviewing last year's open enrollment process and surveying employees for what they would like to see coming up.

Let me show you a few ways to make open enrollment better — for your budget, your employees, and your HR staff.

Open enrollment doesn't happen only once a year.

I had a wonderful boss a few years before starting my own firm who gave me great insight into how to communicate new ideas, The Rule of Eights. At the time, I was managing a new product line for our company that had a radically new, different set of processes to execute. I spent a significant amount of time explaining new procedures to seasoned professionals used to managing projects their own way. I am not a patient person and expressed some frustration about my colleagues not following the new guidelines.

The rule was that I had to explain something eight times. If, on the 8th try, the new procedures were not followed, I could complain. It was an effective lesson. Most of my colleagues adapted to the new processes slightly before I reached my eighth at bat. I still use this method today when explaining new concepts.

Open enrollment is similar. Even if you've made no changes to your plan; there are new ways to manage an old concept and employees need time to learn.

The best time to start thinking about the next open enrollment is right after the last one closes. If you've just wrapped up another chaotic and ineffective open enrollment, you probably feel like you never want to do that again! I used to be wiped out - just in time to celebrate the holidays with my family. And then I didn't want to think about open enrollments again for as long as possible.

As much as you might feel the same way, let's take this opportunity to reach another outcome.

Right after open enrollment is a great time to survey employees about the benefits plan. You might use Survey Monkey, Typeform or another no or low-cost tool to reach your employees about other issues. Any of these tools will serve you well here.

Sample questions might include:

- If you changed your medical plan, why did you change? What prompted the change to the new plan? How do you feel about the changes?
- Do they have everything they need—cards, certificates, contact information for carrier partners?
- Are there any benefits they would like to see next year?
- Standard "what worked well" and "what didn't work well" questions for the open enrollment process from both a communication and execution perspective.

The data you collect will give you a benchmark for what people understand and what you want to focus on at the next open enrollment. This survey information can be added to the planning process for next open enrollment. I would encourage you to use this information to create an ongoing communication strategy throughout the year to increase the knowledge base. Don't wait for next year!

Surveying right after open enrollment allows you to address any pressing issues as well as reinforce any new plans. Employees increasingly rely on their employer for benefits *and* financial tools (The Guardian Workplace Benefits Study). A simply designed, ongoing communication strategy can increase employee engagement, combat some financial "ill-health" issues and make your employee feel more valued. The best news here is that this is simple to set up and can be automated, reducing the time requirement of already stretched HR staff.

This is a perfect time to hold a contest about any changes you want to make sure everyone understands. There are some great new tools to send a quick quiz to everyone (five questions or less), track the results and then award a prize.

For example, if you have just added telehealth or a direct primary care component to your plans, communication throughout the plan year will help increase engagement in these new options.

Freshbenies, a provider of non-insurance services, has a client (400 lives) that prioritized telehealth services as part of their self-funded medical plan. Over 4 years, they had over 1,000 telehealth visits, saving their employees office visit, urgent care, and employee copays. The net savings to the plan itself was over $600,000.

A significant number of employees do not feel current benefit communication strategies are effective. The old plan of (maybe) a meeting, a benefit guide and turn in a paper form (or make your elections online, on your own) isn't working for most people.

In addition, both employers (66%) and employees (23%) agree that employees are less productive at work when they are worried about personal financial problems (MetLife).

The Society of Human Resource Managers (SHRM), discusses open enrollment challenges regularly. Only 7% of HR leaders are achieving their benefit plan metrics for employee engagement and benefit satisfaction. Their key finding is that employers who use data analytics report 14% higher engagement scores than those that do not. You don't need to fall into this huge group. You can easily set yourself apart using the tools discussed here.

With the data you collected right after open enrollment and are collecting throughout the year, a simple plan can be created and set up in an hour or so, and then delivered throughout the year.

For the first time in 2017, at the Society for Human Resources Professionals annual conference, the top concern was recruiting top notch employees and keeping them — not healthcare costs. Recruiting and retaining was the reason that one-third of employers expanded their benefits package this past year.

Given that it can cost 150% to 200% of an employee's salary to replace him (How Much Does Employee Turnover Really Cost? Jack Altman CEO of Lattice, Huffington Post, Jan. 19, 2017), it makes sense to spend a little time throughout the year to help him feel more valued.

Gearing up for open enrollment

The financial decisions for the new plan year are typically happening with the involvement of the CFO and even the CEO. Appropriately for any company, budget is the top priority usually followed closely by what is considered best for the employee.

Make a few key open enrollment decisions now, and you won't be scrambling later:

- Tentative dates for open enrollment
- What is the goal of open enrollment? Is there a financial incentive to drive employees to or from a plan?

- Are you adding a new concept like Direct Primary Care, telehealth, medical advocacy or a more structured Rx program?

While the C-Suite is working on the financial aspect of the benefits, HR can be working on the plan design and execution areas of the project:

- Who will be communicating new concepts like telehealth, Direct Primary Care, medical advocacy or a more structured RX plan?
    - o   Your staff, your insurance broker's staff, an outside enrollment firm?
    - o   Is this the year you have one on one meetings or do you have an active online only enrollment? What about a call center or email chat?
- Are you satisfied with your current enrollment partner?
    - o   If yes, let them know as soon as possible what your enrollment goals and timeline are.
    - o   If no, begin vetting new partners immediately.
- What is the timeline for delivery of information to your enrollment partner? Who is responsible, you or your broker?
- When does information need to be delivered to carrier partners? Do you manage your own reporting or will this service be contracted out?

The HR team can also be preparing employees for what is coming. We have all heard the expression that "nobody cares how much you know, until they know how much you care." This applies particularly to Millennials who are changing the way we conduct all aspects of our businesses. While their risk tolerance is quite like "The Greatest

Generation," how they like to be communicated to is vastly different.

Take a moment; let people know what is coming. Using some inexpensive (or free) communication tools, it is possible to be ahead of any news regarding benefits for the upcoming year.

- Are you adding an often-requested benefit?
- Are you changing plans?
- Have you had a great claims year, and there is no increase in the employee contribution?

Get the word out!

All generations like diversity of benefits, and will seek out those that suit their needs best, even if they are funding some plans with their own dollars. Don't think that because you have a limited budget, you can't offer a rich and diverse benefits plan to your employees.

SunLife Financial's research indicates that most employees prefer some type of learning- assistance regarding their benefits. Those that received this assistance increased their participation in employer paid, employer-contributed, as well as employee-paid benefits.

Execute, Execute, Execute

Open enrollment is often a chaotic time for HR staff. If you have a solid plan in place, it will be busy, but it doesn't have to be unmanageable.

If you have followed your original timeline, all the heavy lifting has been done, and this can be a time for your HR staff to engage with your employees in a more fun and less stressed out manner.

It is also a perfect opportunity to take advantage of the Rule of Eights! If your employees are going to a meeting, have some sort of personal follow up (one on one, call center, email chat) and must acknowledge their elections, they are well on their way to better understanding of what they have and how to use it.

The "new" open enrollment wrap up

It is finished!

The meetings were well received; each employee is enrolled with a fuller understanding of how their benefits work together, stragglers have been accounted for. Employees have had time to have a neutral party answer their questions.

Since the timeline was followed, all the data have been transmitted to carriers on schedule.

This open enrollment, HR staff have been busy, but not unduly stressed.

Carriers have time to load employees into systems before the effective date, so the "I am not in the system, and I need to go to the hospital" problem has been avoided.

There is also time to audit thoroughly. I know everyone hates this part! However, one complete audit of the first series of invoices can catch any errors or duplications. And this should absolutely be completed by the employer, not outsourced to the broker. Most of these items are easy to correct if caught early. If you don't audit or if you audit in six months' time, most of these minor adjustments cause a large headache, wasting your HR staff's already limited time.

You've learned how (and why) to survey your employees to gauge understanding, communicate with them throughout the year, and deliver a timely enrollment.

All that is left is to set up the communications plan for next year and toast to your success.

Allison De Paoli

President
De Paoli Professional Services
San Antonio, TX

Allison founded De Paoli Professional Services in 2015 to provide outstanding enrollment communication solutions to small and midsize businesses by utilizing best in class technology alongside best in class people to help ensure that employees receive information in the best manner for them.

De Paoli began her insurance career in the Greater Washington DC area and shortly thereafter moved to Florida to work in the family benefits business as Vice President of Operations. After moving to San Antonio in 2000, she began working as an Aflac associate quickly becoming a top 1% sales producer.

After a successful career as an associate and producer, Allison decided to put her knowledge and expertise to work with her own firm, De Paoli Professional Services, allowing her to deliver first class enhanced benefits as well as effective enrollment, implementation and communication strategies.

www.depaoliprofservices.com
acdepaoli@depaoliprofservices.com
210-617-3086

CHAPTER 9

LESSONS LEARNED

*The Power of Leveraging
Data the Right Way*

Robert Gearhart, Jr.

E verything I thought I knew about being a Benefits Consultant changed forever in a meeting with the executive team from a large window manufacturer employing 2,000 people across five states. We had conducted biometric screenings for four years, put wellness coaches in every facility, and were weighing building a primary care clinic for employees. After a 90-minute debate, the CEO flatly stated, "I have gone as far as I'm willing to go based on what we think. Tell me what we know."

After four years — and hundreds of thousands of dollars — all that we had effectively accomplished was use the increased contributions from employees with poor biometrics to fund "Wellness Programs." Even with the best of intentions, the data showed these efforts didn't lead to improved health or reduce claims costs. The CEO's message was simple, yet profound: ***there is a vast difference between thinking and knowing.***

Data is the great equalizer that allows us to bridge the gap between what we suspect is the correct course of action and what we can prove is the best course of action. As a leader in your organization, you use data to drive decision making in almost every aspect of what you do. However, when it comes to employee benefits and particularly the health plan, few business leaders can explain why that expense is rising faster than almost any other line item on their P&L.

The challenge most organizations (large or small) have is an acceptance of a status quo that is simply not in their best interest. This is especially true as it relates to accessing critical data. In this chapter, you and your company will hear the good, bad, and the ugly of leveraging data (or not). After reading this chapter you will have a greater appreciation for utilizing your data effectively to yield happier more productive employees and a healthier bottom line at the same time.

The Usual Suspects

Health Insurers conduct business in three primary verticals; Medicare, Individual Coverage, and Employer Coverage. Medicare reimbursements are based on the Medicare Physician Fee Schedule (MPFS) which is adjusted depending on where the care is rendered. The MPFS standardizes Medicare reimbursements and limits what an insurance company can do to generate higher margins.

The Individual Insurance Marketplaces developed by the Affordable Care Act continues to unravel in large part because of the mounting losses being taken by insurance carriers. In the State of Ohio, where our company is headquartered, Aetna, Anthem, and United Healthcare have all exited the State Exchange for 2018. Insurance Carrier losses in the individual market have been well documented and have resulted in carriers deciding to significantly limit their plans, and in some cases, completely withdraw from participation.

Health Insurer share prices have soared since the outset of Healthcare Reform. The fixed reimbursements under Medicare and turbulence in the Individual Marketplaces leaves only one vertical to drive much of the profits: Employer Coverage. Here are the share prices of the four largest publicly traded health insurers from the outset of Healthcare Reform through the writing of this chapter:

	Share Price April 2010	Share Price June 2017	Share Price Increase
Aetna	$27.28	$150.59	452%
Anthem/Blue Cross	$48.05	$189.96	295%
Cigna	$31.94	$169.08	429%
United Healthcare	$27.07	$181.63	571%

Health insurers utilize insurance brokers as their primary distribution channel to employers and individuals alike. Like any organization selling a product, insurers use commissions, bonuses, overrides, and retention goals to deliver maximum value to their shareholders. Business leaders have always relied on insurance brokers, consultants, advisers, etc. to provide guidance and counsel in managing employee benefits. However, employers do not know how or how much these advisers are compensated.

Health insurance and employee benefits are often overcomplicated by those with the most expertise. I will share three stories outside of the insurance and benefits industry that parallel many of the issues facing employers and consumers of health insurance to illustrate this point. The stories that follow can be read in any order and applied at any time. There are limitations to the data available to employers based on size, being fully insured or self-funded, and rating methodologies. Leveraging the data available to your organization is the responsibility of your broker/consultant, insurance carrier, and your team.

When a 40% Discount Is a Bad Deal

In 2016, a lawsuit was filed against Kohl's, JCPenney, Macy's and Sears alleging that the retailers used "misleading and deceptive false price advertising." In short, these companies were accused of falsely inflating the original price of the item before applying a "discount." For example, the lawsuit against these retailers claims that one retailer advertised a front-load washer with an original price of $1,179.99. In reality, the retailer never sold the front load washer for more than $999.99. Customers weren't getting the deal they thought because no one ever paid the original price the retailer listed for the front-load washer.

Most consumers of health insurance can relate to the example above when reviewing the "discount" they receive when using their health insurance. For years, insurance carriers have touted that their "Network Discounts" save employers huge sums of money between what providers have billed, and what the insurance plan must pay. These discounts appear on each individual's explanation of benefits and in the employer level reporting provided by the insurance carrier.

Employers need to be mindful that the discounts received are far less important than finding the true unit cost of the services being used. A 40% network discount on a $1,000 MRI seems like a great deal until you find that another provider will perform the same MRI for $200.

Carrier Standard Data Reporting Packages do an excellent job showing high-level aggregate data around utilization, cost, discounts, location of care, etc. However, these reports do not show the sunken cost associated with inefficiencies or lack of management within the network. Employers must move beyond the network discount, and engage partners who can drive utilization inside and sometimes outside of the carrier based network to reduce the per employee per year cost of claims.

For Employers: For large, self-funded employers, there are partners that will analyze historic data to uncover sunken costs and work with employers to reduce and recover these lost dollars. Many of these partners will work on performance based contracts where they do not charge fees and only share in the savings with the employer.

If your company is smaller or fully insured, there are numerous Medical Management and Member Advocacy Programs that can increase quality of care, direct members to low-cost providers, and encourage better overall utilization of health plan dollars. When evaluating these providers, search for vendors who will use performance based compensation and set clear, measurable goals that are reviewed often.

The primary responsibility of any corporation is to generate value (return on investment) for their shareholders. For the insurance carrier, controlling your medical costs is only beneficial if done to a level that retains your company as a client. Any further cost containment will compress margins and decrease profit. As an employer, you are re-sponsible for going further to control costs and return value to your shareholders.

Carrier Efficiency, Employer Insolvency

C&D Distributors was a South Carolina based provider of small hard-ware, plumbing fixtures, and electrical equipment to the U.S. Military. In 1997, the company incorrectly entered shipping information for an order that resulted in an overpayment of $5,000 which the company promptly returned. Through this experience, C&D Distributors ac-cidentally discovered a flaw in the government's order system. They realized that shipping charges were entered in a separate database and paid without being tied back to the original order. Investigators un-covered instances where C&D Distributors billed almost $450,000 in shipping for a single elbow pipe that cost $8.75. Over the next 9 years, C&D Distributors submitted 112 fraudulent shipping invoices totaling almost $21M before the fraud was discovered.

As an employer and sponsor of a group health plan, understand-ing how your insurance carrier partner is allocating and spending your premium dollars is essential to containing costs. Insurance carriers will often reference their auto-adjudication rates which minimize issues for employees by paying providers promptly. The higher the auto-ad-judication, the more claims that pass through your plan without ever being reviewed. If you aren't willing to allow your accounts payable team to pay 90% of invoices without review, you shouldn't be partner-ing with an insurance company that does.

For Employers: You must ask your Insurance Carrier about their auto-adjudication rates and any programs available to further review claims. Many carriers set a dollar amount to trigger the review of claims. From an employer's perspective, $10,000 in claims for one employee costs the same as $1,000 in claims for 10 employees. However, insurance carriers may review the claims in the first scenario, but not the second, because $1,000 claims do not trigger a review.

It is important to find Carrier partners who agree to remove auto-adjudication from certain types of services like those performed at outpatient facilities. Many Carrier partners will also engage in physician peer review to ensure that providers are following accepted guidelines and treatment plans. Some carriers even perform these services as standard business practices that will give your employees a virtual second opinion of treatment plans and save the company money at the same time.

The auto-adjudication and billing epidemic has become so bad that there are third parties that will work with medical providers and share in the additional revenue generated, based on their ability to bill your health plan in the most profitable manner. As an employer, if you don't have your own strategies to combat these efforts, you are losing money every time someone uses your health insurance.

Living with Your Mother-In-Law

We were working with an employer who was bound and determined to reduce healthcare costs by improving employee health. Their program consisted of biometric screenings that tested Blood Pressure, LDL Cholesterol, BMI, and Nicotine. The results based on these measures showed that employees could potentially pay $70 per payroll more for their Health Insurance. On-site wellness coaches were brought in to meet with employees. Employees who met and interacted with the coaches a certain number of times could reduce their $70 per payroll penalty.

An employee at the company (we'll call him John), lost nearly 90lbs and quit smoking in the fourth year of the program. John was overweight, smoked like a chimney, and used Budweiser to douse the flames. Frankly, John wasn't all that different from the rest of his co-workers. But the drastic change in John's life prompted us to hear his story.

John began by telling us that his wife was the primary caretaker in the home and completed nearly all the daily tasks to keep the home running effectively. Unfortunately, John's wife required a surgery that would put her out of commission for several months, and John's Mother-In-Law decided to move in with the family to help her daughter recover and fill in around the house.

John's Mother-In-Law observed his after-work routine and chastised him for being lazy, ungrateful, and a few other things we can't publish. John grew so tired of the abuse that one day he stormed out of the house. John made it to the end of the street before realizing that he was out of breath, exhausted, and that maybe his Mother-In-Law had a point.

John began leaving his home each night to walk after work. Not only did the walks improve his health, but the fact that he was not in the house reduced his daily alcohol consumption from 4 to 6 beers to 1 or 2 with dinner. Within a month, he had quit smoking. John described the weight "melting away," and by the time his wife had recovered, he had already lost 40lbs and was helping around the house. It is worth noting that John did not say whether or not he was helping around the house because of his improved health, or if he was trying to get his Mother-In-Law out as soon as possible. I like to think that it was a little bit of both.

John's story illustrates an important point about wellness and lifestyle: it is largely a personal choice. Even when providing employees with the tools to improve their lifestyle and health, the data on the program showed a spike in Blood Pressure and Cholesterol Medication once biometric screenings began. We inadvertently created an environment that encouraged medication utilization over improving health. Making matters worse, this increased medication use showed improvements in the employees' Blood Pressure and Cholesterol, which caused both the biometric screening provider and on-site wellness coaches to claim that their programs were driving improvements in health.

The data showed that nearly all improvements in biometrics were directly attributed to increased medication use. When the wellness coaching data was made available, we found that seeing a coach did not tie to improved biometrics or reduced claims costs.

For Employers: Wellness programs have been positioned incorrectly for years. They are sold as a 3 to 5-year strategy; invariably, the 3 to 5 years pass, yet costs continue to rise, despite vendors showing "improvements." The metrics used to evaluate wellness programs are often limited to those that benefit the wellness provider. Increasing medication adherence provides a nominal benefit but watching medication adherence and strength increase substantially to meet the same health standards means the underlying health of your company is getting worse. Don't let your wellness programs take credit for improvements that are based largely on medication use.

The key to a successful wellness program is the ability to evaluate participants across multiple data sources (biometrics, medical claims, pharmacy claims, workers' compensation, lifestyle programs, etc.) Find partners who will make data readily available and allow their programs to be tested across all the data verticals available to your organization.

If it can't be measured, it can't be managed

As previously stated, the health plan is one of the largest expenses for employers. However, employers typically make these very important (and expensive) decisions with limited data. I bet that you gathered a lot of information the last time you made a large personal financial decision like buying a home, or a car. The same should be true with employee benefits.

Unfortunately, business leaders across all industries and company sizes are at a tremendous data disadvantage when it comes to their employee benefits programs. The brokers and consultants are also under the pressure of the deadline of one policy expiring and another taking its place. The problem is that these decisions are made at renewal, so there is little time for due diligence in terms of evaluating the plan or the carrier because your company is up against the renewal date deadline.

Making these decisions at renewal based on the acquisition cost or annual premium for the benefits ignores the sunken costs associated with inefficiencies at the insurance carriers. Reducing the overall premium by a few percentage points is far less important than making sure those dollars are being spent effectively by your partners. These discussions take more time than the 90 days (or sometimes far less) that your broker/consultant allocates for the renewal.

Knowing exactly how and how much your broker/consultant is being paid in commission by the insurance carriers is also essential. You need to know that you are being presented every option, not only those that benefit the broker/consultant. Remember that all your business partners in this equation are responsible for maximizing the return to *their* company, which doesn't always align with saving *your* company money.

In Conclusion

The moral of these stories is to *demand data*. Many of your current partners may be apprehensive about sharing data, but if any of your current partners won't disclose the level of information that you deem acceptable, it's time to find a new partner. Insurance carriers, brokers/consultants, and wellness providers must earn their revenue by reducing your company's expense and not simply going through the motions. These relationships can only be accomplished by partners who not only share data, but encourage the accountability that comes along with complete transparency.

Our agency no longer quotes insurance policies for non-clients, regardless of group size. Organizations who are willing to decide on a top three expense and who is managing that expense based on the one area that makes every broker/consultant the same (the insurance commodities provided by the carriers) are not ready to do what is necessary to deliver better benefits at a lower cost.

To further align with clients our agency has also moved to full fee disclosure. If we make $0.10 per employee per month as a reseller of COBRA services, our clients know about it. We demand that our insurance carrier, pharmacy, and wellness partners share the maximum amount of data available, so that we can all better measure, manage, and alter our strategic plan with the client.

A funny thing happened when our firm elevated to this level of transparency, *more data meant less competition*. With all the cards on the table and all partners working for the best results for your company, change only happens when it is supported by evidence. Compare this to the status quo where brokers beg for census data to quote insurance products that do little more than raise the share price of the insurance carriers. If you make decisions based on what you *know* rather than what you *think*, you can return those insurance carrier profits to your company's bottom line where they belong.

Bob Gearhart, Jr.

Partner
DCW Group
Youngstown, OH

Bob Gearhart, Jr. is the third generation to lead DCW Group and has reshaped the company into a Next Generation Benefits Firm. He and the team at DCW Group are committed to delivering high performing employee benefit plans to the market, one client at a time. Bob's goal is to reverse the hyperinflation of healthcare that has led to middle class wage stagnation over the last 20 years.

Bob is also a nationally recognized speaker on Healthcare Reform and Employee Benefits. He frequently appears on radio, television, and in print to provide insight into the ever-changing landscape surrounding healthcare in America. In 2017, Bob was invited to El Salvador by that nation's Ministry of Health to provide feedback on the healthcare facilities and providers in their growing Healthcare Abroad Network for patients around the world.

www.dcwgrp.com
bobjr@dcwgrp.com
330-953-2962

CHAPTER 10

THINK DIFFERENTLY!

Grow EBITDA from Your Benefit Plans

Kim Eckelbarger

Does your health plan renewal equal a pay decrease for your employees every year?

Does your attempt to reduce rising costs consist of passing on higher premiums to your employees with less rich benefits annually?

Does your company delegate the benefit plan selection to its Human Resource department, who views this third largest expense line item as an operational cost, and has the *mistaken belief that they have no control over the health care budget*?

It is time to go beyond the status quo. Let's move this conversation from the Human Resources department to an executive with P&L responsibility and financially engineer a few strategic approaches to turn your health and benefit plan into a profit, rather than expenditure.

If you are picking off the shelf fully insured health plans from a carrier grid, and not applying any additional strategy, you are paying the most possible for your benefits. Not only are you paying too much, but you also have very limited ability to hold your vendor carrier partner accountable for the tremendous financial waste in the American health care system.

Not familiar with the waste in the American Healthcare system? You might find it interesting to know that 17.4% of the Gross Domestic Product is Healthcare. We spend more than any other economically developed country, due to increased use of medical technology and higher costs. Even so, we do not utilize more doctor visits or hospital admissions per person.

Despite this excess spending, we have shorter life expectancies and greater prevalence of chronic conditions when compared to these other developed countries. To bring home the overuse of medical technology, the state of Florida has 5 times as many MRI centers when compared to Canada. <u>What strategies do you have to hold your vendor partners accountable, and are they aligned with positive outcomes for the company?</u>

The status quo in America finds mid-sized employers typically offering three fully insured plans to their employees. Generally, a combination of a Low, Medium and High quality/cost plans are offered by the employer. When the employees elect coverage, the young and healthy tend to enroll in the lower quality/cost plan because they are low utilizers of health care. The reverse is also true, in that the older and unhealthy will be attracted to the higher quality plans due to being high utilizers of healthcare, given they can afford the premium costs. The higher quality plan realizes faster-increasing costs as its members are naturally higher utilizers of healthcare; it becomes a more adverse risk pool.

Step 1 — Right Size Your Plans Yourself

If you follow this basic premise I just covered, then it will be easy for you to understand that you can "right size" your plans more cost effectively than the insurance carrier can. It has worked for our clients for years, and it works every time, with every carrier, as the challenge of adverse risk pools on high-quality plans exist for all carriers. This simple thought of right sizing your plan offerings by building them off your lower cost base plan will allow you to realize premium savings every year. It also turns the tables on traditional thinking that to reduce costs, your need to reduce benefits. The truth is exactly the opposite; you have to increase your benefit offerings to reduce costs.

See the exhibit below, a 5-year case study for employers with an average of 101 employees, who saved close to a half million within a 5 year time period by right sizing their higher quality plans themselves.

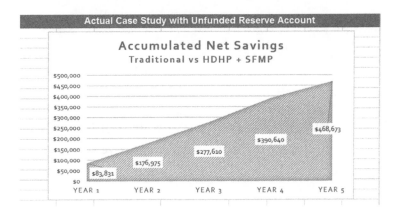

Actual Case Study with Unfunded Reserve Account

Accumulated Net Savings
Traditional vs HDHP + SFMP

I share with you the positive economic impact of utilizing a higher deductible health plan with copays in combination with a 105 plan to allow employees to essentially have the same $3000 deductible. We replaced a $3,000 fully insured deductible plan with a $5000 deductible and added the 105 plan. Savings are shown in the chart above; averaging $920 in premium savings per employee per year. Totaling $468,673 in savings over a 5-year period on a 101 employee company.

Step 2 — Build Profits from Your Healthcare Plan

Dream bigger, and take this concept a bit further to build profits out of your health plan offerings. See Exhibit below, demonstrating the employees funding the buy down of the deductible:

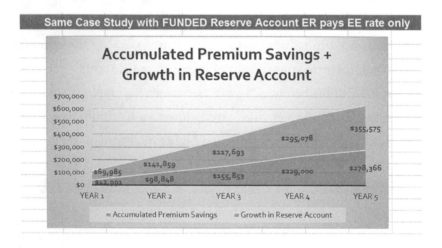

I share with you the positive economic impact of generating $165,268 in profits for this same client over a 5-year period.

Step 3—Apply Strategic Thinking to All Your Benefit Offerings, Then Repeat Steps 1 & 2

If you are still reading, then you are probably already thinking, how can I apply strategy to other benefit offerings?

Dental/vision plans are not currently being marketed as a wellness benefit, but should be. Dental and Vision wellness prevention visits save lives and reduce health plan spend with early detection. These visits are especially valuable for the 35% of the population that skips visiting their primary care doctor each year. This wellness initiative can detect things like Anemia, Diabetes, Kidney Failure, HIV, Cancers, Multiple Sclerosis, Rheumatoid Arthritis, High Blood Pressure and Heart Disease. These plans can be available on a net low/no cost basis due to tax favored status to employees and their families, corporate social security tax savings to the employer, and a little strategy.

Strategic thinking would change the dental/vision benefits plan design to being dollar based, rather than procedure based and offer multiple plan annual maximums (E.g. 500, 1000, 1500, 2000 etc.}. We have the employer contribute to the core lower cost plan and allow interested employees to buy up to a choice of 1-2 more higher quality plans.

Not only is it dollar based, it has a co-pay feature rather than a deductible. The dental community in our area has agreed to pass thru the $10-15 co-pay, plus take a $5.00/claim withhold when our processor pays the claim. The scenario looks like this: You have a $100 service {let's say a cleaning}, and you give the dentist office a $ 10 co-pay. The DDS sends the claim to our processor. The processor removes $100 from the employer's reserve fund, and sends the Dentist $85. The dentist receives $85 from the processor and $10 from your employee, for $95 total, and the dentist allowed a $5.00 withhold. Why would the dentist do this? Because this plan has no discounts involved, plus a simple, easy to understand design with NO EXCLUSIONS, a dentist's dream!

We have a corporately self-funded, dollar based, Freedom of Choice for Provider, dental {and/or vision} plan where 100% of the funding is used to pay for claims or stays in the employer's reserve fund. This competes nicely with the fully insured dental/vision plans that have 35% retention built into the premium. We reversed the roles as follows: instead of 35% retention to the carrier and 20-25 % discounts to the dentists, there is 0 retention built into the funding and no discounts. Our plan has 15-17 % retention, but it is paid by the dentist passing thru the co-pay plus $ 5.00 of their own money, not by the employer.

Bottom line: having a dental/vision plan with a benefit of 100% of the first $250 or more, encourages a visit to the provider. About 30-40% of the insured don't see their dentist/eye doctor each year, but they should. The visit to the provider will, in many cases, find a health challenge, when treated, avoids a large medical claim with early detection. Most participants BUY UP to the richer plan, and the corporate social security savings on the BUY UP funding offsets the employer's funding per employee.

END RESULT ⇒ A NO COST/LOW COST BENEFIT TO THE EMPLOYER WITH A SIGNIFICANT BARGAIN TO THE INTERESTED EMPLOYEES WHO BUY UP.

On to Disability Plans

How about adding a new no/low cost/reserve building fringe benefit offering to round out the benefits package?

Similar to the creative/cost effective dental plan offering that has been a no net cost item for our clients, we designed a plan where our clients contribute $5/month/employee, yet the reserve fund withdrawals + corporate social security savings are greater than the cumulative $5/month/employee corporate contributions. We work from a base insured plan of $100/week short term disability benefits plan and the result in a no/low cost item due to employee contributions for the buy up option (+ corporate social security savings on the contributions).

Specifically, interested employees can buy up to a 60% of compensation benefit. The money collected from the interested employees stays in the client's operating account and is used to pay the corporate self-funding involved, plus offset the less than $5/month/employee corporate premium for the $100/week insured benefit.

This unique/cost effective group insurance plan will replace the current in place voluntary short term individual plans and will save the interested employees an average 50% vs. current premiums being paid.

See Case Study below:

Short Term Disability Case Study 140 employees	
Employer provided a $100/week Short Term Disability Plan for Employees, annual premium costs:	12,050.50
Employer offered buy up option for additional coverage and collected from the employees:	23,302.16
Corporate Tax savings on collected employee premiums:	1,783.00
Claims were corporately self-funded on the buy up option, and claims were paid in the amount of:	12,057.13
Impact: Reserve started on No Cost benefit for 140 employees with savings to employees who buy up.	**$977.53**
Prior to this plan design, only 13 employees had coverage.	

Having Fun with Life Insurance Offerings

Let's walk thru a creative, cost effective Group Life concept designed originally by John Stoner, at The Stoner Organization, that when implemented, would not cost the employer any more money than the current in place off the shelf status quo offerings while positively impacting employees who are interested in buying additional coverage for themselves favorably by 40+%.

Traditionally, basic employer paid rates are composite rated, while in contrast, voluntary premiums are step rated. Traditional supplemental voluntary coverage is generally priced to achieve 35-50% participation. A mentor of mine, John Stoner, recognized that the impact of offering a voluntary design with the employer paying 100% for the first $10,000, and achieving 100% participation. The 100%

participation rate creates a 20-30% reduction in premium costs.

When the rates went down by 20-30%, then the "Average" of the step rates now come back to the same amount as the composite rates typically used for the basic coverage. The cost to the employer doesn't go up. The cost to the employees to buy additional coverage on themselves and family members goes down by 20-30%, and they can now afford more coverage. The 100% participation also greatly improves the amount of guaranteed issue coverage offered by the carrier, creating another win-win for the employer and its employees.

To improve the value further, the IRS allows the first $50,000 of group life to be paid with pre-tax dollars. Given the employer provides for $ 10,000 in Group Life, the next, up to $40,000 purchased by the employee can be paid pre-tax and provide another 20-25% improvement in value to the employee who buys additional coverage. The final kicker is that the employer saves 7.65% corporate Social Security savings on the money paid by employees to buy the additional, up to $40,000 of coverage.

Bottom line: the employer is a lower net cost for the cost of the first $10,000 of coverage, plus a potential 50% improvement in value to the employee buying more coverage.

Step 4 — The Unexpected Result of Advocacy to Control Waste in the Healthcare System

While it is easy to understand the savings associated with virtual or telephone doctor visits, it is the advocacy component which is providing unexpected results for clients by providing additional control and unexpected savings.

You would naturally expect when the advocacy team assists with directing an employee on how to obtain appropriate care and catches them before they utilize the Emergency Room for a Primary care visit, we would reduce the costs inside the healthcare plan. You would also expect the advocacy team to reduce costs by assisting with invoice questions which result from billing mistakes made by providers.

The additional transparency from the advocacy team provides an opportunity to help an underwriter with limited case notes to understand the members' future care plan. Underwriters, like everyone, have multiple renewals going on at any given time, so the time needed for them to dig into the detail behind case notes can be limited. The advocacy team capturing data enables us to better drive this process, and gain control of waste in the healthcare system.

Step 5 — Improvements in EBITDA from Organization Fitness

Organizational well-being is a recent concept inside American business. With the help of others, we have learned how to connect vitality strategies inside companies without the use of financial incentives. We are tracking an engagement level of 75% and higher within the companies that engage. Contrast that with the status quo which engages about 25% even when financial incentives are used.

The rewards of creating an organizational culture that improves the physical workplace and provides an environment, in which people thrive, are in the ability of a company to remain flexible and resilient. It also attracts positive talent to your organization, as like attracts like.

Connecting the concept of wellness to retirement savings and demonstrating that you must put a few things in your "Well-Being 401K" today if you want to have anything to take out later in life, resonates with the work place, as does appealing to the children need for wellness.

We meet the employees where they are, and do not spend resources in areas where the readiness to change is not evident. The status quo wellness vendor will offer things like stop smoking programs if they know your population utilizes tobacco. However, trying to enroll an employee in a stop smoking program, when they have no interest in changing this behavior, is a waste of time and resources, as well as completely annoying for all involved. The key is to understand which employees are ready to make lifestyle improvements, and then have resources in place to assist.

Leadership MUST buy into the program. A couple of champions are needed to step up inside the organization (anyone can step into a leadership role for the program) to get it started, and the end game is creating self-starters inside our organizations. The employees must believe that the program is for their own well-being—not being used purely to reduce health insurance costs, and CONFIDENTIALITY is a MUST.

In the mid-market space, when we demonstrate an engagement level of 75% or more, we are seeing anywhere from a 7-15% return on premium savings from the health plan carrier. Couple that with the other benefits of a healthy, productive, workforce and you have a win for your organization. The high levels of engagement allow us to capture the information needed to develop the execution strategy. The cost of programing runs 1-5%, which leaves us with a 2-10% premium reduction.

A Final Thought...

You will find a common thread in this chapter of challenging the status quo and NOT accepting off the shelf vendor solutions. My hope is that you will move the benefits programing to an executive with P&L responsibility that applies strategy to the third largest line item expense for American employers. We are in an Economic Healthcare Crisis that is unsustainable and requires thinking differently than we have in the past. Strategy with execution will provide employers and America improved EBITDA, and begin to solve our Economic Healthcare Crisis.

Think Differently!

Kimberly A. Eckelbarger

President
Tropical Risk Management
Trinity, FL

As the founder of Tropical Risk Management, Kim Eckelbarger specializes in delivering innovative, strategic and meaningful employee benefits solutions throughout the Tampa, FL region. She was a contributor to the groundbreaking organizational leadership book, *Shared Values, Shared Results*, authored by Dee Edington.

Kim and her team focus on key performance indicators to produce quantifiable and documented results for their employer-clients helping them reclaim significant dollars and bolster EBIDTA.

Beyond strategic benefits planning, Tropical Risk Management also identifies ways to improve opportunity costs, remove redundant processes, document legal compliance, automate processes, and assist with developing internal talent all to maximize the performance and productivity of the workforce.

www.tropicalbenefits.com
kim@tropicalbenefits.com
727-237-5858

CHAPTER 11

INSTITUTING STRATEGIC BENEFITS PLANNING

The Process that Allows Your Benefits Program to Run Like a Finely Tuned Machine

Tim Olson

According to a recent article in *Forbes Magazine*, the number of benefits brokers will decrease by 50% in the coming years. In the past 37 years, I've worked with hundreds of employers and tens of thousands of employees but the employee benefits industry is going through a complete overhaul. It's game-changing and employers settling for the status quo will pay *Thousands* and probably *Millions* more without a strategy in place.

At the time of this writing, the Trump administration has failed a second time to "repeal and replace" Obamacare. As most people know, Republicans have the majority in both the House and Senate, but can't get agreement within their own party on fixing the Accountable Care Act (ACA).

No one can agree on how to fix the problem and despite the reconciliation process which requires a simple majority vote, they're still having trouble implementing acceptable change. The biggest ACA issues include:

- Individual Marketplace policies average a 20% increase every year.
- People can't afford deductibles of $3,000 or more.
- Insurance carriers are dropping out of the individual market like flies.
- Medical expenses are the number one cause of bankruptcy.

While the individual marketplace continues to be plagued with challenges, we've seen considerable growth in the group market, despite the negative impact resulting from many ACA rules.

Obamacare:
It's complex and puts pressure on employers.

Since Obamacare was approved March 23, 2010, the strategies to gain a competitive advantage under ACA have swung tremendously. The emotions I've seen from company owners and CEO's have been off the charts from table pounding to yelling, screaming and making bets with their CFO that Obama was going to be impeached or assassinated!

Over the past 40 years, I've never seen more contempt for ACA compared to all the other regulatory changes combined affecting the employee benefits industry. Consider how Obamacare has impacted employers:

- All 30 hour FTEs must be offered qualifying coverage within 90 days of service.
- They must offer a plan that meets minimum value or pay a sledgehammer penalty of $2,260 per FTE. (2017 and not counting the first 30 employees)
- Even if they offer a plan, the Tack Hammer penalty applies ($3,390 in 2017) for each 30 hour FTE that declines the employer's policy and qualifies for a subsidized Obamacare policy.
- Employers must apply the "measurement" rules for variable hour employees on a monthly basis or "look back" method.
- Employers with 50+ eligible employees must file form 1095-C each year.
- Employer contribution policies are crucial: they impact employees within 400% of the federal poverty level who otherwise could qualify for a subsidy.
- Cadillac Plan tax (delayed until 1-1-2020) applies a 40% penalty of plan cost exceeding $10,200 per year for single coverage and $27,500 for family coverage.
- The required Essential Health Benefits continue to put never ending upward price pressure on group health insurance policies.
- Non-compliance will subject employers to ACA penalties, equal to $100 per day per infraction.

With over 2,300 pages between the House and the Reconciliation bill, the law is so complex (far exceeding the short list above) that many employers purchased software tools to run all the metrics.

Dealing with double-digit increases is only part of the problem — figuring out what rules apply and administering the new requirements added a ton of expense as well. No question, the ACA legislation was a watershed event that changed employee benefits plans and risk mitigation strategies forever.

Evolution in the employee benefits industry

To become a Next Generation Benefits Firm that delivered value, we had to build the infrastructure to help employers gain a competitive edge and stay ahead of the ever-changing complexity of what ACA was morphing into.

At that time, our epiphany moment came: we decided to embrace this game changing legislation and become ACA experts. We started investing everything back into our company and today, The Olson Group has grown from 7 to 27 staff members with significant revenue growth. Our *"why"* is defined as a never-ending passion to understand our customer, bring them all the services available in the industry and dig into every possible risk strategy for them.

This model contrasts distinctly with many agency owners selling out to the big houses and throwing in the towel. We've built the foundation for the next generation and our goal is to bring a culture vastly different that benefit companies with 50,000 employees. Above my office reads, *"Our biggest competitor is the Status Quo,"* and describes how we embrace new strategies to disrupt the incredible hurdles we all face in health care.

Now, the essence of our business model has grown from an ACA software tool into helping employers develop Strategic Benefits Plans that address all aspects of their employee benefit programs.

We've spent the last four years meeting with a mastermind group quarterly to develop cutting-edge strategies and bring to our customers all the innovative ideas that agencies like ours have created around the country. Masterminding with 40 agency owners is very powerful and has helped develop the foundation for a business model, so employers can focus on building a Strategic Benefits Plan that keeps them informed and current with the critical areas.

Strategic Benefit Planning: How to get started

The first step is understanding the critical areas affecting the employee benefit programs that employers offer. You begin by defining goals and objectives—consider how you rate the following questions on a 1 to 10: ("10" being the highest)

- Our benefit programs are integrated, streamlined and focused.
- Our employees understand and fully appreciate the value of the benefits we provide.
- We have a documented 3-5 year benefit strategy where goals and objectives are defined and measurable.
- The presentation, communication and education around our benefits motivates and engages our employees.
- We frequently assess our vulnerability and feel comfortable with our benefit plans compliance.
- Our advisory fees are laid out in complete detail for all the services provided.

- We completely understand all the ACA rules and our plans have a competitive advantage over our competition.
- Our adviser provides member level analytic views and provides clear metrics for measuring performance, progress and return on investment in benefits.
- Our wellness and disease management program is successful and our adviser is able to show the return on investment and help us show improved attractiveness to employees and the marketplace.

The above questions are just a sampling of key discussion points you should be having with your adviser. Over the past year, we've taken a "step back" with our customers to reassess and confirm goals and objectives. The following is a sampling of topics and questions we discussed:

- What are the key performance indicators (KPIs) that drive your company's bottom line?
- What have you done to offset the impact of health insurance increases over the past 5 years?
- How is your company impacted by government regulations?
- What are things you do great?
- What separates you from others in your industry?
- How would you define employee morale and company culture?
- How do you recruit top talent and retain them?
- Describe your 3-5 years strategic company plan that separates you from the competition. Further describe your weekly strategy meetings with managers and key people in your organization.

- Do you have an aging population and can you describe turnover as positive, negative, high, or low?
- Performance based advisory fees — Will your adviser put part of their fees at risk if your health insurance program doesn't perform as expected?

This short list is a good start for company owners and advisers getting on the same page to maximize goals, objectives and to better understand each other. Do your values and goals align?

It is so refreshing and enlightening to be in tune with an executive team and everyone can "feel" they are heading in the same direction moving forward. Year 1, year 2 and years 3-5 goals are laid out in a working document.

Strategic Benefit Planning — The Critical Areas

Our trademarked system is called *BenefitsEdge*™ and it lays the framework for company owners and executive teams to get in front of all the complexities of their programs, evaluate the risk strategies available to them, assure compliance, perform deep dive analysis, evaluate plan performance, understand all the tools in the marketplace and ultimately, maximize plan satisfaction for employees.

Wouldn't it be great to have employees coming into your office saying how much they love working for you and how beneficial the benefit programs have been for them? Don't employee benefit programs fall in the top 2 or 3 expense items for your company? Why not have a plan that maximizes success that employees value?

Five Key Areas

1. **Establishing Goals & Objectives.** To confirm goals and objectives, we utilize a Risk Enterprise Scorecard system that addresses 15 specific components within the 5 key areas — a sampling of the questions was listed in the getting started section.

2. **Deep Dive Analysis.** Once objective and goals are confirmed, it may be time for market evaluations. Typically, we perform deep dive analysis every 2-3 years. Key factors include:

    a. Change in leadership
    b. Market Conditions
    c. Risks to avoid, transfer, mitigate, or assume
    d. Strategic Risk vs. Operational Risk vs. Hazard Risk
    e. Tactical Strategies
    f. Change in objectives
    g. Health Insurance:
        i.   Fully Insured to Level Funded
        ii.   Level Funded to Captive or Coalition Programs
        iii. Captive to Stand Alone Self-Funded
        iv.   Self-Funded to Fully Insured
        v.   HSA/HRA/MERP/Dual Option Strategies
        vi.   Wellness Initiatives
        vii. Spousal Incentive HRA Plans
        viii. Contribution Policy Changes

h. Ancillary Lines

i. Voluntary Enhanced Benefits

j. Retirement Programs

k. Electronic Enrollment Initiatives

l. Technology Innovations

3. **Compliance.** Did you know 95% of employers have a plan out of compliance? When you think about all the Notice requirements, ERISA rules, SPD rules, Plan Document Amendments, Restatement Rules, Fiduciary Requirements, Retirement Plan Fee Disclosure Notices, 5500 filings, IRS Form 720, Safe Harbor rules, ACA Notices, HIPAA, COBRA, FMLA, FSLA, etc. How do you stay ahead of the game?

We found completing a detailed compliance assessment service which addresses all the critical areas is the first step. The next step is documentation and backing up your work with a compliance and HR software tool. Our staff HR consultant puts it all together, so customers are DOL audit ready.

4. **Plan Performance.** Some of the prominent key areas:

a. Wellness Initiatives.

b. Data Analytics software tools — digging into the data and addressing strategies for super utilizers, evaluating modifiable behaviors and focusing on Population Health Management education.

c. Spousal Incentive HRA programs and other strategies to take advantage of Obamacare rules.

d. PBM options—tremendous opportunities exist for RX strategies. Manufacturers offer co-pay assist programs to help employees qualify for huge savings potential. Sourcing prescriptions through foreign countries is another strategy starting to take off in the marketplace.

e. Urgent Care contracts—A strategy where Urgent Care Centers contract with certain employers to waive co-pays and treat people faster.

5. **Plan Stewardship.** The ultimate goal is employee satisfaction with your benefits program. Have you maximized the education opportunities for employees outside of the open enrollment time frame? Maybe it's time to consider off cycle education, or audio power points on your electronic enrollment portal. Sit down with your adviser and discuss how to maximize employee education and increase plan stewardship. Understanding how the benefits work is the first step—teaching them how to maximize benefits efficiency takes them to the next level.

Creating the Working Document

Many times, our meetings are recorded, but at the very least, detailed notes are documented and added to the Strategic Benefits Plan Documentation. Keeping everything in front of the team assures the best opportunity for success. Below is a checklist for the plan documentation you should include:

• Goals and objectives are set for the current year, next year and thereafter. All are laid out with time frames and who's responsible for each task.

- Strengths, Weaknesses, Opportunities and Threats (SWOT) are then developed and discussed at the next strategic planning meeting.

- The Action Plan and Task List is laid out to ensure all projects are identified, time frames are established and who is responsible for each task. Every employer has different priorities and key objectives for year 1, year 2 and beyond varies widely. Recently, we had a meeting where compliance was THE most important goal—they were not compliant with ACA, Notices, SPDs, FMLA, FSLA, COBRA and HIPAA. Penalties are severe, so getting them DOL audit ready was the number one priority.

- Plan performance objectives cover the entire spectrum and include, but are not limited to, market evaluations, data analytic tools, Rx management programs, disease management, education for super utilizers (return on investment for claims related to lifestyle changes and modifiable behaviors), aggressive wellness initiatives, smoker surcharges, spousal incentive HRAs and much more.

- Employee satisfaction with the benefits program is the ultimate goal with respect to education, affordability and how to maximize the value for themselves and family members.

The Employee Benefit Industry: Services & Expectations

Think about your current broker relationship—How often do you meet and how do you describe the discussions? Is the focus about:

1. Products?
2. The bidding process?
3. What census items they need?
4. Price?
5. The renewal meeting?

In contrast, are the meetings focused on:

1. Services that reduce your time spent on the employee benefit programs?
2. Ways to make you and your team more efficient?
3. Identifying key performance indicators that reduce your bottom line expenses?
4. Cutting edge-risk strategies with out of the box thinking?
5. How technology will give you a competitive advantage over your competition?
6. How to maximize employee understanding and satisfaction with the benefits program?

The first example is transactional based, where the focus is grinding through bids and coming up with the lowest cost. We refer that process to old school employee benefits planning 101; it is the default and automatic approach with almost any employee benefits firm. This approach misses the mark on so many levels:

- No focus on services and strategies promoting efficiency.
- Employee meetings are an after-thought.
- Many years, the renewal process is in the 11th hour, putting a ton of pressure on everyone.
- No long range Strategic Benefits Plan.

The second example is goals and objectives focused, in tune with the employer with a long-range plan, committed to evaluating every risk strategy, software tool, compliance module and utilizes both tactical and strategic solutions to maximize benefits at the lowest possible cost to both the employer and employee.

Furthermore, goals are established in all the key areas — some examples include:

- Affordable Coverage
- Improving Member Health
- Assure Compliance
- Monitor Plan Performance
- Ensure Member Satisfaction

Assuming all the critical areas are addressed, employers can expect to demonstrate a strategic leadership model combined with forward looking quality and fiscal measurement capabilities to improve the odds of success for its plan and for the employees and families associated with their organization.

Conclusion

The bottom line is employee benefit programs are complex, ever changing and they continue to be one of the largest expenses to employers. Strategic Planning is essential to stay ahead of whatever the next piece of legislation comes down the pike. It may be healthcare, additional regulations to retirement plans, changes to the tax structure of benefit programs, who knows?

If you commit to a process utilizing the fundamentals in the five key areas, work with an adviser focused on services and create a working document laying out the action plan, you will maximize the chance for success.

Tim Olson

Managing Partner
The Olson Group
Omaha, NE

In 2003, Tim Olson founded The Olson Group—an employee benefits consulting firm with an emphasis in retirement planning and group insurance plans.

Tim's focus on serving his clients holistically garnered him and The Olson Group the honor of being named 2015's Benefit Adviser of the Year by Employee Benefit Adviser magazine. Since then, Tim and his team have set the standard in client service by reinventing and reinvesting in the practice to deliver ACA expertise, electronic enrollment platforms, wellness initiatives, and fiduciary expertise among other vital solutions. Recently developed *BenefitsEdge*™—a game-changing strategic planning process that allows organizations to intentionally determine the outcomes of their benefits investment.

The Olson Group currently works with more than 150 employers participating in 500 employee benefit plans, and covering more than 20,000 employees throughout Nebraska, Iowa, Missouri, and Kansas.

www.theolsongroup.com
tolson@theolsongroup.net
402-289-1046

CHAPTER 12

BEST PRACTICES DEBUNKED

Craig Lack

What if the best practices are not the best? What's wrong with the process? Is there a better way to lower health care costs? I think these are important questions to ask because the best practices that are applied today haven't really changed significantly in the past decade.

It's the same story over and over again — ineffective and reactive. Before we can debunk the best practices, let's first review the various stages of the "status quo" related to the annual healthcare renewal process.

BEST PRACTICES DON'T WORK

The 'Status Quo' Annual Healthcare Renewal Process

Step 1 — Carrier Develops a Renewal Proposal

Step 2 — The Pricing Formula

Step 3 — Broker/Consultant Validates the Formula

Step 4 — The Market Scare

Step 5 — The Employer Decision

Step 1 — Carrier Develops a Renewal Proposal

Sixty to one hundred twenty days prior to renewal (sometimes even farther), a carrier releases to the employer an annual renewal proposal. This renewal proposal contains proposed rates and benefits for the next year. It also provides general information about the account, some summary population data, and perhaps experience or utilization data, if available. The latter is sometimes omitted and a basic renewal exhibit is presented to the client.

The carrier delivers the renewal via electronic or hard copy format to the broker/consultant. Sometimes, the carrier delivers the renewal in person to the broker/consultant, especially if the news is not so positive and the proposed renewal is high. Delivering the renewal in person provides the carrier a chance to explain the basis of their renewal rate development.

The renewal proposal is only an offer to renew. It does not typically represent the final rates until the employer or their broker/consultant accepts the proposal.

Step 2 — The Pricing Formula

The carriers develop health insurance rates using past population and utilization experience. The most popular rate development methods are Manual Rating and Experience Rating. Carriers applies a combination or one of these methods.

The pricing formula and derivatives of it have been around, believe or not, for over 50 years. Its main premise is to utilize past experience as the basis for future expected costs. There may be some adjustments made but the formula has always been the same.

Claim or medical expenses of the past are adjusted to make sure outlier claims are not considered in the calculation. Expenses are trended forward, in simple terms, this means inflationary factors are applied and added to the medical expenses to predict future expenses. Administrative costs and margins are added to determine the final rating. Sounds simple but there are many opportunities to play hide and seek with undisclosed margin. For my article on this go to: *http://insurancethoughtleadership.com/hide-seek-healthcare-profits.*

Step 3 — Broker/Consultant Validates the Renewal

As part of the process, a broker/consultant validates the renewal. This means all of the factors used in the renewal pricing and the formula are once again reviewed to determine whether the renewal rates are fair and reasonable.

Consulting firm and their representatives examine the renewal process closely, questioning every data point, and formula. The end result is quite predictable as almost always the broker/consultant finds the renewal to be unreasonable, too high, or overstated. It's rare that the result is any different. Then the broker/consultant takes a further step and will negotiate down the renewal based upon his/her own underwriting or analytics.

It's all about performing due diligence and to show that an evaluation occurred and the renewal was not accepted in its original version. There are tremendous inefficiencies in this process but yet it is repeated year by year.

Step 4 — The Market Scare

Along the renewal process, if the broker/consultant is not pleased with the proposed renewal and progress of negotiations, the traditional we will advise the client to market approach comes into play. This creates a sort of "scare tactic" which forces the carrier to re-evaluate its position and determine if there is any further reduction or adjustment that can be made to avoid approaching the market for competitive insurance quotations. By definition, it is implied that action is required from the carrier if it wants to eliminate the risk of not renewing the case.

It's the stick of the carrot and stick approach. From a carrier's standpoint, the moment a case goes to market their chance of losing the business increases. Or, if the carrier retains the case, the pricing may be greatly reduced.

This market scare technique is quite effective. In my opinion, most renewal reductions are attained by this basic technique. The main downside to this is that artificially lowering the premiums down through scare tactics means eventually the true utilization and cost of the program will reappear. Think of it like squeezing a balloon where pressure at one end results in expansion somewhere else. At some point, the renewal will be cost prohibitive and no competing carriers will be interested in quoting the group—leaving you trapped.

Step 5 — The Employer Decision

Under the traditional process, the employer receives the final proposal from the broker/consultant. The employer most likely accepts the recommendation. Additional changes may be made such as benefits changes or other adjustments that could contribute to further reducing the final renewal.

Debunking the best practices

So what's wrong with the current process? The main problem with this best practice is that it doesn't truly manage costs. It considers health care as a liability, something to be reduced and bargained down. There is no holistic approach and only symptoms are treated, not causes. It ignores the most important factor that affects cost — the health status of the users of medical care.

When carriers develop the renewal, the data that is utilized is old. It doesn't matter whether it was last month or 12 months ago, it has passed and may not accurately reflect the future. Additionally, brokers/consultants and employers are fortunate to obtain any meaningful data from carriers. Even if the data is available, how can we know they are correct and reflective of the population that will be using the benefits in the future.

Carriers rely solely on utilization of the past incurred and paid claims. It is not sufficient information to base future rating on. Many of today's high utilizers in a given group may not have even shown up last month or last year. How do we know who will have a heart attack or organ transplant? Yes, of course, an older population will have increased tendencies to have these expensive procedures, but it is not unusual to happen with a younger population. An older person perhaps may be married to a younger person or have a younger dependent.

Demographic variables that are often ignored and can also impact the claim forecast include provider selection and utilization, product and plan design, Medicare eligibility and other payer eligibility.

The pricing formula is another big question. Let's suppose all the data is available and correct, then we have the issue of accepting the carrier's formula to be the most effective in pricing the health plan in the future. The formula hasn't changed much in the last 30 years and many of the factors are based on subjective values.

For discussion purposes, let's imagine that it is the most accurate. But accurate pricing doesn't manage the cost and make it reasonable. A high utilizer is still a high utilizer. Nothing in the pricing formula incentivizes the actual user to pay more or less. The group rate is averaged and all employees get the same rates. So the low utilizers basically are subsidizing the high utilizers. Not sure if employers are aware of this, let alone individual employees. One of the big disadvantages of fully insured plans is the fact carriers charge the risk of a few high utilizing members on to the entire group membership rates...every year...forever.

The broker/consultant certainly is a valuable resource in validating the renewal. Once again, what is the purpose of a drawn-out renewal evaluation when the final outcome is already certain that the carrier pricing must be reduced. Additionally, the renewal sometimes is requested so far in advance of the effective date that by the time the negotiations are completed the trend adjustment lowers the cost. The challenge always remains that negotiating lower pricing doesn't impact the utilization. More importantly, the true costs driving health care is not addressed. The prices charged by the health care providers are the largest culprits to perpetual increases.

The market scare tactics only complicates the process even more. Making the relationship among the broker, consultant, and carrier too dependent on bargaining and negotiation rather than looking at one of the largest contributors to cost—frequency and severity of services utilized by the members. It becomes a temporary approach to solving the symptoms and not the real problem. Like masking the symptoms rather solving the cause…like most prescriptions!

Come to think of it, it's an exact reflection of our government lobbied politicians who refuse to address the primary issue facing health care in America—the wanton and unscrupulous charges billed for medical and pharmacy treatments by the Health Care Supply Chain.

The employer then is at the receiving end of an antiquated analog legacy process that doesn't solve the cause of health care cost increases. Cost will eventually creep up and correct itself. Most likely, the outcome will be a significant increase to the premium rates. In the end, nothing else can be thrown at the problem but cutting core benefits and shifting costs to the employees as a desperate reaction to lower the health care liability. When the population is over utilizing and the premium is underpriced, reducing benefits will not matter much. Drastic cuts must be made to make a difference. Consequently, the result over time is that the coverage is more expensive for the organization and the employees, there is reduced access to care and fewer covered benefits.

THE BLACK BOX

The elephants in the room

The elephants in the room are obvious but not easily understood— health status of the membership and the prices charged by the providers. All health care pricing is ultimately based upon each member's utilization, health status and the cost of accessing the medical delivery providers. Unfortunately, too often the prices charged by medical providers bear no relationship to the actual cost to deliver the treatment because of perverse incentives built into the system.

It is apparent that the traditional renewal and quotation process of health insurance doesn't address the problems at all. The system keeps avoiding the cause and creates a distraction to focus consumers and buyers on the financing cost of accessing medical treatments.

The ugly truth is that carriers hide behind HIPAA and refuse to release meaningful data to employers. Employers don't know their medical utilization, biometrics data or have meaningful claims data that may be indicative of future claims. Employers are in the dark when it comes to knowing what is driving their healthcare costs and the carriers provide no way of assisting employers in managing their emerging health care risks. Why is that?

As an employer, if you don't know what your risks are, all you can do is react to your renewal every year and hope it's competitive (a less bad rate increase than your peer benchmark). The renewal process is like déjà vu every year—hope, shop, spread sheet, compare, shift costs, reduce benefits, limit access to care and add Best Practices that don't work and repeat every year.

Effective strategies that can impact the frequency and severity of the claims should reveal actionable intelligence on adherence, trigger claims that indicate future large claims, gaps in care and purposeful case management. Additionally, all controllable medical and pharmacy claims should be avoided, transferred, and evacuated whenever possible in a manner that is suitable to managing health care risk management to a fiduciary standard.

Big Data—Little Insight

Besides the elephant, carriers also remain reluctant sharing meaningful and reliable information in predicting costs. They look at the past 12 months, past 24 months, past 5 years. There we go, it's like driving to New York from California but only using the rear-view mirror for directions. Their front view is always uncertain because the predictive and meaningful data analytics are hidden in a carrier's box. And, don't assume the carriers' legacy claims systems are even remotely capable of producing insights because they auto-adjudicate the majority of their paid claims to contracted hospitals and providers.

CHANGE YOUR PERSPECTIVE, TO SEE EMERGING HEALTH RISK!

The myth of national consulting firms

The perception of buyers is that large national consulting houses can negotiate better rates and are most likely to set the standards of best practices in health and welfare benefits strategies than smaller agencies or consulting firms. If size were a proxy for quality then clients of national consultants would never have a rate increase. That bears repeating. If size were a proxy for quality then clients of national consultants would never have a rate increase.

Employers often feel confident that their benefits are in the best hands possible because of the name recognition of these large national consulting firms. Some even have offices all around the world. As you look deeper to examine the offering of these firms, you find that everything is not as it appears. For example, the primary growth model of the top national firms is M&A. This includes the acquisition of dozens of small agencies, boutique firms and the occasional platform agency.

The reality for employers is that practice variability and the broker you work with from the national firm is only a piece of the whole picture the firm presents. The recommendations you receive are predominantly a function of the experience of the specific broker you work with on an ongoing basis.

True confidence and certainty in purchasing health care should be measured on the outcome produced as a result of the consulting message, and not based on the size of the messenger.

Managing health care as a liability is not risk management

Managing health care as liability is not risk management because once health care is considered as an expense, like buying supplies and equipment, there is very little management of risk. The traditional way of procuring and renewing insurance includes few components of risk management. It's supply side thinking. Healthcare liability basically is reduced to the cheapest price and this is definitely not the best practice of applying risk management.

However, the new reality of health care in America is that the demand side (self-funded employers) can control the pricing of the delivery of medicine. Think of it as supply chain management for health care. The future belongs to solution providers who can meaningfully reduce the frequency and severity of medical and pharmacy claims while improving the quality of medicine for employees and their families. Anything less is just wasting money on activities that don't work! Health care purchasers should focus on measurable outcomes that predictably reduce claims. And, consultants should be prepared to risk all their compensation if their recommendations don't work.

Craig Lack

President
ENERGI
San Juan Capistrano, CA

Inc. magazine calls Craig Lack, "the most effective consultant you've never heard of." As the creator of Performance Based Health Plans®, Craig consults with public and private C-level executives and independent health care consultants to eliminate employee out-of-pocket expenses, measurably lower health care claims, and drive more EBITDA to the bottom line.

He is a leading authority and a sought-after speaker at national conferences, business coalitions on health and to C-suite groups. Craig has appeared in *Forbes, Inc., Fast Company*, Huffington Post, *Success*, and Yahoo Finance and has been featured on CBS, ABC, CW and FOX.

His mission is to help employees eliminate $1 billion in out-of-pocket expenses.

Inc. says, "Craig Lack is the most effective consultant you've never heard of." http://www.inc.com/logan-kugler/this-entrepreneur-gave-up-nba-dreams-to-make-millions-off-healthcare.html

Forbes calls Craig Lack a "Broker Whisperer for independent healthcare consultants." http://www.forbes.com/sites/davechase/2016/06/26/if-you-want-to-see-the-future-of-healthcare-watch-the-cable-industry-what-happened-to-newspapers/#3af3a2a16bb1

To learn more go to: www.craiglack.com
Engage Craig Lack in a conversation at: www.meetme.so/CraigLack

CHAPTER 13

EMPLOYEE BENEFITS

Measuring Affordability,
Return on Investment, and Results

Rudy R. Garcia

The employee benefits landscape

There is no doubt that the C-Suite and Director level position in Human Resources has become numb to ever-increasing premiums and the ongoing need to reduce benefits, specifically health insurance benefits, to make ends meet. Many businesses already have hit a dead end with no significant savings remaining in the race to the bottom of the benefits bucket. The standard spread sheeting of plans and premiums as a renewal strategy has long been dead, yet the status quo persists. Even after changing brokers one or more times, most businesses are still up against the same challenge: "Where do we go from here?" The uncertainty and lack of confidence in what the government can accomplish has only grown more apparent.

It's no wonder that most employee benefits decision makers have retreated to the storm cellar to wait out the health insurance industry storm that has been raging on since the late 1990s. We are nearing 20 years of steady, and sometimes surprising, increases in the costs of health insurance. That many have given up hope, settling for annual rate increases is a fact of life in the business world. The benefits industry is at the end of the death spiral when looking at options under the status quo approach to employee benefits, specifically the health insurance component.

At this very moment, a movement is afoot. A small, yet courageous and growing group of employee benefits agencies, employers, innovative health insurance solutions and technological advances have given rise to strategies that are reducing costs, improving outcomes, simplifying HR and benefits administration, and improving the health and productivity of the workforce. In this chapter, we describe this grassroots' local effort that is reinvigorating hope; ensuring employees know, understand and value their benefits; and realigning incentives for employees, advisers, insurers, providers, and employers in order to get results that most employers have long since given up on. For those who have the capacity to reignite hope and think outside the status quo box, this chapter is for you.

Rethinking the employer/broker relationship

Since around the year 1998, health insurance premiums have tripled. It may come as a surprise that the income for each benefits broker working on a commission basis has tripled. This should be a huge problem for employers, because the job of the broker is to provide their clients with a better deal, not spoon feed them to the carriers. If a commissioned broker can convince a client to continue on this ever-increasing premium path, they get a raise out of the deal...EVERY TIME.

When was the last time your broker shared how much they earn in commissions in contrast to the value of the services and strategies they are providing? In most cases, this has never been offered as a point of reference because most status quo brokers do not know how to demonstrate their value in comparison to the invisible commissions they are earning from the insurance carrier. It's a conversation they hope never comes up.

The fact is, a new breed of broker exists. The next generation broker is, by all standards, a consultant. They focus on a deep understanding of their client's business mission, vision, goals, and culture. They thrive on transparency and alignment of incentives. They stay on top of current issues and innovations, and deliver solid insights to their client base that drive well-informed decisions that get results. They recommend solutions that bring compliance, benefits, employee engagement, and systems integration together to maximize the client's return on investment through appreciation, efficiency, and effectiveness that can be measured. Later in this chapter, we show how to identify a NextGeneration Benefits Firm.

In order to begin to understand the importance of the benefits package to a business and break the status quo, a paradigm shift is required, regarding the way employers and employees view their benefits, especially health insurance. Our goal here is to give decision makers enough hope that it is worth moving beyond the status quo to give this refreshing approach the opportunity to make a difference that has been so long in coming.

Building a competitive benefits package

Building a competitive benefits package begins with an understanding of a few key pieces of information:

- What is the benchmark standard for the employer's specific industry?
- What strategies can be implemented that minimize employer's expense while maximizing the employees' benefits?
- How well are employees engaged to understand and value their benefits compensation?
- How are results measured?

Today, most businesses believe that simply slapping in a health insurance plan, regardless of the level of benefits and employee cost share accomplishes the minimal standards of reducing turnover and improving health and productivity of the workforce. *This simply is not the case.* Most businesses, sad to say, are simply throwing away large sums of money into premiums with little to no impact on their business goals.

In a given industry, it is important to maintain at or slightly above the standard offering in terms of benefits. If a company is offering a package below the industry standard, they immediately lock themselves out of some employees when it comes to hiring and, in fact, will likely be in a risky position where they could lose their current employees to other businesses who *are* offering benefits at or above the industry standard. To create a benefits program that provides more value than the money, effort and time invested requires attractive benefits, reasonable cost share, effective employee engagement, and well designed & integrated systems to reduce errors & redundancies married with transparency, performance-based compensation, and smart medical case management.

Simple changes in the following area are all part of a strategic offering that produces desired results for your business:

- Offering choice of plans and carriers that meet a wide array of employee needs
- Incentivizing opt outs when employees have other valid health insurance options
- Including a suite of low cost/high value enhanced benefits both voluntary and employer sponsored options
- Establishing effective communications that improve employee engagement
- Ensuring employees see and understand their total compensation statement at least two times annually
- Explore the possibility of moving from a fully insured solution to an employer coalition of proven self-insured solutions that have been consistently reducing health insurance costs by 25 to 50 percent, and keeping it there year after year.

In terms of choice, not all employees are the same, so one-size-fits-all policies are not ideal. If a program is not offering what some employees need, they will be placed at a disadvantage. It makes sense to offer multiple plan levels, all of which meet the same basic criteria, but which are also tailored to provide extras to those who want to take advantage of them.

Enhanced benefits are frequently perceived by employees as a greater value than health insurance. The main reason for this is that employees tend to use enhanced benefits more frequently than health insurance, so they have first-hand value experience. Dental, vision, chiropractic, acupuncture, pet insurance, critical illness, cancer, hospital, and accident coverages tend to fall into the voluntary options where employees simply pay premiums via payroll deduction. Other enhanced benefits like disability insurance, long term care insurance, and life insurance better fit into an employer sponsored strategy. Together, these benefits combined with health insurance make up a robust benefits package that allows smaller businesses to offer a benefits package rivalling even the best offered by larger corporations.

Most employers have never had employee benefit statements, also known as total compensation or "hidden paycheck" statements, which state in hard numbers the full value of compensation packages to employees. When total comp is communicated well to employees, employers have more leverage when negotiating, and employees can see exactly what it is that they are receiving in total compensation before they jump ship for another employer. Until now, the only way to create those benefit statements was by manually compiling and entering data, but today, next generation agencies bring automated and integrated solutions to employers that make producing a benefit statement as easy as a click and view.

Today, many employers with 20 or more employees have discovered the solid results they can get from coalition-based, well-managed, self-funded solutions that have demonstrated the ability to lower and maintain premiums that are 25-50% lower than the fully insured industry average. While the average cost per year per employee under a fully insured product hovers around $12,000, the properly managed self-funded coalition model has been reducing the overall net costs to employers to between $5,500 and $7,500 per employee per year. Unlike the self-funded solutions of the past, new technology paired with the right combination of health experts, data analytics, and aligned incentives has freed up much of the waste that is now buried in the non-transparent system of fully insured medical plans, plan administrators, providers, and broker compensation that has run the status quo up against a wall.

The truth is that there are strategies and well-managed solutions that can restore affordability and effectiveness to the employee benefits world. Once the status quo thinking is broken, the possibilities bring a new sense of inspiration and vigor to business decision makers.

The true employer cost of employee benefits

Return on investment (ROI) is not always as straightforward as it would seem in the realm of employee benefits. Though there are some hard metrics which can be looked at, many of the returns are indirect, yet still very valuable. The intangible returns are some of the most important, however, and they are often the ones which are overlooked by employers who are overly concerned with the bottom line price of employee benefits.

The top two line item expenses for most employers are going to be payroll and benefits, with little variation. Sometimes, marketing budgets or cost of goods may slide into second place. Consistently, employee benefits are in the top three expenditures.

Many employers think of payroll and benefits as two separate items. Benefits would better be thought of, however, as *a function of payroll. To be clear, a function of full-time equivalent (FTE) payroll.* By calculating benefits as "per FTE per hour" (PFPH), employers get a fresh perspective on how benefits can be seen as a function of payroll compensation. From there, costs are better explored, and options can be weighed more thoroughly. Offsetting benefits costs through adjusting raises can now be done accurately. When done well, a complete and attractive employee benefits strategy can be done for under $1 per FTE per hour. An extremely robust employee benefits package can easily fit into less than $2 per FTE per hour. A next generation agency has the specialized knowledge to guide any employer through this exercise.

While the end cost to the employer can be less than one or two dollars per hour, the actual perceived value from the employee far exceeds the investment when properly communicated and reinforced through effective employee engagement and the use of total compensation statements.

Any CFO can tell you that $1 invested in employee benefits is much more cost effective than $1 invested into hourly pay or salary. When an employer utilizes a well thought out employee benefits package, the cost is usually only 70 to 80 cents on the dollar. When a dollar is added to payroll, the true cost is closer to $1.20 to $1.30. The cost to invest in benefits at first blush is, at least, 45% less expensive than adding a dollar to payroll. When you factor in systems integration and employee engagement, many times, your investment in benefits is far exceeded by the increase in employee engagement, health, and productivity. Yes, a benefits program, if properly implemented and managed, can be a profit center instead of a cost center for the business.

PFPH Calculation Formula

- (Total Monthly Premiums – Employee Contributions) x 12 months = Employer Gross Annual Outlay
- Employer Gross Annual Outlay – Payroll Tax Savings – Workers Compensation Premium Savings – Corporate Tax Write Offs = Employer Net Annual Outlay
- Employer Net Annual Outlay/Total Number of Full-Time Equivalents (enrolled or not) = Per FTE Per Year Employer Net Outlay
- Per FTE Per Year Employer Net Outlay / 52 weeks / 40 hr/ wk = Per FTE Per Hour Employer Net Outlay

Keep in mind; this calculation does not take into account the indirect impact of a well-designed and communicated benefits package effect on absenteeism, presenteeism, morale, productivity and employee turnover, and training costs. Once these are factored into the equation, a strategically designed and communicated benefits package not only pays for itself, but drives additional business revenue. It's time to turn your employee benefits into a profit center.

Once an employer begins to look at things from a PFPH perspective, it becomes more clear what changes can be made. Many employers currently stick only to medical because it is typically the largest expense. Can things be shifted to include enhanced benefits both voluntary and employer sponsored? A simple change in perspective can not only drive effective outcomes, but can also take the sting out of the gross premiums associated with employee benefits.

With a thorough understanding of PFPH and what the company needs from its plan to remain competitive, finding and funding a plan becomes easier. There are two primary types of funding for benefits plans. Fully insured comes with lack of transparency and is conducive to fraud, waste, and abuse. It is characterized by having only premiums, copays and coinsurance handled by employees, with everything else being covered by the insurance company. While this sounds less risky, the fact is that most employers are overspending due to the lack of transparency in the fully insured area. Self-funded solutions must always be strategically designed and managed with incentives aligned with transparency and demonstrable results. These solutions are in existence today and are getting results employers have all but given up on. A next generation agency can properly guide employers along the path towards well-run coalition self-funded solution with the proper cooperation and break from the expensive status quo that exists today.

How to measure indirect ROI

There are a few ways which ROI can be financially measured: premium savings, lowered administrative costs, reduction in turnover, improved employee engagement and system/process efficiency. Employee turnover can also be a killer for small businesses. The cost of acquiring and training new employees is enormous. Thus, hiring the best talent possible and retaining those employees is essential. Keeping employees happy with a competitive benefits plan is one way to do that. Smart metrics that measure current turnover, employee satisfaction, and other indirect impacts and compare it to metrics taken after implementing a next generation benefits strategy can further identify successful outcomes and places where adjustments can further increase desired outcomes.

Indirect ROI is more difficult to measure, and requires resolve and consistency. The only real metrics an employer has to go on are surveys and their general sense of what is going on within the company. Managers, executives, and even general staff are usually very aware of the morale of the employees in a company. If that morale is low, it can lead to issues of absenteeism or presenteeism (coming to work but not being "present" mentally, checked out). These are all signs of employee dissatisfaction which, in turn, can lead to a desire to leave or at the very least, to decreased productivity.

Performance metrics are an essential aspect of designing a solid benefits program. In terms of carriers, metrics could include the speed at which phones are answered, how the customer service fares, the ability and speed at which appointments can be scheduled, etc. On the financial side, premium costs are the primary measure. Unfortunately, for most businesses under 1,000 employees, fully insured carriers do not offer performance guarantees. Self-funded coalition solutions, on the other hand, allow for access to all metrics so that employers can redesign and tweak the offering to get better results year after year.

Working with a NextGeneration Benefits Firm

Traditionally, employers were left jumping from vendor to vendor to get all of the professional services they would need. A broker would handle their policies, but wouldn't answer legal questions. HR would either be internal or outsourced, but wouldn't have effective communication with brokers or the law team. An IT team wouldn't understand the boots-on-the-ground needs of employees. On and on, it would go. Why couldn't it all be rolled into a comprehensive, integrated solution with aligned incentives? That's where NextGeneration Benefits Firms come into play.

The agencies who are leading the charge take a consultative approach, reveal their compensation, negotiate multi-year compensation, agree to measurable performance guarantees and get results that most employers have all but given up on. Though they can differ in their approach, the core values are the same:

- A complete, strategic and holistic approach employee benefits
- Commitment to Transparency for Agents, Providers, Insurance Carriers and Third Party Administrators
- Best in Class Systems and Smart Integrations (HR Onboarding, Benefits Admin, and Payroll)
- Client-driven rather than carrier driven with aligned incentives
- Willing to place a portion of compensation at risk based on results and performance guarantees
- Willing to offer multi-year fee guarantees by disconnecting commissions from health insurance premiums
- Present options for self-funded solutions for consideration
- Stay at the leading edge of industry news and innovation to bring the most relevant solutions to the table

Traditionally, a company would do the opposite of many of these points. For example: With fully funded programs, the kind typically used for businesses with under 100 employees, carriers do not provide their utilization data nor fee schedules. Program integration is unheard of, with companies being left to deal with information coming from all sources on their own, leading to a significant amount of data entry redundancy, the same information being passed from Human Resources to Benefits Coordinator to Accounting back to Carriers and often being stored in physical locations as printed documents and within multiple systems. Likewise, brokers and agents are incentivized to deliver rate increases to the clients by receiving compensation from carriers as a percentage of premium, which is actually to the detriment of the clients themselves.

One of the largest ways to decrease and offset benefits program costs is through the implementation of automated and integrated support systems. Rather than working separately with a payroll company, human resources department (internal or external), and a benefits coordinator, the data from all three can be funneled into a single system or integrated best in class systems through which everything can be accessed. Technology to do this simply was not offered to small businesses in the past, but with the growth of Software as a Service (SaaS) programs, it is becoming more and more prevalent, cutting down significantly on administrative overhead and redundancies, while also freeing up man hours and lowering the workload for employees.

A NextGen Firm finds ways to attend to client needs without requiring additional workload and sometimes decreasing existing workloads. For example, by integrating HR systems, benefits programs, and other employee data into a single or integrated databases which can be accessed by employers, employees, and other parties as necessary, Overhead is lowered, efficiency is increased, and the amount of redundancy is dramatically decreased.

Total Compensation Statements are not new, but they are beginning to become more ubiquitous in the business world as people realize their value in onboarding and maintaining employee relationships (and ensuring clients are getting what they expect).

Bringing it all together: Transparency, valuable benefits, maximized return on investment & measurable results

The future of benefit packages revolves around three things:

1) Client driven and complete
2) A holistic approach to integration
3) A thorough look at metrics and ROI

Benefits packages do not have to be a money sink for your company. Rather, they can become a profit driver if they are implemented in the right way. Whether that profit is direct or indirect is up to the person setting them up, but the pros of realigning your benefits with the help of a next generation agency far outweigh the cons. Traditional group benefits methods simply can't remain competitive going the way that they have been for the last few decades. The lack of transparency, race to the bottom mentality and, frankly, greed of some companies, has priced out many small to mid-sized businesses which would benefit from these programs. That has hurt not only the businesses themselves, but also the brokers and the carriers that are committed to serve them. The problem is exacerbated by the lack of transparency that many companies choose to make the norm.

The key to maximizing benefits is through the analysis of metrics and the ROI of the package. By measuring financial aspects, including premium costs and plan levels, and intangible aspects, including employee satisfaction, reduced risk of regulatory penalties and fees, and others, a clear picture of the value of the plan begins to come into focus. Armed with that, employers can better make decisions for their company moving forward and the staff is not only more efficient, but also happier.

The idea that employer-sponsored benefit plans must be a cost center simply isn't the case. The problem is that many employers do not have the time, resources, or knowledge to accurately judge how large an impact their benefits plan is having on their company. By shifting perspective and reviewing the financial and intangible ROI of the benefits plan, it becomes clear how valuable it is and where to make adjustments. Employers can then demonstrate to not only themselves, but also their employees, what value the benefits are actually providing using hard numbers. Armed with that knowledge, employers can shift their status quo benefits from being a cost center to a profit center. The help of a Next Gen Agency is essential to making that transition.

Rudy Garcia

President & CEO
Qandun Insurance Agency
Glendale, CA

After 17 years of working his way from receptionist to senior account manager for Kaiser, Rudy Garcia launched Qandun Insurance Agency in 2012 to fill what he saw as an underserved opportunity in the small business realm. In 2016, Rudy began re-inventing Qandun to incorporate strategies that not only create robust employee-centered benefits but elevate the insurance industry to a new level of strategy, results, and transparency. Qandun has now grown to six employees and is on target for over half a million in revenues for 2017.

Rudy is a member of the Agency Growth Mastermind Partnership—an exclusive national network of strategic, forward-thinking business consultants and benefits advisers. In 2017, he was honored by the Association for Insurance Leadership for his "impressive efforts in the reinvention of his agency as a NextGeneration Benefits Firm that can provide a superior and more cost-effective benefits plan for employers and enhanced benefits for employees."

www.qandun.com
rudy.r.garcia@qandun.com
818-233-8918

CHAPTER 14

BENEFITS ANONYMOUS

*Breaking the Cycle of Employer
Addiction to Healthcare*

Bill Hughes

With average health insurance premiums as high as $7,500 per employee annually, and double or more for a family, any savvy CEO or business owner has to be asking themselves, "when will health insurance premiums surpass salaries and wages?" The answer is the elephant in the room and, if employees make $12 per hour, at some companies, premiums for a family already cost as much as that $12 per hour wage. What can an employer do?

Believe...it starts with a belief that there is another way. It starts with an openness to hear out of the box strategies. These are not typically born of big corporate structure, but of entrepreneurialism and a maverick spirit that bucks every tie-down that holds our crazy health care system in place. But there *are* answers that can provide dramatic bottom line changes that help both employers *and* employees & their families. But it will not happen if we continue down the same path we have been on for 50 years or more.

Go ahead, speak the truth aloud…BENEFITS are BROKEN (Employer-sponsored Health Insurance). And they are broken because the health care system is broken. Now, the insurance industry certainly has contributed to the breakdown, but its cost structure reflects the cost of health care in our society.

Now, if you are there and can admit the truth of BROKEN BENEFITS, you can join my Benefits Anonymous (BA) group and break away from the crazy addictive cycle we are in, which begins with admitting the system is broken. Now that you can speak the truth, it can set you free…if and only if you can take appropriate action from this new truth you have acknowledged.

We will commit ourselves in this BA group to never allow hospitals, insurance companies, or the medical community—or government—to dictate all our choices as free people. We will use our brains, which are God-given, to think of better ways and systems to provide better care and lower costs. And it will always be completely transparent, so we can know the real truth of what is driving these crazy costs.

You will discover strategies you have never heard of or considered, and that's because no expert has taught you. And of course, every company's benefits expert knows it all and does it all, which is why the cycle continues, correct? But if you can lift your head above the fray for an moment outside the feedback loop that passes for benefits dialogue, there may be some ideas that will threaten the profit of insurance companies, brokers, hospitals, and medical providers...and their relationships with you as well. We have to shake their world to the very core to keep you from literally perishing (the current trends unabated will overrun every other expense category and profit in your company eventually). If you are a CEO, the long-term survival of your company, your ability to retire very possibly depends on this very thing being properly acted on.

This is the beginning...but if you would like to know more about a different way, we will first look at "where does our money go?" We must address that in order to fix the problem. Stay Tuned for more about "how to break the cycle." But it starts with recognizing; acknowledging and acting on the truth...it will set you free.

In Volume One, I Discussed the never-ending cost spiral of Health insurance and how it will eventually surpass the cost of salaries and wages if left unchecked. If your plan has had an 8-10% annual cost increase for 10, 20, or 30 years, you must admit that no one in your wheelhouse has an answer to stop the runaway cost spiral.

If this is you, speak this TRUTH to yourself..."My Benefits are Broken...and there is no one to save me!" It is troubling to face this reality for sure, but having faced the truth, it allows us to open ourselves to new conversations. One such conversation we should have is "my assortment of lawyers, CPAs, HR, Benefits Consultants, and risk MGRs have simply been unable to navigate this in a controllable way." Now maybe no one can, but what if someone could?

So if you want to be a self-proclaimed member of what I call "Benefits Anonymous," you may enter my 12 Step Program to break free from this tyrant called Health Insurance, not from its benefits, mind you, but breaking free from the control it now has over you, your group, and your bottom line.

Benefits Anonymous — 12 Steps to Freedom from the Control of Employer Healthcare Over My Company:

Step 1 — I choose to exercise my choice as a free person to never allow hospitals, insurance companies, the medical community, or government to dictate my choices.

This is about being aware, being involved, and being informed. In order to be informed, you must look under the rug, under the hood, dig deeper, and address the elephant in the room. You must let your vendors, medical community, politicians, insurance carriers, and consultants know what you want, need, and even demand.

Even as we pontificate about a 12-step program to break free from the tyrannical monster of healthcare, the cost spiral of employer health plans continues. A never ending upward spiral, that if unchecked, will eventually outstrip and overwhelm all profits and margins in your business, if you allow it to, that is.

Step 2 — I will use my God-given intellect to participate in creating a better way for healthcare in my family, company, community, and nation.

The act of the Human will is powerful. And that power from an Almighty God should never be underestimated. For years, employers have sat on sidelines, while healthcare providers and insurance companies held their fate.

Then the hope was in Government. And we all know how well Obamacare has worked. We must step up to the plate and be counted! We must choose to use the intellect God gave us, the creativity He endowed us with, for after all, we are made in His image! So let's acknowledge our ability, our power, and our intellectual capital to resolve the problems facing us. It may start with some out-of-the-box thinking and listening.

If your advisers have you in programs that year upon year go up 8-10%, would it benefit you to hear some other ideas? Solutions are out there, and putting multiple minds together to achieve a common goal is powerful stuff.

Step 3 — I demand full transparency of all expenditures, so that I will know "where my money goes." This is the first step in directing action.

CLUE: Most employers cannot comprehend the hidden issues in their health plan that they are unaware of. What would possessing that knowledge of the hidden mean? Virtually no one is looking for these things. Like the deep dive into medical spending and Rx spending and how much, why, and is it consistent? I am not referring to reviewing claims reports. They typically are not in transparent formats.

Transparency…Digging deeper into the real meaning so that you have knowledge in order to choose, and choose well, I hope. What the heck do I mean?

Few employers know how the money in their benefits plan is spent. Employers believe they have access to Loss Runs and reports. But do those reports really tell you what you need to know about how the money was really spent? For example, knowing how much my plan spent on a drug is not sufficient! Rather, when my plan is supposed to pay the average wholesale costs of drugs, why did it pay $83 one time, and $300 another time for the same drug on the same day? Is your insurer providing that kind of information, and if they are not (hint 99.5% odds are that they are not), why not? In the end, to a large degree, transparency is putting all the cards of knowledge on top of the table, and helping you understand it.

Transparency is also a choice; a choice you have to make as to whether you will allow people to take your money and exclude you from the inner sanctum of knowledge about how healthcare dollars are spent, or know exactly how, not just where it is spent! For instance, does your insurer make you aware of fees paid by providers to be on their network (can be 30-40%)? Are they divulging clawback fees from Pharmacy Providers? Why not? The secrecy stops here and now, and I demand to know exactly how my money was spent on health services. Sometimes, that message is best sent with a change in how you spend your money, and what insurers or administrators you choose to spend it with, and being proactive about that, rather than reactive about that at renewal time.

Step 4 — I accept that as little as 15-20% of the insured population in a group health plan account for as much as 80-85% of costs. The percentages vary from group to group but the basic ratio causes you to shine the spotlight in the right place.

No one has likely shown you how and where to shine the light in the past. Most benefits advisers do not know how to find these dark crevices and corners and put them in perfect daylight. After all, they are usually paid to sell insurance. They know that well. Insurers at the high levels know how their part of the game is played, but they have no bottom line interest in sharing those tactics with you.

You cannot deal with your costs without bringing these cost drivers out into the light, in order to fully understand the dynamics of what is driving costs in your plan. If you do not understand the cost drivers, it is nearly impossible to take appropriate action to control those expenditures. If I accept that a very small percentage of my population consumes most of the budget, it guides me to a question: what is the next step? The next step is to ask the right questions.

Step 5 — While medicine has made tremendous advances, it is still woefully inadequate to treating many chronic diseases, while waste and overspend in the treatment of chronic illness are rampant. I will use this knowledge to provide sensible options to employees.

CLUE: There may be options.

Health plans limit very inexpensive chiropractic care that helps solve the root problem without invasive surgery, which often leads to further complications down the road. A discectomy and fusion can be $30,000 or more. But that is probably the beginning of several surgeries for many people. The point is, employers often limit inexpensive options and drive employees to the most expensive options that create a whole new set of problems down the road. That is penny wise and pound foolish.

So allow your plan to cover the chiropractor. He is cheaper than a surgeon. Insurance companies are driven by Medical Directors who are M.D.s. They often do not appreciate the value of chiropractic. Do not let their bias hurt your plan or your employees.

Another issue revolves around chronic disease treatment. Cancer, diabetes, auto-immune illnesses, ADD, arthritis, Lupus, and on and on…can often be impacted by diet, detox, and a host of integrative medicine options that cost a fraction of traditional medicine. Our medical system is poorly suited to treat most chronic illnesses. So, if your employees want options that can save 60%-90% of the cost, why not let them?

Step 6—I will endeavor to inform my group about integrative medicine approaches that can lower costs of chronic care by as much as 70%, while creating an underlying foundation of health and prevention with widespread impact on health and prevention.

CLUE: This is not just a wellness program. They are also woefully inadequate. Integrative medicine begins to erode the high-cost structure of services.

This requires covering services traditionally NOT covered by most health plans. But therein lies the power! More of the right things is more healing, less money.

Traditional wellness plans are mostly like the urban cowboy: a very showy cowboy hat and no cattle to back up the cowboy or the hat! I am going to talk about creating health and that is much more comprehensive than a wellness plan.

Integrative Medicine is often the only path that corrects root causes. Most doctors are taught very little about diet. Diet is the very foundation of health, and combined with the knowledge of integrative medicine and its whole-body approach; you can avoid most chronic diseases including cancer, heart attack, and stroke, or hold them off till very late in life. We will all die, but we do not have to live sick and tired as many of us are now doing. Life style and diet change are critical. But the real knowledge of how to pull this off is not widely known, and what is pandered as the diet or weight loss program of the day is not enough.

Let food be your medicine, and let medicine be your food. This is the foundational truth of health. It is impossible to be healthy without practicing this truth. To practice healthy diet and lifestyle takes the knowledge that practically no one is teaching. But knowledge and practitioners are out there.

Step 7—I will implement programs to provide options from the traditional way Pharmacy Benefits Managers buy drugs.

CLUE: This is the second major cost saver, and can SAVE 50% of RX costs.

Pharmacy costs are high. No revelation there. But when we find out that foreign governments buy the same drugs for 90% less than we pay…I get upset. I call it "The Fleecing of America." Some of it is on the back of Big Pharma, and some of it is on the back of Insurance Companies

Insurance companies worsen the problem by clawback. What is clawback? Clawback is basically like a fee that is charged the retailer for being in the insurance company network. I have been told it is as much as 25% to 40% of the cost of a drug. So who pays for it? You do, in an inflated price of drugs you purchase. So how do we collectively do an end run?

- Remember that 15% to 20% of plan participants who drive 85% of the costs? Some high-cost specialty drugs can be $50,000, $100,000, $150,000 annually. We can source those from tier one countries like England, Netherlands, and Canada (not a Canadian Pharmacy). You can save 50-70% there.

- For the more everyday variety of drugs, Walmart has a cash program where cheap generics can be bought for cash for $5. This same drug may have a $20 copay on the drug card. That is a 75% savings, and no expense hits your plan. Educate your employees and help them sign up.

- One doctor told me that she was getting $75 generics for $18. Teach employees how to save money out of their pocket and use these first as their best option. Insurance does not make everything cheaper, and we can stop some of the fleecing by getting the insurance company out of the way for everyday care.

These strategies alone can save your plan 15% of the total plan spend (75% of drug spend).

Step 8 — I will endeavor to arrange education for my employees about all their options to cover their risks.

CLUE: Some employees have better options outside your plan. These options reduce risks of some of the 15% budget busters discussed earlier. They may not be aware of what is available.

How do we educate employees?

- Employee/patient advocacy programs must be implemented to provide employees transparent information about their health care. For instance, information about costs and normal outcomes for a surgery at their chosen provider before surgery can be performed. Typically the best outcomes come from surgery centers that do very high volumes, and costs can vary by facility by 30% to 70%. This is shocking… a better result for far less money. You can pay for the patient and a family member to travel to a high-quality provider with lower, bundled costs. With better outcomes, the employee reduces the risk of complications and the plan saves money on the initial surgery and unnecessary complications. Better results at a lower cost.

- Direct Primary Care (DPC). A direct primary care physician does not take insurance, Medicare, or Medicaid but provides unlimited visits, office care, and even after-hour emergency phone visits for a fixed fee per employee per month, usually $50-$100. This capitated approach removes all the risk and overhead of insurance and admin from your plan, saving 10%–15% of your plan cost. The accumulation of savings strategies are now starting to build like a tidal wave of cost reductions!

Step 9—I will consider new paradigms in pay and benefits that will revolutionize my healthcare spend, while helping employees improve outcomes.

If you keep doing what you have been doing, you will keep getting the same result. Let's change the paradigm. For example, consider the possibility of choosing not to cover Rx that cost under $100, and give the employees the buying tools to get it for cash directly. Some amount could be reimbursed by an HRA. Use HRAs and create a defined contribution to limit your spend, encouraging employee participation in money saving tools discussed previously. Carve Primary Care out of your plan and provide Direct Primary Care. There are some issues around compliance but there are strategies that will make it work.

Use a planning advocate who is highly trusted as a gatekeeper to guide employees and provide pre-certification of procedures. They also can educate employees about centers of excellence, integrative medicine, and health options for chronic care.

Consider carefully the percentage you pay, and how you can pay employees more for lower cost and better health outcomes. Reward good behavior. Much of our current system rewards bad behavior and bad outcomes. Flip the tables!

Don't accept status quo on anything, ever.

Step 10—I will implement SIHRA programs that help reduce member and dependent risks.

CLUE: Do I even know what SIHRA is? Maybe I should find out?

Dependents are, as a group over time, the worst risks. Healthy spouses working are usually on another plan. If you choose not to allow spouses to be covered under current ACA rules, they are eligible for coverage under individual Obamacare plans, and subsidies if income-eligible. When the spouse is on another plan, an option is a highly successful program to incent the employee and dependents to join the spouse on the other plan. The large claims it saves drop to your bottom line. This may impact a small percentage of your population, but effectively deals with some very large potential risks and may save some very large claims from your plan.

Step 11—I will consider alternative funding arrangements and implement them when they make sense.

Another risk is paying too much for administration and insurance. If you can cut your plan's cost of care in half or even 30%, one of two options should be considered.

- Self-Funding. Not to be confused with self-insurance, the employer now basically insures a large deductible. Easy funding can be guaranteed that looks like a monthly premium. You get to save the claim costs.

- Captive Arrangements. You can participate in Captive Insurance Companies that are owned by the participating employers. The insuring mechanism has stop loss like a self-funded plan, but the big deductible layer is shared by several employers. This can help level the year-to-year experience, and with a group of like-minded employers sharing these strategies, it will definitely beat the street plans available. The employers pocket the savings.

- You save 4% on taxes. Every rate increase takes the taxes up.

Step 12—I will not pay brokers or advisers, or be party to an arrangement (such as commissions) on any agreement that pays them MORE when they do not act to minimize my cost. I will consider incentive-based pay to benefit consultants that work for my best interest. I will audit my expenditures and will know how and where my dollars are spent. With transparent detail.

CLUE: How do I do that?

- Brokers are human. If you pay them more when your costs go up, you very well may find yourself paying more. If you pay them more when you pay *less*, you may very well find yourself paying less. It is that simple, but true. Incentives are important.

- Hospitals pay to be in networks (as much as 30% to 40%). Consider contracting directly and tying it to a percentage of Medicare reimbursement. A hospital that gets 50% or so reimbursement from Medicare may likely be happy with Medicare rates plus 30%. That will be 40% to 50% less than your insurance company is paying. With direct contracting the hospital does not have to pay the network fee. So it works. And you have effectively done an end run on your insurance company!

- Audit your expenditures! Demand complete transparency of expenditures with real specificity. Most insurance carriers do not provide it without a serious fight (getting it is likely a losing battle). However, most Third-Party Administrators (TPA) will. Do not allow an insurer to continue without an agreement to provide transparency. They have that kind of information…and hope you never get it. TPAs simply work to administrate your claims. They usually have no interest in camouflaging the numbers. Consider who is working in your best interest. Then go that direction.

Conclusion

As you can see, I have given you multiple strategies to save 4%, 10% 15%, 20% 25%...eventually, a combination of these will ruthlessly slash your medical spend into submission. The key is in knowing and understanding how these dollars are spent and how these systems work, so you can work ***against the system instead of being a willing subject to it.***

Never, ever allow large corporations to control your fate and rob you as part of a high-tech fleecing, ever again!

Bill Hughes

President
BenaFix
Waco, TX

A graduate of Baylor University Hankamer School of Business and an innovative benefits consultant, Bill Hughes has been proactive in reengineering the purchase of healthcare. To that end, he is a published author of multiple books on the topic of Employer Healthcare Management. Bill is passionate about transparency and the reform of healthcare on the national landscape as well as helping employers manage and navigate new ways to purchase healthcare.

Bill is a Charter Member of the Agency Growth Mastermind Partnership—an elite national network of strategic, forward-thinking business consultants and benefits advisers.

www.BenaFix.com
bill@benafix.com
254-218-4600

CHAPTER 15

A CEO'S GUIDE TO MEASURABLY REDUCING HEALTHCARE COSTS RIGHT NOW

John W. Sbrocco, CSFS

Stop Gambling

Atlantic City is a wondrous place; I remember visiting years ago, when the casinos were filled, and the players were waiting in line for a table. Today, most casinos are closed, and those remaining are empty with $5 tables on weekends. As I sit down at the roulette table and watch the ball run around the track, you can see the eyes on players filled with nothing but hope.

This look of hope is what I see from too many employers come renewal time. Unfortunately, most employers' hope lands on green double zero as they watch the insurance carrier win their ante for the next twelve months. If the employer strategy is to annually interview consultants in a grand search for the lowest cost fully-insured carrier, how can the future be bright? If an employer does not address the major issues as to why healthcare costs are spiraling out of control, they are simply gambling with the future of their companies.

Managing Risk

Employers manage risk for every aspect of their business. Whether it be vetting the new drivers for their fleet or a work place safety program to avoid accidents on the job, they must take into consideration these risks that could hurt their bottom line and even put them out of business if they are not strategically managed and accounted for. This is called supply-chain management.

It is very clear why the C-suite is in control of these decisions and strategies in place year after year. However, when it comes to the management of the benefits package, I don't see the C-suite involved. My question is how many other multi-million dollar departments in your company do you let HR manage? Is your HR/Benefits manager the right person to manage the 2nd largest item on your P&L? After all, this individual is typically adverse to change and disruption to employees.

It continues to surprise me that almost all employers that I meet with do not have ANY risk management strategies in place for their health plan that is doubling in cost every nine years, and reducing the value of the company. So why is it that so many employers don't have strategies in place to reduce this rising cost? It seems to me that the status quo mindset has led them to believe there is nothing they can do about it since they have been failing for so long at curbing this financial burden. If you are reading this book, there is good news. Its contents should help you break loose from the grips the status quo has on your organization.

Employers and their employees have become accustomed to believe the story the "BUCAs" (Blue Cross/United/Cigna/Aetna) have been beating into their head for decades. "You have to be enrolled in our networks because we negotiate big discounts on your behalf, and you would go bankrupt without us."

What if I told you that their discounts are typically over 50% and that can sound appealing. However, it's based off an imaginary number no one pays. A 50% discount on a $5,000 cell phone still nets out to you paying $2,500 for a cell phone. So not only are they over-charging you for health care services, but they are charging you a fee in your premiums to access these overpriced contracted providers. You see, this is not the insurance carrier's money they are playing with; it is the member's money they use to pay providers, and they get to keep a percentage of what is paid. The more they pay out, the more the carriers and providers make.

That doesn't even factor in the hidden revenues streams in the system. Sound like collusion? That's exactly what it is. I have seen my secretary negotiate better discounts on surgeries than PPO networks with no pushback from the provider after saying we don't participate in your network and will pay cash. Add that up and what you pay for is a network that over pays its providers and facilities on average 300-400% of what Medicare pays, and in some cases, as high as 1700%!

Now please, tell me the reason you need them? Is this starting to get you mad? I sure hope so, because you have been taken advantage of for years. If you are too busy for this to be of concern to you, then just close the book now. The solutions I will be talking about requires you to change your "there is nothing I can do" mindset. I want you to get ready for the inside secrets on how to take control of your health plan and beat the insurance carriers at their own game. I am talking about strategies to cut healthcare costs today, not by managing member's health, but by strategically slashing the unit cost of care.

Overpaying for Services

How can we expect to reduce the cost of our insurance premiums if we aren't addressing the main factor driving the increases? 90% of the premiums you pay are directly or indirectly related to the claims.

So, ask yourself what you are currently doing today to control the claims spend inside your health insurance plan. If one of your answers includes the big discounts provided by PPO networks, you can just start the chapter over. How can a PPO network, that overpays its providers and makes more money as claims spend increases, reduce the cost of your healthcare spend? These PPO networks have contracts on services like MRI's that pay in the range of $400-$6,700 for the same MRI, depending on what facility you go to. So, if they wanted to pay out less, wouldn't they list the prices and direct you to the lower cost facility? This example is how you should be managing your healthcare spend if you want to control the cost of your claims.

Unfortunately, employers have been led to believe the insurance carriers are doing this for them. Take a minute to think and realize how silly that is…this is the health insurance equivalents of letting the fox guard your hen house.

Are you looking to cut claims spend by 15-25%? Our most innovative employers are providing employees medical services at 1/3 of the cost for most procedures and of higher quality. If an employee buys healthcare services at a lower cost without sacrificing quality, an employer can start to bend the curve on rising health insurance costs. Is it really that hard to have this type of strategy in place for healthcare services? Take a look at how many Amazon boxes are sitting outside your neighbor's door on a weekly basis. You see the forward-thinking employers are providing employees with free care for major services when they make smart healthcare decisions.

Providing an employee a knee surgery for $20,000 from the best surgeon in the region compared to a surgeon recommended by your primary care doctor who did three knee surgeries last year at $60,000 a pop, will certainly start to bend the health insurance curve. Sometimes, you will find doctors performing surgeries at three different facilities; however, they vary in price by five times the amount. Is it starting to make sense as to why your health insurance costs continue to spiral out of control? You have been providing employees with an unlimited credit card to use for healthcare expenses. Is it their fault that their spending habits are out of control?

Now that you know the C-suite should be more involved with the healthcare program than a few hours annually, let's look at some numbers for motivation. Stop accepting the BIG house ABC brokers' less bad renewal increases that are below industry average. Those "Legacy Best Practices" have not helped you beat the system; it's helped keep their pockets lined with the products they represent. Now I know it's easier for your organization to be wrong with the group, then right by yourself. I can only help if you are willing to step outside the box the status quo has most employers trapped in.

Our firm, Questige, is so confident in the strategies we provide; we are placing our consulting fees at risk. I dare you to ask your BIG house ABC broker to do that. Don't be surprised if they change the subject. We recently implemented one of our leading strategies that tailored eligibility, added incentives, and transferred risk, for a lower cost than retaining the risk. The employer was spending 5 million dollars a year on healthcare and saved 30% compared to expected utilization. All we did was exploit Obamacare laws that exist today, and by doing that, we drove new revenue to the bottom line. Using risk management can dramatically reduce your spend, then why are you allowing a benefits manager to make the decision on what solutions could have an immediate positive impact to your bottom line?

Is the Cartel Controlling your Prescription Cost?

In the 70's & 80's, Pablo Escobar was the most powerful drug lord and the leader of the Medellin Cartel. He was earning as much as 420 million a week! His trade flourished so much that he was smuggling nearly 15 tons of cocaine every day. Some would ask how one person could become this powerful and so rich without being stopped. It was quite simple: eliminate competition, get the support of the people, and become a politician. If you didn't go along with it, then he would kill you.

Fast forward 30 years, and take a look at the BIG 3 Pharmacy Benefit Managers/Cartels: These companies made 280 billion dollars last year by passing drugs from the manufacturer to the plan members. Their business model has been very similar to the Medellin Cartel. They started by getting the support of the people to help lower the costs of drugs by buying in bulk.

Unfortunately, they now have grown to the size that they can control the manufacturer by manipulating their formulary lists since it covers so many members. They also built a lobbying group that is the largest in the country (bigger than the next 3 combined) to protect them from competition outside of the US, which creates a monopoly and keeps prices sky high! The lobbying group was able to put a law in place with politicians that make it illegal for Medicare to negotiate drug prices with the manufacturer. How is it that the largest payer of healthcare is not allowed to negotiate prices on bulk buying? We can buy fish from Japan and lettuce from Mexico, but not our medication from Canada?

We have a system that's incentivized upon rebate value. If you eliminate the competition and hold 80% of the market, you can control the manufacturers by requiring them to provide monster rebates back to the Cartel for filling their medication. If the drug manufacturer does not provide the rebates the Cartel wants, they can simply drop them from their list of covered meds and potentially kill the patients taking that medication.

Who is paying for these rebates? The members of course. Harvoni, the newest Hep-C drug spreading like Castro's distribution of cocaine in the 70's, costs about $94,500 per treatment in the U.S. Somehow, the exact same drug costs a measly $900 in India. Who is picking up the difference...the Cartel.

I recently reviewed a drug filled for toenail fungus remover that provided a $700 rebate back to the Cartel for one fill! Now, if the member paid cash for the prescription, they would have paid $500 vs. $1,200. The Cartel has the incentive of a $700 rebate to make sure that prescription gets filled. You see they earned the trust of the people and now the members aren't educated enough to realize who is the one ripping them off.

When the Cartel is removed from the system, we can provide employers solutions that cost the plan typically 30 cents on the dollar for high dollar meds. A recent employer spending $700,000 a year on prescription cost cut their spend to $300,000! What could your company do with $400,000 more in EBITDA?

How Do You Fix It?

Unfortunately, most employers have accepted the status quo and believe if their renewal comes in below trend, they are getting a bargain. They are now budgeting for 8-10% increases annually!!! To me, that kind of mindset will blow up your company's profits and empty your employees' pockets in no time.

Today, the average employee is spending 20% of their income on healthcare costs. So, what can be done to break this trend? If you are not using risk mitigation strategies to manage the internal spend of your healthcare costs, you need to wake up. Our solutions are lowering employers PEPY (per employee per year) spend down anywhere from $2,000-$5,000 annually. For a 1,000-life employer that comes out to **$40,000-$100,000** per week! It's time to get passionate and start winning!

If you have made it this far, then go to **www.questige.com** to see if you qualify for one of our risk management solutions. We are reducing premiums and claims on self-funded and fully insured companies by 15-25%. Although our solutions are not for everyone, the initial conversation will determine if you qualify.

#breakstatusquo

John W. Sbrocco

Principal
Questige Consulting
Madison, NJ

John W. Sbrocco, CSFS is a healthcare strategist and founder of both Questige Consulting and Achieve Health Alliance. He began consulting in 2005 and specializes in bringing innovative risk management solutions to self-funded employers. John holds a designation as a Certified Self-Funding Specialist.

John recently visited El Salvador as a guest of the Ministry of Health on a fact-finding mission to evaluate that country's healthcare facilities and physicians for their Healthcare Abroad program for patients around the world who travel for superior medical outcomes at substantial savings over domestic healthcare.

An in-demand speaker at industry events & conferences, John has been featured in industry publications including, most recently, *BenefitsPro* magazine. He is a Charter Member of the Association for Insurance Leadership and a member of the exclusive Agency Growth Mastermind Partnership—an elite group of high-performing benefits consultants and advisers from around the country.

www.questige.com
john@questige.com
908-444-4064

CHAPTER 16

YOUR NEW PLAYBOOK

Follow These Six Rules to
Win the Benefits Game

Dawn Sheue

**Are you managing your employee benefits
or are they managing you?**

Have you ever wondered why you began offering your employees benefits in the first place? As a fellow business owner, I know I have. I currently own a growing group of insurance offices in the Rocky Mountain West. Most of my offices are in small, resort and rural communities. Believe me, finding deer and buffalo is easier than finding a quality employee where my offices are located. However, in the current economic climate, to not provide basic benefits to my employees would dramatically reduce the already limited hiring pool my company has to choose from. So, it goes without saying that I, like you, have found myself between the proverbial business "rock and a hard place" when it comes to the choice of whether to offer benefits or not.

Like many established business employers, employee benefits have become a hiring and retention tool. To acquire quality employees, you must provide more than a decent wage and a positive work environment. More importantly, the days of simply paying employees a few dollars per hour more to get "best in class" employees are long gone. Potential new hires have become more business savvy. They recognize the value of a full hiring package and have come to make benefits an integral part of their career decisions. As such, employers are now finding that offering benefits has become a business necessity when it comes to their bottom line instead of simply an "add on" value to their employees.

Since March of 2013 when the Affordable Care Act was implemented, employers have seen their healthcare spend increase at an alarming rate. Double digit increases have made this normal business line item go from a manageable part of running the business to an unmanageable financial hemorrhage to the bottom line profit. Cutting benefits and cost shifting to the employees has quickly become the norm which dilutes the purpose of offering benefits at all for the small, mid-size and even larger employers. Strategies such as minimizing work hours, moving employees to part time and cutting services have been used to avoid having to pay additional insurance costs and ACA penalties. Many employers are now spending enormous amounts of time trying to lower their healthcare spend versus concentrating on their business strategies. It begs the question…

Are you managing your benefits or are they managing you?

In March 2013, President Barack Obama's newly signed mandate, commonly known as Obamacare began. While this new law fell short of a true universal healthcare system, it has done little to soften the blow to the American employer. Quite the contrary, many employers have found themselves in a strange new landscape where coverage is required, they are required to pay more, and the added burden of reporting and administration has caused employers to live in fear as to whether their business can survive this huge burden.

The American public is faring no better. The mandate requires all Americans (with some minor exceptions) to carry health insurance or face a penalty in the form of extra taxation. Now, more than ever, employer sponsored health plans have become a desired commodity by potential employees. While America is not in the middle of a Great Depression, our highly trained and loyal workforce is minimized by the retirement of the baby boomers and the influx of the Millennials (a generation that has been identified by the word "entitled" whether right or wrong). This is a whole new ballgame and an entirely new playbook for the American employer.

So let's learn the rules…

Rule #1 — Benefits Are Like the Opposite Sex…you can't live with them, but you can't live without them.

You may want to give this rule a test drive by eliminating your benefits altogether. We have all given this thought a passing glance at one time or another. After years of experience, trust me, it doesn't work and the years of rebuilding a quality workforce will be a nightmare to your business future and your reputation. Save yourself this unenviable experience and move on to Rule #2.

Rule #2 — Adopt New Rules to Win the Game.

No matter how long you have offered benefits, the status quo is no longer working! Every sport from football, baseball, basketball and beyond, has had to update and change their rules (think instant replay) over the years. It is no different with employee benefits. If you are maintaining the same benefit strategy from 3, 5 or even 10 years ago, please STOP THE MADNESS. The current benefits climate requires you to adopt "think out of the box" plays, to manage your healthcare spend. If your current vendor is not adopting cutting edge strategies, it may be time to replace your vendor with a true adviser. (see Rule#3).

Rule #3 — Change Your Players.

Has your current insurance vendor brought you new strategies lately? Like coaches in the NFL, sometimes the same old plays no longer are working for you to win the game. Your team needs to shake things up a bit. Sometimes a new coach can bring in a whole new set of strategies and plays. But be careful, if the vendor still plays by spread sheeting your options with the same old carriers, and he thinks you can achieve different results because his relationship with the same old carriers is "different" — look out!

Ask your potential new insurance partner some of the following questions:

- How have they helped their other clients to actually reduce their claims activity?

- What additional value adds can they wrap into your plan, to cut your surgical and pharmaceutical costs (generally your #1 and #2 largest areas of costs in your insurance plans)?
- What is their transfer of risk strategy? 0. Do they have a proven strategy that will stabilize your benefits spend to a 1-3% maximum insurance renewal every year without cutting benefits?
- What is their 3-5 year plan to stabilize your costs and improve your overall employee health while adding benefits during those years?

If your current insurance partner cannot provide viable solutions in these areas, replace your vendor. (Yes, they are your favorite golfing partner, and you don't want to hurt his feelings—I get it.) But seriously, this line item has to be better managed to achieve a different and better outcome. Find a strategic partner who can do that for your business or face Einstein's definition of insanity: Doing the same thing over and over and expecting a different result. You cannot win the game using old strategies. Onto Rule#4.

Rule #4—Change Who Wins the Game.

In a traditional insurance plan (one that is fully insured where you pay premiums monthly and the carrier takes the risk), who generally wins at the end of your plan year? Believe it or not, it's usually the insurance carrier.

Let me ask you this question. When was the last time your insurance carrier refunded money back to you at the end of your plan year? (I am imagining the Jeopardy soundtrack playing in the background as you think). Okay, what is your answer? Most employers would sadly answer, "Never." So, what happens to unused claims dollars left in your claims bucket at the end of your traditional insurance plan year? It becomes the insurance carriers property to keep, and goes to their bottom line profit.

If you are starting to feel your blood pressure rise, you are not alone. You are thinking that that money should belong to you and your company's bottom line. Well, with all due respect to the fully insured carrier plans, I wholeheartedly agree with you. But, in a fully insured insurance plan, it's kind of like Las Vegas...the house always wins. So how can we change that rule and begin to stop the flow of money out of your company? Let's move onto new Rule#5.

Rule #5 — Implement New Plays.

Generally, fully funded insurance plans are grossly overcharging your group. They don't ask medical questions, so they don't know whether your group is super healthy or not. They don't look at your group demographics (such as age, gender, and behavioral habits like are your employees more sedentary or do they exercise regularly?). Without asking these questions, they have no idea whether your group is more or less preferred in its health risk from the next business down the street. They will charge a set amount whether your group is going to file a lot of claims or not. It's like rolling the dice in Vegas.

The true art of managing your company's health insurance risk is understanding where you stand on the Risk Spectrum. Your benefits strategist should be helping you assess your company's risk on an ongoing basis. Consider the following:

1.   Whether your group is small, medium, or large, a male dominant group will almost always have lower claims costs than

a female dominant or equally mixed employee group. Why? Well, because most men don't like going to the doctor. Now, you might be thinking, "Well that's not good, we need to catch things when they are small." And you would actually be right. But you can't easily change human behavior. Like it or not, if your company is in a male dominant industry, you need to test the law of underwriting averages and see if your group is healthy enough for a level funded premium plan.

2. The younger the employee group, the more immortal they are. While this may sound like an old wives tale, current medical underwriting will back up both the thinking process of the younger employee (I am too young to get sick or hurt) and the medical history of the same group. Younger employees tend to cost less and experience far fewer critical care claims. While this should in no way change your hiring practice or imply any age discrimination, should your workforce already include the younger age bracket, learn to use it to your benefits advantage. Composite rates will bend toward the lower age group reducing your premium spend, as well as potential claims.

3. Medicare Age Employees—The American workforce is aging. While many baby boomers look forward to retirement, many more are continuing to postpone retirement in favor of a steady paycheck and continued benefits. Employers cannot discriminate against employees who work beyond Medicare age when it comes to salary or benefits. However, there are alternatives to insurance coverage beyond just offering them your group sponsored plan. Company education on how

Medicare can benefit employees who qualify due to the attainment of age 65 has proven invaluable to many employees who are confused about what choices to make when it comes to group benefits vs. Medicare. Your benefits strategist should be able to provide onsite education to all employees turning age 65 (including spouses). With proper education about Medicare Parts A, B, D and a full Medicare Gap plan (such as the G or F supplement), along with Employer participation in those costs under the new tax ruling, this can end up being a win-win for Employers and Employees alike.

If your overall Risk Spectrum is at a low level, it is certainly time to step out of the traditional plan design and learn the rules of some of the newer plan strategies. Whether it's consumer driven healthcare such as an HSA or HRA program or the winning strategies behind a level funded plan, begin to implement strategies that better fit your employee population. Any insurance vendor who tries to steer you away from a level funded program discussion is one who doesn't understand the subject matter material or someone more interested in their bottom line, not yours. Either one of those is unacceptable in today's changing landscape. Get a second opinion from a level funded expert in the industry.

Rule #6 — The "Hail Mary" of Employee Benefits.

The famous college and NFL quarterback, Doug Flutie, has long been known for the famous "Hail Mary" pass when his team, the Boston University Eagles beat the University of Miami Hurricanes in the final seconds of the game back in November of 1984. For those of us who watched that game, Flutie's precision pass along with Gerard Phelan's amazing catch has become one of the most memorable moments in sports' history.

For the past 20 years, I have been using a similar strategy to reduce employer and employee costs as well as exposure to medical and financial risk. I call it the "Hail Mary" of the benefits industry or better known as "Baking in the Gap."

Back in the early 2000s, benefit strategies largely relied on increasing deductibles, high deductible health plans such as HSAs and any other type of strategy that would lower the employer/employee spend on health insurance premiums. Gone were the days of $100, $250 and even $500 deductibles. They were quickly becoming too cost prohibitive for most employers. In addition, the flaws of the HMO system were too noticeable to ignore, and many employers were making a mass exodus from HMO plans to the more popular and flexible PPO plan strategies. However, a new dilemma was starting to put pressure on employees, and a little-known group of benefit programs walked out of the shadows. Voluntary benefits had found its place in the game.

Now, for many years, I had advised against voluntary benefits. After all, your employer and I had designed the most "state of the art" benefits plan out there. It should take perfect care of you in your time of need! Or did it?

Now begins the story of a neighbor friend of mine who I'll call Sarah. Sarah was employed by our county, and I had managed the County benefit plan for many years. I was focused on providing the very best benefits at the lowest costs, and I had a track record of keeping annual renewals to a 1-3% increase year after year. The county was generous enough to cover 100% of both employee and dependent premiums. I thought I was doing a great job! That is until the day I had a conversation with Sarah while we watched our kids play together in the neighborhood. Sarah had been diagnosed with a rare form of cancer. Her treatments took her out of work for weeks at a time. In addition, she had to spend thousands of dollars to and from a special treatment center in the Midwest. She had to call in her parents (who lived in another part of the country) to come and watch her kids so her husband could travel with her during her treatments. Now, they were out two monthly incomes! She mentioned to me that they were considering having to file a medical bankruptcy.

I asked Sarah, how could that happen? After all, she had the best medical plan in the area. Her response stopped me cold. She agreed her medical expenses had been well taken care of through her work plan, but it was the non-medical expenses that she had never considered. My heart broke that day for Sarah and her family. I made it my mission in life to explore what type of program could have forestalled this threat to Sarah's family. And then I found the meaning of voluntary benefits. You know, those "add-on" benefits that pay you money if you have an accident or hospital stay or a critical illness. Only after hearing Sarah's story, I decided that these voluntary benefits weren't so voluntary after all.

I began a systematic inclusion program that quickly changed my long-term strategy with my clients. If I could reduce their premium spend monthly and manage their level-funded benefits well enough to refund them unused claims dollars at the end of their plan years, what would they do with that extra returned claims money? They couldn't put it back into operating funds, as it would become a tax liability. How about using it to fill the gap between their employees' medical and non-medical costs if/when something unexpected happens? And so I went into research mode to find "best in class" programs that actually filled in the benefits gap on high deductible plans. I also focused on low-cost programs that would pay the employee money for travel and lodging when a serious accident or critical illness occurred.

Dawn Sheue

President
Summit Insurance Services
Jackson, WY

An employee benefits professional with more than 30 years of experience in the industry, Dawn Sheue has continuously been named one of the top analytical benefits consultants in the Rocky Mountain area. She has founded two successful insurance agencies that focused on tailoring quality, cost effective programs, and expanded benefits for both groups and individuals. Growth in both agencies has been based on education and client advocacy.

Dawn has been widely recognized by the industry. She was honored by *Employee Benefit Adviser* as one of the Most Influential Women in Benefits Advising in 2017 and she was featured in the August 2016 issue of *Employee Benefit Adviser* as the cover story. In 2017 she was honored by the Association for Insurance Leadership for her strong business growth into several states in the Mountain States region. She serves on the board of the prestigious Workplace Benefits Association.

www.summitinsurancejh.com
dawn@summitinsurance.org
800-261-7612

CHAPTER 17

OVERDOSING ON PRESCRIPTION DRUG COSTS

Gary Becker

am not ok with the status quo...and I am a disrupter. I am trying to help re-engineer the healthcare delivery system.

Prescription Spend is the Fastest Growing Cost Impacting Healthcare Budgets

The fastest growing cost impacting healthcare budgets are prescriptions and they're punishing employers. Brand name scripts have skyrocketed at an annual rate of 13% and the 50 most popular generic drugs have increased 373% the past 4 years. The numbers are shocking and it makes offering affordable healthcare coverage a huge challenge.

High cost specialty meds account for 25% of prescription spend and are predicted to spike to 50% by 2020. Hepatitis C meds cost $1,150 a pill, $94,500 for a 12-week treatment. Employers are getting pounded by these bills and the list of specialty meds is growing. Employers are bleeding money and it's crippling their ability to be profitable and it's sapping employee morale. Employees are now functionally uninsured. They have insurance, and they simply can't afford their deductibles, copays and out-of-pocket expenses, so pill skipping is a growing epidemic.

20% of hospital admissions are related to medication non-adherence and it's a ticking time bomb with an average 3-day hospital stay costing $30,000. 20% of an employer's population has at least 1 chronic condition and takes 4 or more medications. Non-adherence can be toxic to an overall health plan.

Financial Challenges and Medication Non-Adherence

- 70% of US households have less than $1,000 of savings; half of these households have no savings at all
- 25% of first-time scripts for chronic conditions are never filled
- 20% of hospitalizations are due to medication non-adherence

Consequences of Medication Non-Adherence:

- employees feel lousy
- employees are less productive at work
- employees end up in the emergency room where the cost of care is highest

A new solution

The time for innovative approaches to lowering the cost of prescription drugs is long overdue. There are now pharmacy cost-mitigation programs (PCMP), such as my company, ScriptSourcing, which are built upon sound business principles that finally are solving these issues for employers throughout the country. A PCMP helps self-funded employers slash the cost of maintenance name brand meds and specialty meds. On average, clients are saving 70-90%.

Simply put, a PCMP is a solutions and engagement company. Its job is to identify opportunities to mitigate Rx spend, engage and educate, incentivize, and help enroll members. When a PCMP is able to help a member with their medication, it's a win/win situation … the employee Rx copay is $0 and the health plan saves money.

The Results

Decision-makers are interested in results, so I thought I'd share a "snip" of a ScriptSourcing invoice. This employer saved 93.9%…an $84,448 savings.

The Methods

A PCMP can offer several programs to help mitigate the cost of name brand and specialty meds (ScriptSourcing offers all three):

- International Pharmacy Program (IPP)
- International Medical/Prescription Tourism (IMT)
- Manufacturer Assistance Program (MAP)

Incentive Drives Behavior … a $0 copay solution is a big deal

Pharmaceutical Items

Date of Service	Item Name	Dosage	Qty	Days Sup.	MAP /IPP	PBM Cost	SS Cost	Savings
01-Jun-17	Tudorza Pressair	400 MG	360	90	IPP	$1,764.33	$403.90	$1,360.43
01-Jun-17	Neupro	2 MG	84	84	IPP	$1,829.94	$318.90	$1,511.04
01-Jun-17	Januvia	100 MG	84	84	IPP	$1,144.31	$257.90	$886.41
01-Jun-17	Ventolin HFA	90 MCG	600	100	IPP	$165.05	$64.90	$100.15
08-Jun-17	Pataday	0.20%	8	4	IPP	$1,426.24	$168.90	$1,257.34
13-Jun-17	Zetia	10 MG	90	90	IPP	$937.34	$264.90	$672.44
15-Jun-17	Crestor	40 MG	90	90	IPP	$519.85	$122.90	$396.95
20-Jun-17	Relpax	40 MG	36	18	IPP	$2,026.87	$340.90	$1,685.97
20-Jun-17	Cambia	50 MG	36	36	IPP	$2,155.55	$531.90	$1,623.65
20-Jun-17	Myrbetriq	50 MG	90	90	IPP	$965.83	$210.90	$754.93
27-Jun-17	Xarelto	20 MG	84	84	IPP	$1,167.34	$345.90	$821.44
27-Jun-17	Elmiron	100 MG	400	100	IPP	$3,550.20	$615.90	$2,934.30
30-Jun-17	Januvia	100 MG	84	84	IPP	$1,196.58	$257.90	$938.68
30-Jun-17	Welchol	625 MG	540	90	IPP	$1,764.49	$886.90	$877.59
30-Jun-17	Lialda	1.2 GM	180	90	IPP	$1,668.94	$355.90	$1,313.04
30-Jun-17	Humira Injections	40 MG / 0.8 mL	12	90	MAP	$26,232.00	$0.00	$26,232.00
30-Jun-17	Xarelto	20 MG	90	90	MAP	$1,218.00	$165.00	$1,053.00
13-Jul-17	Janumet	100 MG / 1000 MG	180	90	MAP	$1,141.57	$165.00	$976.57
13-Jul-17	Humira Pen	40 MG / 0.8 ML	6	90	MAP	$14,616.09	$0.00	$14,616.09
19-Jul-17	Orencia Injection	125 MG / mL	12	90	MAP	$11,312.90	$0.00	$11,312.90
19-Jul-17	Enbrel Injection	50 MG	12	90	MAP	$13,123.80	$0.00	$13,123.80

Totals: $89,927.22 $5,478.50 $84,448.72

% Savings: 93.9%

There is no doubt that a PCMP can achieve significant savings for health plans. The challenge is most people do not like disruption.

Members are motivated to consider alternative Rx sourcing options because:

- prescription advocates take the time to engage and educate members
- prescription advocates provide financial incentives (often a Visa gift card) for enrolling
- prescription advocates help members enroll
- employees pay a $0 Rx copay for their maintenance medication(s)
- employees understand that healthcare is expensive and "we're all in it together" and to the extent employees can be better consumers of healthcare … future premiums, copays, and deductibles will be lower

Dickinson College

I'll never forget introducing our ScriptSourcing solution to the employees at Dickinson College in Carslisle, PA. A teacher came up to me after an enrollment meeting to tell me how grateful she was to have our $0 Rx copay program. She said that, although she worked for the employer of choice in Carlisle and had a fantastic health plan, she was "functionally uninsured" and had been pill-skipping because she simply couldn't afford her copays.

In just the first six months of ScriptSourcing working with Dickinson College, the college saved over $160,000 and we helped over 40 members with their medications.

Big Pharma Corruption

Big Pharma spends more money on lobbying in the US than the oil industry, the gas industry, the defense industry, the aerospace industry, and the education industry...COMBINED.

Big Pharma's interests are aligned with their shareholders. They are funding politicians so they can protect what's most important to them...the status quo. Medications in the US are grossly overpriced and are two to ten times more expensive in the US than other countries. Big Pharma does not want global competition.

International Pharmacy Program (IPP)

The IPP program is pretty simple. The PCMP works with 4 "Tier 1" countries...Canada, United Kingdom, Australia, and New Zealand. A "tier 1" country is a country deemed by our Congress to have the same or higher pharmacy and drug standards and regulations as the U.S.

These four countries speak English, have socialized medicine, negotiate directly with the pharmaceutical companies, and are paying 5% to 50% for the exact same name brand meds that are being sold in the U.S.

These meds are factory packaged and sealed by the same manufacturer, they're sourced though "brick and mortar" pharmacies, and these pharmacies have real pharmacists that are serving their own citizens. A 90-day supply is shipped to members for a $0 copay and the TPA is invoiced for the cost of the medications.

IPP Safety Standards

There are lots of safety protocols which include:

- all pharmacies employ licensed pharmacists and are routinely inspected
- pharmacies only source maintenance name brand medications
- personal importation up to a 90 day supply
- meds are for personal use, not to be commercialized
- no personal importation of heat/cold sensitive meds
- no personal importation of narcotics or lifestyle drugs
- generic medications are not available
- a licensed US doctor must write the script
- meds must first be purchased through the PBM; no "new to you" medications
- initially must have a 30 supply of meds on hand when initially ordering because it takes a few weeks to set up an account

The FDA wants you to think importing factory-packaged and sealed name brand meds from Tier 1 countries is a health risk but that's simply not the case. Big Pharma influences the politicians that control the FDA.

We don't hear the FDA having health issues importing:

- lettuce from Mexico
- fish from Japan

Drug Name & Drug Strength	Quantity	PBM Per Pill Cost	SS Per Pill Cost	Per Pill Savings	Total PBM Cost	Member Paid	Plan Paid	SS Cost	% Savings	Gross Savings
WELLBUTRIN TAB XL 300MG	510	$44.13	$1.75	$42.38	$23,305.12	$797.11	$22,508.01	$894.21	96.2%	$22,410.91
CRESTOR TAB 20MG	1560	$4.65	$1.15	$3.50	$12,182.47	$4,929.11	$7,253.36	$1,793.36	85.3%	$10,389.11
GLUMETZA TAB 1000MG	150	$52.00	$1.57	$50.43	$7,979.36	$180.00	$7,799.36	$234.86	97.1%	$7,744.50
ELMIRON CAP 100MG	1350	$6.67	$1.51	$5.16	$9,565.55	$555.00	$9,010.55	$2,044.55	78.6%	$7,521.00
LIALDA TAB 1.2GM	1080	$5.20	$1.92	$3.28	$8,407.44	$2,792.34	$5,615.10	$2,072.70	75.3%	$6,334.74
ELIQUIS TAB 5MG	1560	$4.00	$2.45	$1.55	$8,977.06	$2,730.59	$6,246.47	$3,828.47	57.4%	$5,148.59
STRIBILD TAB	180	$87.04	$60.25	$26.79	$15,868.06	$200.00	$15,668.06	$10,845.86	31.6%	$5,022.20
CRESTOR TAB 10MG	540	$5.13	$1.02	$4.11	$4,058.21	$1,286.22	$2,771.99	$552.59	86.4%	$3,505.62
INVOKANA TAB 100MG	390	$10.85	$3.24	$7.61	$4,685.13	$455.00	$4,230.13	$1,262.23	73.1%	$3,422.90
SPIRIVA CAP HANDIHLR	390	$10.73	$2.67	$8.06	$4,293.91	$110.00	$4,183.91	$1,040.51	75.8%	$3,253.40
LATUDA TAB 60MG	120	$26.32	$5.79	$20.53	$3,437.96	$280.00	$3,157.96	$694.36	79.8%	$2,743.60
BREO ELLIPTA INH 100-25	900	$4.38	$2.22	$2.16	$4,506.15	$566.82	$3,939.33	$1,995.33	55.7%	$2,510.82

IPP Savings Analysis

If an employer is interested in a savings analysis, the first step is to determine their "overspend." A PCMP requests a report from the PBM called a "Detailed PBM Report" and is able to analyze eligibles for the IPP program. It's not unusual to see savings of 90% for certain meds.

Multiple Sclerosis Medication Savings

Multiple Sclerosis medications are grossly overpriced in the US and there is a huge opportunity to help employers...and employees.

Tecfidera
$83,356	240 mg	Annual US PBM Cost
$35,095	240 mg	Annual IPP Cost
$48,261	Annual Savings	

Gilenya
$66,699	0.5 mg Annual US PBM Cost
$28,013	0.5 mg Annual IPP Cost
$38,686	Annual Savings

Data Analytics

A PCMP works closely with the employer's TPA and PBM. Data feeds are established to help identify all members who are taking eligible medications. PCMP advocates are able to identify opportunities to engage members and encourage adherence.

Rogue Internet Pharmacies

The FDA is cognizant of and has taken action against rogue internet pharmacies that do not have pharmacists and/or are dispensing counterfeit medications.

Every pharmacy that a PCMP does business has been in business for decades, has real pharmacists, and are routinely inspected … including by governmental agencies. Furthermore, there is a $2 million dollar Lloyds of London liability policy to protect consumers (there has never been a claim) and Lloyds of London inspects the pharmacies as well.

International Medical/Rx Tourism (IMT)

We've all heard of "destination weddings." Well, "destination healthcare" is now available. There are opportunities to travel to places like the Cayman Islands where the cost of expensive medications is significantly less expensive than the US, saving tens of thousands of dollars per patient.

Health City Cayman Islands has one of the most impressive and efficient hospitals in the Western Hemisphere. They are transforming healthcare similar to how Henry Ford transformed the automotive industry.

A PCMP is able to create a win/win situation for employees and the health plan by sending employees to the Cayman Islands for an "all-expense paid treatment/vacation" including flights, beautiful hotel, and meals. The employee receives treatment and their meds at no cost. The health plan savings are impressive. Here's an example:

Gary Becker

CEO
Becker Benefit Group, Inc. & ScriptSourcing, LLC
Baltimore, MD

Gary Becker has been a benefit consultant specializing in self-insurance since 1985 and is the CEO of Becker Benefit Group, Inc. and ScriptSourcing, LLC.

In 2009, Gary created the first benefit captive in the Mid-Atlantic area, helping like-minded mid-sized employers transition from "fully insured" to self-funded" to achieve transparency, control, and risk management.

His impressive success in risk management led to the formation of ScriptSourcing, LLC—a pharmacy cost-mitigation program providing solutions and engagement to help employers slash the cost of maintenance name-brand meds and specialty meds by 70-90% while providing a $0 copay for health plan members. In 2017, Gary established Achieve Health Alliance which is an exclusive benefit consortium for highly proactive benefit consultants and employers.

In 2016, he received the "Innovation Award" from the Association for Insurance Leadership in recognition of his "contribution to the advancement of innovation in the employee benefits industry."

www.scriptsourcing.com
gary@beckerbenefit.com
410-902-8811

CHAPTER 18

BREAKING THE ¾ COURT PRESS IN BENEFITS

Randy K. Hansen

Ever feel like the health insurance industry, the annual rate increases, your broker, and the never-ending list of government compliance requirements have you working against a well-orchestrated ¾ court press? You're not alone! Many business executives and HR managers feel the intense pressure, yet have no way to break the press or ability to go on the offensive. It's one of the few areas in business where you purchase a product from a vendor, and then have little to no say in the product, its cost, or how it is delivered. Remember, they are called *employee benefits* for a reason...they are supposed to benefit employees! And, the employees are supposed to appreciate them.

Even our government has gotten into the act, trying to save us from this runaway train known as health insurance. But we have discovered that the problem is too big for a simple or canned solution. Over the following decade or two, both political parties will have their chance to "fix" the problem. While the eggheads and the talking heads are working on it, you still have a problem: How do I continue to offer affordable, quality coverage for my employees and their families? And I mean coverage that they will appreciate.

Let's start with the view from your level. You generally deal with a broker or consultant in whom you must put a lot of faith. Remember, depending on the size of your company, this may be a top five or even top two spend annually. The choice on who to allow to guide you is an important one. Understand, bigger is not always better. What's the old saying? "If biggest was best, elephants would rule the world."

Big or better?

With the ever-changing environment of health insurance, you want to make sure that you have a professional...but one who will care enough to get to know you, your business, and your employees. Small enough to care, big enough to get the job done.

The big, beautiful office towers are filled with brokerages who want the big fish — and do a great job in those waters. End result at those big brokerages is that the smaller fish get the "up and comer" assigned to their account until he/she has "up and come," then he/she gets promoted to bigger, more profitable accounts. What happens to you? You get a new "up and comer," and the process starts all over again. Just when you think you have someone who knows you and your wants and needs, they move on where there are bigger fish to fry.

Why do you think Ace Hardware has built such a successful business? Think about it: When you walk in, it is not a 200,000-square foot building with ceilings 60 feet high. My local Ace Hardware has had the same group of people working in it for years. I walk in and they know my name. People who over time have earned my trust. I get in, get what I need, and get out confident that I have the tools to get the job done. Does it cost a lot to have this elevated level of service? Nope.

So, do you want to be treated like a Fortune 500 company? Find yourself an Employee Benefits firm where you get the benefits of the 60-story office building, from a firm that intimately gets to know you and your company (your employees, too!). Owned and managed by an entrepreneur who understands a clear picture of the customer.

Ace Hardware keeps its promise and delivers what you expect, time after time, without fail. They do this in a small, comfortable environment. You can get that same thing, through a firm small enough to bring you the consistency you want. So, when you are looking for a broker/consultant relationship, look where you can deal with the same person, year after year. No hand off, no intern, just an experienced consultant who wants to bring a program your employees will like and again...appreciate. Personal relationships will get you more loyalty, more quality communication, and better service—every time!

Now that you have found that consultant, what are you looking for? Today's successful employers are asking for and deserve something more than a rate quoter. Sure, you want the best plan at the best rate. But there should be more to your personal RFP (Request For Proposal). This personal RFP is not a list of meaningless details that might apply to a group the size of the City of Los Angeles. What is meaningful to you?!

HR technology

Technology is your friend. Used to be that you had to be one of the "big fish" to get services like online enrollment. Find someone who will treat you like a "big fish"! Online portals come in all shapes and sizes, and can help you by going paperless, simplifying enrollment in just one step. Do you have multiple carriers providing you with multiple products? That probably means that you are sending paper enrollment forms to multiple locations, on every new employee you enroll. Then, at termination, you repeat the process by sending multiple termination requests. Add to that the notice that you send to your COBRA administrator, so you stay in compliance, and you have made a lot of stops. Now, multiply that times the number of employees you hire or employees who leave your employment each year.

You can save a tremendous amount of time with online enrollment. Add to that 1095 reporting at the click of a button, reports at your fingertips, and integration with payroll providers. Getting an idea yet of how you must have technology? The savings will help pay for those plans that you have to offer to stay competitive in the job market.

At a renewal, ever hear "Here is your current deductible, if we increase it, we can save you some money." Isn't that what everybody does? Raise deductibles, copays, benefits in general...to lower the renewal rates and attempt to keep the premium at a reasonable increase. The net result to your employees is less benefits, slightly higher costs, and anything but a feeling of this being an *employee benefit* to them. How about some creativity? Are there other ways to lower costs without stripping benefits away from your employees? With "trend" running at 5% - 9% for many years now, rates are going to increase. Time to demand more! Bridge plans...GAP plans...HRAs, demand to be shown and know more strategies.

Alternative funding

Take off the blinders and discuss your alternative funding options: level funded and some forms of self-insured plans. Are they a good fit for every company? Absolutely not! Some small companies thrive on plans other than fully-insured, cookie cutter plans. But imagine actually seeing claim information (limited based on privacy rules, but claims none the less). No more guessing as to whether you are the company that has low claims and is helping keep the profits up at your local insurer, or whether you are the goat of their insurance pool. Many times, when you are the goat, they figure out a way to communicate that, as they try to encourage you to find another carrier. When you receive that rate pass or very small rate increase, don't you wonder if, in fact, you should have gotten a 20% rate decrease based on your actual claim experience?

There are a lot of factors that go into rating a group, including the size of your group. Most smaller companies (for this example, let's use 500 lives or less) are too small to be 100% credible. So other factors (like how the pool they are in is performing) must be considered. But, if you are that small retail running shoe and clothing chain that hires primarily 20 to 30-year-old people who also happen to love running....wouldn't you think that you would be a profitable risk for an insurer? Other than the physical therapy benefit being used for sore joints and muscles, that is probably a pretty healthy group of employees!

Benefit options

Demand to see more benefits! Most of these can and should be set up as voluntary, and the employee has the option to pick and choose what plans fit his or her lifestyle (Note: the employee pays for these additional benefits—no cost to the employer). Research shows that employee satisfaction of their benefits increases with the offering of voluntary benefits, such as life, disability, accident and critical illness insurance. Take this as an example. How many times have you seen a "Go Fund Me" announcement because someone either had an accident and cannot afford the out-of-pocket maximum from their medical plan, or a young person dies and their family needs money to give them a proper burial? More and more, I see employees making a quick, easy decision to purchase voluntary life insurance in the amount of $20,000 to $30,000 for the sole purpose of funding their own burial, if needed. Nobody wants someone else to be burdened with that sort of a cost. Nor do they want to be asking for money while they are laying in bed, slurring their words and unable to feed themselves. They would have nothing but time on their hands, time to think about the financial burden their family now has to address.

So, demand to see those extra benefits. You can always decline to offer them, but as a successful business person, you need to know about them.

A benefits partner

Lastly, find a business partner (benefits consultant) who thinks like you, and who will be there ten years from now. This is a RELATIONSHIP, not a vendor! With all the chaos in the healthcare system right now, you can't find the time to know all that you need to know. Find someone who, as I mentioned earlier, is *small enough to care but big enough to get the job done!*

I warn new clients of one very important detail. For good or bad, they get me from here on out. No losing a consultant because of a promotion in their corporate world. My promotion is getting to work with that client, getting to know their business, their employees, and…what is important to them. Not just an annual meeting to deliver a rate increase. Your healthcare and employee benefits dollars are a big spend for the business each year. Trusting it to an emotionless machine is not good business. Find someone you can trust, and stick with them.

Randy K. Hansen

President
PSG Washington
Everett, WA

Randy K. Hansen is president and founder of PSG Washington. His 30+ years of advising clients on employee benefits, HR legislation, and buy-sell & estate planning have made him a valuable adviser to business leaders across Washington.

Randy is a popular guest speaker at numerous estate planning functions, including local county Estate Planning Council meetings. He's also been a featured lecturer at local CPA firms' continuing education workshops, focusing on the use of life insurance in estate planning.

In 2017, Randy & PSG Washington were honored by the Association for Insurance Leadership for their "impressive progress in the reinvention of their agency as a NextGeneration Benefits Firm that can provide a superior and more cost-effective benefits plan for employers and enhanced benefits for employees."

Contact Randy:
www.psgwa.com
randy@psgwa.com
425-258-1768

CHAPTER 19

"BEST IN CLASS"

How to Identify the Right Adviser for Your Organization

Cathy Aitken

"Do I really need a benefits adviser? And if so, whom do I select and how?" These are vital (and often daunting) questions for executives and HR professionals of both large and small organizations.

If you look back on your past experiences, would you answer the question with a resounding "yes", or would you take a few seconds before you answer? If you didn't answer in the affirmative or have reservations about the value you're currently receiving from your existing adviser, then read on.

The investment your organization makes in your group benefits programs is huge, and every company deserves to have the "best in class," right advice. It is a big investment, and making a wrong decision can end up costing the company lots of money not to mention lost time and talent.

In the era of health care reform and other compliance priorities, a strong benefit adviser relationship takes on a greater importance more than ever. As key elements of health care reform have taken hold over the last several years, employers need (and should be demanding) an adviser to help guide them through the constant changes, and plan ahead to deal with new employers' responsibilities.

Of course, the definition of a good adviser will depend on the employer's needs and what the adviser can do to meet those needs and concerns. Not all advisers are equal, but what is it that separates one adviser from others?

Advisers that take a consultative approach, focusing on finding solutions to employer challenges rather than on selling products, can provide employers with the knowledge and tools to effectively manage their benefit plans, costs, communication strategies, and compliance obligations.

An adviser's willingness and ability to provide this type of value should be a key consideration for employers. That means looking for an adviser that can provide advice to support client's decision-making as issues arise throughout the year and not just at renewal or open enrollment. For example, a multi-unit restaurant company that is having trouble getting the attention of their low-paid employee population might look for an adviser that can provide strong benefits communication support specifically for the restaurant industry.

Another key misconception that has resulted in massive unwarranted costs is that "bigger is better" when it comes to an advisory firm. The reality is that an adviser's firm size is not inherently indicative of the level of service and support a company can expect. The focus should be on expertise, meeting needs, and solving problems, not on how many employees a given benefits practice has.

Most companies fall into the common trap of asking several firms to "bid" your business through what seems to be a reasonable and highly technical RFP process. In the industry, we call this the "dog and pony show." Nice glossy presentation, PowerPoint, all the bells and whistles, expertise, reports for tracking claims, customized communication, customer service, etc. You are "wowed!" It all sounds great right? The problem is gloss often is designed to glaze over a lack of strategic expertise and insight.

This is a status quo process and historically, it worked fine. However, in today's chaotic and ever-changing landscape with rising costs, more competition, etc, pretty, cliché-filled presentations with little to no substance are not going to produce meaningful change for your organization. Shouldn't the adviser be interviewing you and your team, asking pertinent questions to you, just like you want to ask them?

You want to work with an adviser that is going to find solutions to your ever-changing needs. What is the point of talking about the adviser's capabilities if those capabilities don't serve your company in a meaningful way. Too often, organizations (perhaps yours) are left with a great presentation, "we do this, and we do that" and little else.

Of course, first and foremost to select the right adviser, you need to first know what you are looking for specifically and be open to the education that the best strategic advisers are capable and obligated to provide. This entire book is based on the concept, "moving beyond the status quo," meaning it is time for employers and advisers to think "outside the box." If you are not ready to embrace innovative thinking, then you can stop reading now. If you are happy with the "status quo," of your adviser doing very little, getting compensated handsomely by the carrier, while you pick up the bill in the dark, then the rest of this chapter and the others won't serve you.

Are you still reading? Excellent — then I assume you are ready to "move on from the status quo," and work with a "best in class" adviser. Let's get to it. How do you move on from the status quo?

I have already mentioned, the adviser should be asking you questions so they can focus their strategies on your concerns and challenges. The adviser should have a specific process in place to help you identify and articulate those issues. The best process begins with some sort of "exploration" assessment or questionnaire to help find out your areas of concern. After that, the adviser will want to complete a more detailed "evaluation" with you before making strategic and tactical recommendations.

A "best in class" adviser is going to ask questions like, "Why do you and your employees feel that way?" It might surprise you to find out that often, the employees are not dissatisfied with their benefits — they just don't know what their benefits are in the first place! The adviser might ask, "Do the employees truly understand the plan in front of them and how it works? Do you think your employees would be more engaged if they experienced a better outcome when utilizing their benefits?" You can see how that conversation is far different from the "status quo" conversation you've likely had in the past.

Good communication mentioned above works at open enrollment, but what happens 2 to 3 months down the road, people forget what was said, the spouse has questions, the employee now goes to the HR department, or the owner, depending on your size. What happens with new hires throughout the year? This all amounts to a bigger and bigger burden on you and/or your HR staff. Therefore, a worthy adviser might offer up a solution after open enrollment, so employees do experience a better outcome.

Imagine the following…

- Instead of having to go through a medical healthcare system alone, your employees are guided through by a health care concierge service, assisting employees & spouses navigate through the healthcare medical system.

- An employee gets an EOB and is trying to figure out, did I pay too much, thought I already satisfied my deductible? The employee either does it on their own, or they come to HR. What if they simply call the concierge who can assist, help negotiate, and resolve the issue leaving HR or the employer out of the picture, thereby freeing up valued employer's time and resources.

- An employee being diagnosed with knee surgery & having access to multiple second opinions that may suggest a different course of treatment, saving costs for you the employer and employee, and the trauma of going through a major surgery.

These are the kinds of results that a "best in class adviser" can bring to your company!

When a "best in class adviser" meets an employer that is ready to move beyond the status quo, the value that can be created is immense.

Once you've moved through the "exploration" and "evaluation" phases, it's time for the "education" phase where you should look to the adviser to provide a detailed report that will educate the employer on the value and cost, if any, for the recommended solutions. A strategic plan should be included within this report, illustrating a timeline and a clear path of how the adviser, their team, and the employer's team will work together to produce and achieve the process-driven solution.

You have now shifted yourself away from the "status quo," and you will be thinking "outside the box."

There are many proven strategies and concepts out there in our ever-changing industry, knowing those strategies and concepts and working with an adviser that shares the same strategic thought process as you and your organization, will make you both the "best in class."

Here's a quick recap to ensure you're working with a "best in class" adviser:

Finding Your Needs — The adviser should have a process in place that asks the proper questions to find out as much information relating to your specific challenges and concerns. You are not looking for an adviser who still offers up spreadsheet after spreadsheet, promoting the lowest rates. You are looking for an adviser who applies a truly consultative approach, asks strategic questions about your company, and looks beyond the scope of your benefits situation.

Changing Industry — Our industry is changing constantly so it's vital you have an adviser who is up to date and keeps you consistently informed. Communication is key in this area, and the adviser needs to put your mind at ease by illustrating their proven process-driven solution. This might take the form of email alerts as legislative changes happen, monthly newsletters, employer access to specific software, just to name a few.

Problem Solving — In the past, cookie-cutter solutions and services were enough; one size really did fit just about everyone, but no more.

You are looking for customized solutions and a specific approach to your company's situation. This does not necessarily mean the adviser will suggest different services and solutions to each of their clients, but rather they will ensure their recommendations are intentional and appropriate for your company. Before recommending a strategy or service, the adviser will determine through the evaluation process the employer's specific needs, and then suggest a solution and/or service with an implementation strategy based on that same evaluation process. Keep in mind not all advisers have direct access to all specific solutions that may be required. The best advisers are not just solution providers; they are also solution finders. If the adviser does not have access to it, they can help you find and acquire it for the benefit of your organization.

You have the choice of choosing who you want to work with. My best advice is to get to know your current adviser and put them through the interview process that was discussed earlier. If the interview falls short, you will immediately know you are not working with the right person.

If you have been given this book by one of the contributing authors, you are one step ahead of the game. As you read this book, you will find many different variations of strategies available to all employers, regardless of your size. While the insurance industry will continue to change and evolve, so will the concepts and strategies, and so will the best advisers becoming more and more valuable to the clients they serve. Working with an adviser that has their "ear to the ground," who is not afraid of change, understands the complexity of the industry, and is always looking for the right solutions, will make your organization a healthier, more productive, and more profitable one.

Cathy Aitken

President
Corporate Benefit Analysts
Nashville, TN

Cathy Aitken is the president of Corporate Benefit Analysts, Inc. (CBA) an employee benefits advisory firm devoted to helping organizations small and large design and implement strategies so they can contain costs and maximize their human capital.

Cathy has a rich background in the employee benefits world having helped clients throughout the United States and Canada on a variety of issues ranging from basic plan design to full benefit strategic planning, employee enrollment, detailed plan communication and beyond.

With a strong focus on non-profit organizations, CBA is well-equipped to deal with budget restrictions and unique challenges that present themselves.

The firm's ability to communicate with its clients to determine the client's specific needs and desires combined with a very pragmatic approach makes CBA an attractive benefits consultant and partner with companies and organizations across the country.

www.CorporateBenefitAnalysts.com
caitken@corpbenusa.com
615-331-0888

CHAPTER 20

DEFINED CONTRIBUTION

*Regain Control on Cost
& Increase Employee Options*

Brian Tolbert

Transitioning to a Defined Contribution Benefits strategy isn't a new idea. Employers could have been doing it for decades. So, why haven't you?

Status Quo

Once upon a time, employers used to offer $0 deductible health plans and pay 100% of the premium. It was a magical time. But after years of employers swallowing the increases passed on by insurance companies, they've reacted in two ways:

1. <u>Change Plan Designs:</u> Introduce higher deductibles, out of pocket maximums, office visit and prescription copays, narrower provider networks, FSA's, HSA's, HRA's, etc.
2. <u>Increase Payroll Deductions:</u> First thought was to charge employees 2% of premiums, then 5%, 10% and so on.

The majority of employers we meet with have been doing this for so long that they fall into something I like to refer to as the **Status Quo**.

Specifically, they're offering two plan options—"Base" and "Buy-Up"—and paying 80% of the Employee-Only coverage on the Base plan. Sound familiar?

The funny thing is that the Status Quo works pretty well when you get a 2-3% increase. Employers can keep the same plan designs and both Employer and Employee can afford the nominal increase. No big deal.

But things get tricky when the plan receives a 22-23% increase. Those years see an all-hands-on-deck approach to the renewal! The HR professional, CFO and business owner roll up their sleeves with their broker / consultant / adviser / golfing buddy (whatever title you want to give people like us) to pour over spreadsheets comparing plan designs. Hours and hours of collaboration and of course a strategy to communicate the plan changes to employees.

Through hard work, the Executive Team ultimately gets the renewal down to 12%, and feels pretty good about it! Sure, they "tweaked" the plan a bit by increasing the out-of-pocket maximum, making a

onto your employees. So let's move into how you're increasing options to employees.

1. Maximize benefit options available to your employees
    a) Let's say your "Base" plan is a high deductible plan and your "Buy-up" is a lower deductible.
    b) Stop telling your employees, "*We're offering a Base and a Buy-up Plan.*"
    c) Start telling them, "*we pay the first $300 towards the cost of your health insurance.* and you can choose from 4 plans (or 5 or 6 or 7, etc).
    d) Here's what the plans should look like in your transition year:
        i.   <u>Option 1</u>: Match the *plan design* of the "Status Quo" Base Plan
        ii.   <u>Option 2</u>: Match the *payroll deduction* of the "Status Quo" Base Plan
        iii. <u>Option 3</u>: Match the *plan design* of the "Status Quo" Buy-Up Plan
        iv.   <u>Option 4</u>: Match the *payroll deduction* of the "Status Quo" Buy-Up Plan
        v.   <u>Option 5</u>: An HSA-eligible plan (if not included in one of the first 4 options)

Let's do a quick Q&A:

1) **Question**: Are employees happier with more options, or are they just confused?

    Answer: Your concern of creating more confusion is a valid one, but theoretically offering employees more options merely increases the probability of meeting everyone's needs.

Instead of worrying about possible confusion, challenge your benefits adviser and their ability to clearly communicate and help match employees with the plan that best meets their needs.

2) **Question**: What can I expect enrollment numbers to look like?

   Answer: What's hard with the Status Quo is that you didn't want to make too much of a plan design change because you were thinking about the employees that really utilized the plan. Meanwhile, you were over insuring everyone else. Following the 80/20 rule, you'll find that 80% of your employees will enroll in a plan that costs less than either of the Status Quo plans you've offered in the past.

3) **Question**: What do my renewals look like every year?

   Answer: Each plan offered will receive its own renewal. So one plan might get a 5% increase, while the other could get a 25% increase. For the plan options that receive reasonable increases, keep them. The ones that get big increases, work with your adviser to find suitable replacements.

4) **Question**: What should I do in a year I get a 40% increase on all plans.

   Answer: The likelihood is really low but if it happens you'll have to go to market possibly making dramatic changes. Bear in mind you'd be doing that if you stick with the Status Quo anyway, so you're no worse off than where you would have been.

The Catch

Defined Contribution isn't a new concept or strategy. You could have been doing this for the last 10 years if you wanted to. The trouble is that it's impossible to implement using paper processes.

If you haven't already adopted a technology platform to streamline your processes, you've got to do that — or ask your adviser to help you do it. To put a finer point on this, let's compare logistics around our Status Quo and Defined Contribution scenarios.

Process under the Status Quo:

1) You're giving employees paper forms that explain the benefits and illustrate payroll deductions. Those forms ask employees to communicate who is to be covered, birth dates, social security numbers, etc.

2) In a worse case scenario, you're handing them the insurance company enrollment forms and asking them to enter this same information over and over (one form for United, one for Guardian, one for Unum, and so on.)

3) Employees review the information you've handed them and make an Employee-Only, Employee-Spouse, Employee-Child(ren) or Family election, for either the Base or Buy-up Option. That's 8 different payroll deductions any one employee could have.

4) Once you add ancillary benefit elections for things like dental, vision, voluntary life, short term disability, long term

disability, accident, critical illness, cancer… more forms and more payroll deduction combinations—which is likely why you aren't even offering all of these benefits to your employees in the first place(!)

5) Now it's someone's job to collect and review all the forms in order to communicate benefit elections to insurance companies and calculate payroll deductions and then key into your payroll system.

6) We should also acknowledge that it's not easy to get these forms back from employees by the deadline and can be even harder to read their handwriting. Not to mention many of them are incomplete, missing dependent birthdates and SSN's.

Defined Contribution is attractive because you're able to offer employees so many options—but you will never be able to implement without technology.

Process using Technology:

1) Employees log into a Benefits Administration system and can view benefits, payroll deduction amounts, and if necessary download Benefit Plan Summaries and Provider Network lists.

2) The Ben Admin system already has employee age and salary information, so when employees view benefit options that are reliant on those data points (Voluntary Short Term Disability,

Voluntary Life, Critical Illness, etc.) their cost share shows in real time.

3)   Employee information is always legible and error proof. Specifically, an employee won't be able to add their daughter to the dental plan without also providing her date of birth and SSN.

4)   Once enrollment is complete, you can export an excel spreadsheet illustrating enrollments to your insurance companies, or even better communicate through an integration of some sort. Updates to payroll can be made similarly.

Let's Wrap It Up...

Save Money: Because you've moved to a Defined Contribution strategy it allows you to better project healthcare costs in future years which means you've regained control of one of the fastest growing line items on your P&L.

Happier Employees: Offering more benefit options to employees allows them access to more options than they ever had before giving them a higher probability of enrolling in a plan that more closely fit their needs.

Save Time: Moving to Defined Contribution has forced you to move your benefits administration process online—which is a good thing since that's where you conduct every other part of your business. And because that process has moved online it allows the communication and election of all benefits to be more streamlined giving your organization more time to spend on things that are mission critical to your customers.

Brian Tolbert

Principal & Benefits Practice Leader
Bernard Health
Nashville, TN

Brian Tolbert has over ten years of experience in the health and benefits industry and is one of the founders of Bernard Health. Based in Nashville, Bernard's mission is to be the world's most trusted adviser when it comes to helping people plan for their healthcare. Today, they provide employer advisory services in multiple markets and license their proprietary all-in-one HR software, BerniePortal, through other trusted benefits advisers all over the country.

Brian received his BS from Vanderbilt University and earned his MBA from the Owen Graduate School of Management.

He and Bernard Health were honored with the 2017 Summit Award from the Association for Insurance Leadership in recognition of their creating a NextGeneration Benefits Firm that provides a superior and more cost-effective benefits plan for employers and enhanced benefits for employees. Most recently, Bernard Health was named to the Inc. 5000 list of fastest growing companies in the U.S.

www.bernardhealth.com
800-505-0750

It is clear that change is needed. As principal of an employee benefits consulting firm that leads with risk management, we have a front row seat to the impact employers are gaining from new strategic approaches to proactively identifying employee health risk profiles and implementing programs for improvement. The pathways to improvement include building an employee's personal awareness of current and likely future health as well as crafting automated approaches that incent employees to engage with health professionals, to improve and manage their risk profile.

Claims statistics (2) confirm that close to 40% of the overall increase in medical plan cost is due to the 5% of the employee population referred to as "high flyers." These employees often have health risk conditions triggered by markers such as high blood glucose (diabetes), high blood pressure (hypertension) and high cholesterol (hyperlipidemia) which in combination can lead to heart disease, stroke or kidney failure.

Surprisingly, many health plan participants are not aware of their risk conditions or vital numbers. Of the 25 million people with diabetes in the United States, over 7 million are unaware of their condition. Similarly, 15 million of the 75 million Americans with high blood pressure are unaware of their condition, and 46% overall do not have their condition under control.

While many employers have focused on holistic wellness plans that address all medical plan participants, our benefitSMART process starts first with participants with multiple conditions that combined, place them at highest risk of extreme medical cost in the next 6-12 months.

A 2016 RAND wellness programs study lends support to this approach. This study of over 600,000 employees from 7 companies found that the preventive wellness measures spread over the entire population provided an ROI of only $.50 per $1.00. In contrast, the

ROI for targeting members with currently high-risk conditions such as heart disease and diabetes returned $3.80 per $1.00 of investment.

Our firm's proprietary benefitSMART process addresses these issues with a proactive and analytic approach. While some employers look to intercept high-risk participants prior to them becoming high claim, we feel this approach is inherently flawed due to relying only on current medical or pharmacy claims.

The R2 or statistical probability of identifying future claimants based only on current claims is just 28% as it represents a fraction of the total plan population, as well as changing year over year. Statistically, 30% of the employees will have no medical or Rx claims in any given year while 30% will spend $500 or less. Hence, very little information can be gathered on 60% of those on the medical plan by relying only on claims data. However, the predictive capacity can be increased up to approximately 75% by including additional data points such as health risk assessments and biometric reporting.

Health risk assessment data can be gathered in less than ten minutes by means of our proprietary benefitSMART online survey. The value of this methodology is in helping intuit the trajectory of the participant's future risk. Wayne Gretzky, an all-time great hockey player, credited his success to "skating to where the puck is going to be." In the same fashion, a participant with a significant family history of heart disease, breast or colon cancer can build a narrative of potential impending disease. Risks due to ethnicity, participation in smoking tobacco and over usage of alcohol are other valuable indicators that can be discovered through self-disclosure in an HRA.

Biometric data is another valuable source of health risk currently taking place. It most typically is gathered from participants at both open enrollment, and new hire eligibility for participation in the medical plan.

An example of the value that can be gathered from biometric data is in the area of blood glucose risk. High blood glucose is difficult to manage, if not measured biometrically; due to its ability to lurk at dangerous levels before breaching into Type 2 diabetes, in the same fashion that water can press dangerously close before destroying a seawall or dam. Once breached, Type 2 diabetes can be managed, but not truly reversed.

In the United States, over 79 million adults over age 20 are classed as hovering close to type 2 diabetes in a classification of pre-diabetes. The outcome of diabetes is a gradual wear down of the heart and other organs such as the kidneys as they are forced to work overtime. Grim statistics show that 68% of heart attack victims over age 65 were diabetic.

Blood pressure or hypertension is an additional area where biometric data can provide a predictive lift to high-risk situations. Mean arterial pressure is a clinical term to describe in essence, the RPM's of the heart. Unfortunately, the body does not provide a feedback loop of either a dashboard gauge or the roar of an engine like an automobile. However, biometric tests can provide an early warning.

A medical colleague of mine recently described an interaction with one of his plan participants that brings this to life. Acting in the role of risk manager for the plan, this medical professional was presented with the risk score of a plan participant with an elevated mean arterial pressure rating of 152. Since any score above 110 is problematic, he called the participant to create a call to action. The risk manager spoke briefly and asked how the participant was feeling. Upon hearing that he felt poorly but was not quite sure why, the risk manager impressed the need for an immediate visit to his physician and asked for feedback after the visit. Ten days later, the risk manager received a call from the treating physician advising that the patient had been admitted to the hospital directly from the office visit, as his body was in the early stages of stroke. Opportunities like this are the validation of the value of early risk interception by proactive risk scoring.

Vision exams can be an additional source of early warning in regard to high blood pressure. As high blood pressure is genetic, it often goes overlooked. Once high blood pressure crosses a specific threshold, it can only be managed by weight loss, avoiding salt, and prescriptions. The advantage of establishing eye screenings for prevention is the fact that the eye is the smallest organ. As such, the pounding of the internal organs caused by blood pressure will show up first in the eye. This is the data that can be harvested and used in our overall predictive health risk analytics.

A trending data point is consumer model data, without healthcare data, similar to data used by Google to sell products to consumers. This technology can be used to predict concurrent risk, which is highly correlated with cost. Using commercially available purchasing data resources, strong correlations between consumer data and prospective risk scores and costs can be inferred. While this is a new field, it holds high promise.

Once human resource leaders and CFO's determine that building a health risk interception program using analytics is of value, key elements must be established to maximize the process.

We find that starting or re-establishing a consistent meeting schedule as benefits committee is highly valuable. We find that our clients are more interested in meeting regularly outside of the renewal cycle as actionable data that is de-identified is now readily available for review and actionable steps.

Items that will naturally flow from these meetings will encompass items as diverse as how an employee's illness affects department scheduling, how leave effects reinstatement rights through FMLA or

ADA, or how prescription drugs such as opiods or opioid withdrawal treatment impacts safety at work or OSHA responsibilities.

A significant and natural outcome of enhanced awareness of high-risk health profiles will be the need to hire a care outreach team that is both skilled clinically and capable from a psychosocial motivation standpoint. Guarantees of both timely outreach, as well as significant results from their outreach, should be expected and monitored for impact.

In addition, there will be an enhanced ability to target high use and high-cost areas such as substance abuse, specialty prescription access, and price or other items that become apparent. As benefit committees follow the data, they will be amazed at what they find. We have found items as diverse as lifestyle drugs being utilized at a cost of $18,000 annually with no medical necessity, as well as pockets of opioid abuse and subsequent medication for recovery that exceeded $12,000 annually, but was not being monitored adequately to ensure recovery included appropriate weaning from the recovery drugs.

One of the most rewarding areas benefits committees will now be able to generate results from is the increased leverage health risk data will provide in negotiating renewal pricing from insurance carriers, and stop loss vendors. As current and future risk can be independently validated from the claims, risk and care outreach reports the leverage with financial partners will be significantly stronger.

Benefits committees will also need to consider how best to incent employees to participate in the health risk profile improvement process. A good starting point is to brand the program specifically to the employer to ensure it fits the culture of the organization and resonates with the employee population. A common practice is to tie participation in biometric screening and health coaching to either monthly premium contribution levels, or out-of-pockets levels.

More novel approaches will use elements such as vanishing deductibles to incent participation. A year two or year three approach may well involve moving from participation based criteria to outcomes based criteria, which involve employees measuring up to expected norms in regard to blood glucose levels, blood pressure, cholesterol, and body mass index. Employers need to weigh the impact on employee morale before moving in this direction.

Financial incentives typically average a $50 monthly reduction in medical premium and are the starting point for participation based measurements. Subsidies can be structured as cost neutral if wished, so that those who choose not to participate subsidize those who do.

An alternative to providing direct subsidy is to tie access to unique programs to participation in the health risk data gathering process. We have found that many of our best cost containment programs can be leveraged to get participation in the health risk program. Many of our clients who participate in our proprietary RX Advocate or Facility Direct Discount programs are able to provide shared savings for employees who are willing to be more engaged as purchasers in paying for hospital events, scans or prescription drugs. Often, employees can earn a zero out-of-pocket experience by following our process in these areas.

An effective way to garner better participation in biometric screens or health risk assessments is to tie qualification for our zero out-of-pocket facility, scan and RX program, to participation in the health risk process. An additional benefit of starting with tying admission to the zero out-of-pocket shared savings programs is that employers will typically get the highest users of prescriptions drugs and hospital facilities and scans on board early as they have the most to gain from the reduced out-of-pocket approach.

Employers moving toward a proactive health risk analytics and coaching approach such as our benefitSMART process will need to compare the cost of the program to the relative impact. We find the cost to implement is usually less than 3% of annual premiums plus the cost of employee incentives, if any.

The impact will depend on the effectiveness of each employer in engaging participation from employees. However, with 40% of the average employer plan spend tied to high risk and high-cost claimants, it is clear that the impact will typically far exceed the investment.

It is notable that in the 2015 national study seen below, that 70 employer plans utilizing the same analytic tools, processes and care outreach vendors as our benefitSMART process, achieved results in the aggregate of 33% lower per member cost per month. Each employer facts and circumstances are different, but it is clear that a competitive business advantage is achievable for employers willing to develop and execute a similar approach.

Finally, we hear that the greatest value to employers of the benefitSMART program is the human impact generated by those like the 42-year-old single mom coming home to her kids every night and managing her business unit with excellence—opposed to missing six months of work, impacting family members and spending $120,000 of the plan claim fund.

Truly, health risk profile improvement can create a competitive business advantage by reducing business cost and maintaining the health of employees.

Pete Scruggs

Principal
Golson Scruggs
Battleground, WA

Pete Scruggs has provided risk management and employee benefit solutions to employers for over 25 years as Principal of Golsan Scruggs Insurance & Risk Management. Golsan Scruggs' proprietary benefitSMART process improves employer finances and employee health risk trajectories by leveraging data transparency, risk management and custom strategies.

Pete is also a recognized expert in providing corporate and board room training for human resources leaders and CFOs regarding legal compliance with applicable state and federal employment and benefit laws.

Pete received the 2017 Innovation Award from the Association for Insurance Leadership for his contributions to the advancement of the industry.

www.gsirm.com
pscruggs@gsirm.com
503-267-9059

CHAPTER 22

THE SEVEN PILLARS OF FINANCIAL WELLNESS

(And How Employers Can Use Them to Help Create More Productive Employees)

Mark Snider

Financial wellness is a hot topic these days among HR profession-als. What exactly are the main components of a financial wellness program and why are many employers endorsing them? We'll explore why companies are adding this to their suite of benefits, and also look at some of the major components, or "pillars," that should be considered to build a program designed to foster a more productive workforce.

Several major studies have documented the relationship between employee financial stress and productivity, including the following:

- An American Psychological Association study found that "70% of employees are seriously concerned, if not seriously worried, about their finances."
- A 2012 SHRM Research Spotlight on Financial Education Initiatives reported that "60% of HR professionals say financial stress is having some impact on employees' work performance."
- A 2013 AON Hewitt Consumer Health Mindset Survey of 2,800 workers found that "51% of workers surveyed said (financial) stress caused them to be less productive at work."

While many employers already have or are planning to implement an employee financial wellness program (33% in the above AON Hewitt study), the focus and the content delivery methods vary, depending on the philosophy and culture of the company and the characteristics of its employees. Therefore, each employer should customize their financial wellness program to suit the organization's unique nature and goals. However, all employers would do well to consider the following seven pillars when designing a financial wellness education plan. Each pillar includes some "braces" that are critical to hold the plan together.

Pillar #1 — Budgeting / Lifestyle Planning

Having a system to track expenses and eliminate unnecessary items in an employee's budget is an essential first step towards financial wellness; keeping outflow less than inflow is critical. A budget is the cornerstone in building a solid financial structure. Whether one uses a simple budgeting software package, tracks it the old-fashioned way on paper, or creates separate bank accounts for specific financial areas, being able to accurately account for both income and expenses is important. As Ben Franklin wisely proclaimed, "Beware of little expenses. A small leak will sink a great ship."

Pillar #2 — Debt Management

It is important to carefully manage debt and be sure it is used wisely in any financial plan. Debt can be classified as "good debt" or "bad debt."

"Good debt" is used for positive financial leverage, which means an investment's return is increased by borrowing to finance it. The debt may be incurred to buy an appreciating asset (e.g., real estate) with a reasonable interest rate (a rate less than the expected investment return), and the interest is often deductible from income taxes, as is true of rental properties.

"Bad debt," on the other hand, is debt that is often used to fund a depreciating asset (e.g., sports car, clothes) to support an employee's lifestyle. The debt is frequently loaned at a high-interest rate with no tax benefits. A survey by Alliant Credit Union underscored the need to keep bad debt under control. Thirty-seven percent of the survey respondents listed paying off credit cards as a top goal, and 22% said staying afloat with debt obligations is a major concern. When consumer and credit card debt is adequately managed, it is much easier to find money in the employee's budget to begin building assets, starting with our next pillar.

Pillar #3 — Savings

It is important to accumulate funds to cover emergencies, and have available for investment opportunities — and for peace of mind. The emphasis of a savings plan is on the return _of_ money rather than the return _on_ money. Keeping an adequate source of liquid funds, i.e., money that is readily available without penalties or taxes, and with no risk of principal fluctuation, is often overlooked. Having funds available in a bank account or money market fund for emergencies or unanticipated investment opportunities will relieve the employee from worry and sleepless nights, allowing him or her to be more focused on the job. Life insurance cash values and loans from a 401(k) or 403(b) plan (where interest is repaid to the employee's own account) can also be considered as supplements to savings; however, they should not replace liquid savings in a bank account or money market fund.

Pillar #4 — Adequate Insurance Protection

A well-designed insurance program plays the role of protecting assets, through homeowners, auto, and other property insurance policies, reducing liability through personal and professional liability policies, and replacing and supplementing income through life, disability income, health insurance, critical illness, and long-term care policies. Employer provided benefits such as medical, dental, life, and disability coverage, provide a base of protection.

Every well-designed insurance program, however, will require that the employee seek assistance from outside advisers with expertise in property and liability insurance, and life, health, disability and long-term care plans, in order to ensure the employee has the proper level of protection for all facets of his or her life. An adviser with the proper experience and credentials will help design and secure the appropriate protection plan for the employee, and will help coordinate individual policies with company-provided benefits and government benefits such as Social Security.

Pillar #5 — Investments

The investment pillar is the key to building long-term wealth, and is also the most complex, as there are many types of investments, each with its own risks as well as unique opportunities or upside potential. Some people are suited to a "do it yourself style," with a hands-on approach to investing. This type of investor may buy and manage real estate rentals, start a business, or take an active role in creating an online brokerage account, buying and selling stocks, bonds, ETFs, or mutual funds. The employee who actively manages his or her own investments, of course, needs to invest the time and effort necessary to learn how to be a successful investor.

Many employees would prefer to work with an investment adviser to create a plan to help guide them through the often confusing maze of investment choices. Investment professionals work either on a fee basis (flat fee, hourly rate, or asset-based fee) or on a commission basis, where they are compensated based on the products purchased. The method and amount of the investment adviser's compensation should be disclosed and transparent. Employees should choose a financial adviser based on his or her reputation, area of expertise, and a sense of trust and comfort with the adviser. It is prudent to look for recognized credentials, like the Certified Financial Planner (CFP) designation, as well as experience and referrals.

Pillar #6 — Retirement Planning

Although many people think of investing as retirement planning, retirement planning is named as a separate pillar for several reasons. A retirement plan includes a number of lifestyle issues, such as what age the employee plans to retire, where he or she plans to live, whether he or she will work part-time and semi-retired (or start a new career), when to take Social Security or other government benefits, the company's retirement plan (if the person is fortunate enough to have one), the health and family situation, as well as many other factors.

There are a number of tax incentives to invest in retirement accounts, typically with an upfront deduction on either an employer-sponsored plan (401(k), 403(b), 457 plans) or on an individual plan (IRA, SEP-IRA, etc.) Many of these same plans will offer a ROTH option, which allows the person to take the income tax benefit in the future when money is withdrawn at retirement, instead of having an upfront tax break. The ROTH option gives the employee the opportunity to maximize tax benefits. ROTH options may be available with an IRA or an employer-sponsored 401(k) or 403(b) plan.

There are many online planning software programs that project an employee's future retirement income including Social Security, a spouse's retirement income, and personal investments. A qualified retirement planning adviser also can assist by providing information on the impact of inflation, and planning for medical and long-term care needs. It is critical to start retirement planning early and to review the plan regularly.

Pillar #7—Estate Planning/Tax Planning

Whether an employee's financial plan will result in sizable wealth or a modest estate, it is important to plan a legacy to leave hard-earned assets to the people or institutions the employee chooses—and to have those assets transferred efficiently and with the least cost in taxes, probate and attorney fees, and other expenses. Most individuals seek advice on reducing income taxes during their life, either by working with a CPA or other tax preparer, or by using tax software to help identify all the deductions available to them.

Professional advice is equally important in planning estate and gifting, and the advisers should include an attorney as well as an accountant, investment adviser and life insurance agent. In addition to a properly drafted Will, Power of Attorney (POA), Healthcare POA, and Living Will, an experienced attorney will advise on the proper titling of assets and whether a Trust is advisable to accomplish planning goals and/or reduce taxes. Again, it is important that the employee looks for expertise in this practice area when choosing the attorney and other advisers, as well as special credentials and reputation. Proper estate planning can make certain that a lifetime of work and planning can continue to provide value for the people and causes the employee cares about most.

Another Key—Supporting the Seven Pillars

In addition to these seven pillars of a financial wellness plan, there is another important factor that is the essential "brace" to hold the pillars together: DISCIPLINE. Discipline is essential to execute the plan and keep it on track and current. The "perfect plan" that initially had all seven pillars would soon begin to crumble and be ineffective without regular monitoring and updating. As our lives, our situations, our goals, our income, and our assets change—and as legal and tax provisions change—employees need the discipline to review their plans, modify them and keep them current. Discipline braces the seven pillars to keep the financial wellness structure strong.

The employer can play a major role by creating a financial wellness program that provides education and tools to help employees stay focused, minimize stress, and be more productive as a result. The 10th *Annual Study of Employee Benefits Trends* by MetLife (2012) found that "A clear majority of employers (57%) say they believe that financial education boosts productivity." A financial wellness plan can be delivered in many ways, including through "lunch and learn" seminars, providing financial technology platforms, or arranging for qualified financial professionals to meet with employees one-on-one, either at work or offsite.

As we see convincing evidence of the advantages, more employers are adding financial wellness components to their suite of employee benefits. The payback of a well-designed program can be a significant impact on the company's bottom line, as employees achieve financial health!

Mark Snider

CEO
Snider, Fuller and Stroh
Athens, OH

Mark Snider is a founder and CEO of the prestigious insurance advisory firm Snider, Fuller and Stroh.

He started his insurance career in Athens in 1971. With his wide range of experience in the field, he has served as chairman and an Ambassador of Ohio AIFAPAC, and as a National Board member of the Association of Health Insurance Agents (AHIA). He was honored as a life member of the Million Dollar Round Table and Top of the Table.

Mark is a board member of several business, government, and non-profit boards and he been an adjunct faculty member of the Ohio University College of Business since 1976. In recognition of his regular contributions to many civic activities, Mark was named Chamber Person of the Year in two different years and was awarded the Ohio University Honorary Alumnus of the Year Award in 2010 and the Distinguished Service Award by the Athens Area Chamber of Commerce in 2012.

www.sniderfullerstroh.com
mark@sniderfullerstroh.com
740-594-8385

CHAPTER 23

LEVERAGING STRATEGIC RESOURCES TO CUT BENEFIT COSTS: SHORT & SWEET

Will Glaros

How would you like to make a renewal decision that accomplished all of the following results for your company?

- Renewal options that could reduce your costs by 15%.
- Further cost reduction with benefit changes but minimal impact on your employees.
- Less cost out of pocket for medical and RX claims for the employer and employee.
- Providing coverage to employees who previously could not afford to pay.

- Access to high-quality provider services with good outcomes.
- Access to high-cost drugs for minimal expense.
- Simplified on-boarding for new employees.
- Simplified benefit enrollment at open enrollment.
- NO DIRECT COST TO YOU—THE EMPLOYER.

You are probably thinking "who on earth can make a claim like this in a world that seems to have run out of options for employers and employees alike?"

We have been delivering on these promises when the circumstances and geography work. With over 30+ years of operating within the employee benefits environment, we have learned that being a good steward of available resources is the key to our success and our clients' success.

First, someone has to take the time to be constantly looking for resources that maximize benefit performance.

Second, you have to have the expertise to identify those resources and develop a plan for their implementation.

Third, education of the employee and employer is paramount to initial and ongoing success.

Fourth, you must have a consultant who understands the resource and has taken the time to develop relationships within the organization.

Let's use a just completed acquisition of a new employer group for our firm as the case study for review of these points. We'll call them The Very Smart Company, Inc. and for short, VSC, Inc.

We were introduced to VSC, Inc. by a mutual client four years ago. It was obvious that their current consultants were a good firm and that the client was only looking for price relief. As most people know, if it's price you are looking for and everyone gets the same data and information, the price will be the same for both advisers.

For us, that is a walk away situation as we don't like to disengage a relationship if the client is happy with the broker and we cannot improve their situation.

Advance three years and a new request by our firm to present a new strategy we developed after analyzing strategic resources in a new light. We determined that this engagement was worth the effort as we had several positive outcomes that we could deliver that their existing brokers had not discovered.

One, the competing brokers were from outside of the area and were not aware of small changes in a carrier network offering. This enabled us to engage a slightly smaller network option with minimal disruption and a 15% reduction in cost and still offer the larger network at a 5% reduction. The other broker had shown the larger network, but had no idea the other option existed.

Advantage — Local Knowledge.

Two, knowledge of a secondary provider relationship based on healthcare reform changes to the system. The secondary provider was a local Federally Qualified Health Center (FQHC). This knowledge was helpful for a variety of reasons:

- The FQHC provided the navigators for presentation of a state Medicaid expansion called HIP 2.0 which would extend coverage to the employer's lower paid employees. HIP 2.0 is unique to Indiana. If you are located in a state which has not extended Medicaid or one which has, you will need to check with your consultants to verify.

- They provided a sliding scale payment system based on
  income with reduced payments by the employees who
  met the income qualifications. This included insured and
  uninsured employees.

  A more in-depth look at the sliding scale will provide an
  even more compelling value this can have for the employee. In
  the case of a High Deductible Health Plan (HDHP), the full
  negotiated net allowable cost goes fully toward the deductible,
  while the amount owed could be as low as 25% of that price.
  This gives even more validity to using an HDHP as a plan
  alternative.

- The FQHC provided access to a drug program only available
  through Disproportionate Share Hospitals (DSH) and
  FQHC's. This program is available to insured and uninsured
  alike, as long as the person is a patient of the clinic. The
  discounts are significant, and the advantage is that the claims
  for RX when purchased through the FQHC do not pass
  through the health plan, thereby reducing claims.

  The program we uncovered was a program basically
  unknown to the general public. The program is called 340 B
  and traditionally has provided access to discounted medications with large savings through DSH hospitals.

  The 340 B program was extended to FQHCs when it
  began in 1992, but until recently through resource review, we
  uncovered the potential use of the combined FQHC / 340 B
  option for other users.

  The finding was unique in that the reviews we had been

doing for FQHCs, and the potential value to our customers was primarily related to uninsured and lower paid employees. Qualifications for benefits were seemingly based on income requirements and the sliding scale, but on a deeper dive, it was revealed that the discounted prescription drug benefit was not governed by the income relationship. It was governed by the patient relationship to the provider, meaning that anyone using a FQHC had access to these lower cost drugs.

- The quality of care and forward thinking of this FQHC is providing excellent results and significant savings on claims. This is for those employees who utilize their services.

  Their providers are a mix of Primary Care Providers, Nurse Practitioners, and nurses including some facilities access to dental and vision providers. Work is ongoing to expand access through virtual visits and community access through high visibility employers.

  In the case of the FQHC we utilized, they were working to identify the use of resources, in order to provide more cost effective care and patient outcome.

- The FQHC also sent out a team to the employer's worksite for a health and wellness fair. They assisted employees with becoming patients and signing up for wellness exams. Those that had insurance due to the ACA received those exams at no cost, and the employer used some of their savings to pay 50% of the screenings for their uninsured employees.

  In addition, the medical director made presentations to the employees, talking about wellness, health awareness, and the 340 B drug program.

Once the global biometric data is available, our team works with the FQHC to deliver ongoing informational output relating to the risks of the group. This further activity can reap ongoing results with potentially lower claims costs.

- One final benefit which was an outlier was that during the wellness fair, the employees of the firm became familiar and comfortable with the FQHC team. This comfort led to a subsequent situation where an employee, who was considering taking their life, called the FQHC people and was talked down and put on a path of action.

Overall, the use of this resource, previously undiscovered, gave the employees of VSC, Inc. access to more services at a lower cost and saved a life.

Advantage—Local Knowledge, caring people and ongoing research.

Three, implementation of an electronic onboarding and enrollment system. This change to our mode of operations was a cumbersome and a significant time commitment that included identifying the proper system, then putting it in place.

This was an effort for our firm, a challenge for our clients who were the first to act, but an overwhelming success for ALL.

Once the system was put in place, it not only simplified our administrative burdens, but it also made for a more streamlined onboarding and enrollment process for our clients.

The system you utilize should provide the dual use of being integrated with direct connection to the carriers and for firms under 100 where live feeds are not normally approved, manual submission of all changes.

Consultants who provide you with an electronic process similar to this have every right to be paid for the access to these systems. In our case, we have never charged for access as we have either made it part of our fee or the standard compensation, provided the insurance carriers provide ample reimbursement.

The system works in two phases as follows:

Phase 1: <u>ONBOARDING</u>

All new employees are on-boarded thru the electronic system, providing access to I-9s and W-4s, as well as applications and whatever other information the employer wants to gather.

The employee can also have access to the system for their portal, in order to pull any of the information they have provided.

Phase 2: <u>ENROLLMENT & ADMINISTRATION</u>

New Employees—For all new employees, when they enter their data for onboarding, much of the information is used to populate the enrollment system and forms.

Existing Employees—For all current employees insured and waivers, will either be accessing the system to enroll at open enrollment or for a special qualifying event. This is also done on the portal by the employee's with the assistance of HR if necessary.

The use of the electronic portal reduces the time it takes to enroll new employees, and for open enrollment that used to take weeks can be done in days. In one case, an employer with over 100 employees was able to complete the enrollment in three days.

Another benefit of the system is that all annual renewal notices required by ERISA are provided on the portal with sign-off needed. This provides additional protection to the employer for meeting those requirements.

Finally, the system is date sensitive, and that benefits the employer for proof of application dates, if there is any pushback by the carriers regarding adding or deleting employees.

Overall, the reduction in time required by HR to manage this part of the process is greatly reduced, and Employees spend far less time off the job enrolling and understanding their benefits.

Advantage –Technology.

The VSC, Inc story is not isolated, and you as an employer can reap the same benefits by having representation which is looking to the marketplace for concepts and ideas which can benefit your firm.

In summary, you should secure diligence by your consultant by asking them to provide you an ongoing stream of new ideas and educational processes for your employees. In addition, they should be able to demonstrate their capabilities with systems and processes built to reduce your time and effort in the administration of your benefits.

Will Glaros

Managing Partner
Meyers Glaros Group
Schererville, IN

For decades, business owners in Northwest Indiana have relied on Will Glaros to deliver the highest quality benefit services to companies throughout the region. Will founded Employer Benefit Systems (EBS), which was one of the largest locally owned employee benefits firm in Northwest Indiana until the company merged with HIA Insurance in 2014 to form the Meyers Glaros Group.

In his current role as managing partner at Meyers Glaros Group, Will continues to work with the area's leading employers to develop their benefit plans. Very active in the healthcare industry, he has led the Northwest Indiana Wellness Council, served as past president of the Northwest Indiana chapter of the National Association of Health Underwriters, sits on an advisory board for the Indiana Department of Insurance, and is a member of the Leading Producers Roundtable and Anthem Broker Advisory.

Will has been interviewed by numerous news outlets for his wealth of knowledge about healthcare reform and speaks to organizations about trends in healthcare. Throughout his life, Will has also been involved with many community and civic organizations including serving as past president of Habitat for Humanity and current board member for the Early Learning Partnership (formerly Parents as Teachers).

www.meyersglaros.com
will.glaros@meyersglaros.com
219-865-6447

CHAPTER 24

SAVE MONEY, MAKE MONEY & MITIGATE RISK

Proven Benefits Strategies from North of the Border

Ron Hansell

Beyond the stereotypes of hockey players, year-round snow, and the overuse of "eh" and "sorry," Canada is the United States most mutually beneficial trading partner, with approximately $300 Billion dollars crossing the border each way every year. That is over $1 million crossing the border every minute.

As a result, many US companies have Canadian subsidiaries or are thinking of starting one.

This chapter will help innovative companies like yours, break the status quo when it comes to your Canadian subsidiary's benefits plan. We will help you change your benefits game, helping your employees, and boosting your bottom-line. We will unite the well being of your company and your employees, saving you money, making you money, and mitigating risks in ways that you never knew possible.

To do so, the chapter is broken down as follows:
- Canadian Benefits Landscape
- Cost Effectiveness
- Fiduciary Responsibility
- Employee Appreciation and Understanding
- Case Study—how we saved a client $200,000 with one solution

Canadian Benefits Landscape

It is a common misconception that because of the public healthcare system in Canada, there is no need for private employer benefits plans. Almost all Canadian employers need to provide a benefits plan to be competitive. In fact, a recent industry survey found that 4 out of 5 Canadians do not want to work for an employer without an industry standard benefits plan.

If you aren't familiar, the public health plans in Canada vary slightly by province and territory, but all provide hospital and physician coverage for their residents. The private group health benefits plans provide coverage for the following:
- Prescription Drugs
- Dental

- Long-term and short-term disability
- Paramedical services like chiropractor and massage therapy
- Vision
- Group life insurance
- Medical supplies and services
- Out of country coverage
- Semi-private hospital

Co-pays and deductibles are low or non-existent. The average cost per employee is $3,000/year and to be tax effective, the employer will often pay the premiums for all benefits except group life insurance and disability. The result is an annual employer cost of $2,400 per employee and an annual employee cost of $600.

This cost certainly pales in comparison to your US benefits plan, but ensuring the Canadian plan is cost effective, fulfills your fiduciary responsibility, and has a high-level of employee appreciation and understanding is crucial to your success north of the border.

Group health benefits are just part of the landscape; the other part includes group retirement plans.

The Canadian group retirement landscape is going through a comparatively high level of change. As in the US, there is a significant shift from defined benefit plans to defined contribution plans, and most employers share a similar contribution limit to US companies, of 3-5%. Additionally, the federal government is increasing the contribution requirements for the federal plan, and The Canadian Pension Plan. These changes are requiring more intensive and extensive reporting, and more strategic governance policies. Cross Border Benefits is equally focussed and specialized in group retirement plans, but due to the nature of this book, this chapter will focus exclusively on group health benefits for your new or existing Canadian subsidiary.

For more information on the Canadian group health benefits and group retirement landscape, please visit www.crossborderbenefits.ca and for our current Canadian benefits manual, contact us at advisor@crossborderbenefits.ca

Cost Efficiency

Despite our lower cost benefits plans and public health care, we are not immune to the major increases caused by high-cost specialty drugs, increased incidence of disability, and low-interest rates. Double digit increases are fast becoming the norm, with an industry trend of a 10-12% increase in premiums per year (threatening to double the average cost in 5-7 years). It is for these reasons that when we refer to cost efficiency as a primary factor to the success of your Canadian operation, we are not fixated on the price today, but instead, focussed on the cost tomorrow.

As we often say, "doing what you've always done will get you what you've always got," and in today's environment, that simply is not acceptable. Sustainably reducing the cost tomorrow demands that you take an innovative approach, are willing to break through the status quo, and take a serious interest in changing your benefits game—it is paramount in helping your employees and boosting your bottom line.

The most proven way to operate by this philosophy is to choose a best-in-class adviser who understands the challenges and opportunities you face as a US owned company with your Canadian subsidiary.

This adviser will ensure you have proper:
- Your corporate vision is reflected across the border
    o   Creates consistency and equitable relations
    o   Crucial for any employees transferring cross border
- Government integration

- o To prevent gaps and overlaps
- o Shift costs and responsibilities from your private plan to the government plan when possible
- Consumerism driven plan designs
  - o Incentivize employees to make smarter purchases, in turn stabilizing long-term benefits costs
- Innovative vetted products and services
  - o Access to the solutions that will help make you money, save you money and mitigate risks in ways you didn't know possible
  - o Only implement strategies and solutions that are practical, and whose level of disruption will never outweigh the benefit
- Fraud detection
  - o Eliminate unnecessary claims and abuse
- Renewals aligned with your fiscal planning period
  - o Ensure that the proper care and attention are spent in the planning period.
  - o No surprises

For our cost-effective assessment of your program, contact advisor@crossborderbenefits.ca

Fiduciary Responsibilities

As a fiduciary, you understand and appreciate your responsibilities in Canada. But, Canada is a unique place with many different, existing, and pending, regulatory, and legislative changes.

Your time and resources to learn these differences and stay on top of these changes are limited.

So, without the right advising firm, you and your company's **fiduciary responsibilities** can quickly turn into you and your company's **fiduciary liabilities**.

To avoid this, you need:
- Concise governance & quarterly reports
- Timely updates on pending changes with workable proactive strategies
- HR resources
- Third-party disability management
- Benchmarking
- Optional third-party administration

The consequences of failing to fulfill your fiduciary responsibilities can be significant. For our proven fiduciary fulfillment assessment, contact us at advisor@crossborder-benefits.ca.

Employee Appreciation & Understanding

Low turnover and attracting top talent is crucial to your company's success.

Having the right group benefits and group retirement programs will help you achieve that.

In fact, a recent Sanofi study found that 66% of Canadian employees would rather keep their group benefits program than have a $15,000 raise—this is staggering, considering the average Canadian benefits plan costs $3,000 a year.

Having a strong benefits program is part of the equation, but equally important are:
- Proven communication strategies

- Employee education sessions
- Online and phone support
- Concierge advice
- Employee and family assistance programs
- Well-formatted employee surveys

Breaking the status quo on employee appreciation and understanding to positively impact employees and the company's bottom line, isn't always easy but to succeed with your Canadian subsidiary it is absolutely necessary.

For our 5-step guide for well-formatted Canadian employee surveys, contact us at advisor@crossborderbenefits.ca

Case Study—How we saved a company $200,000 with one solution

Over the years, we have worked with Canadian subsidiaries as small as 1 employee and as large as 5,000 employees. Including new ventures, mergers and acquisitions, and long-standing Canadian subsidiaries. In this case study, we will focus on a 1,100 employee long-standing Canadian subsidiary. It will demonstrate how we were able to bring greater cost effectiveness, fulfill fiduciary responsibilities, and increase employee appreciation and understanding. For confidentiality, we will refer to this company as ABC Inc.

Please note this group is on an Administrative Service Only arrangement with a $10,000 stop-loss and has employees in 5 of Canada's 10 provinces. The solution outlined below can be applied to groups as small as 3 employees, and can be applied in a fully insured environment. We have defined high cost specialty drugs as any drug costing more than $10,000 per year.

We were referred to ABC Inc. from their US benefits adviser with a mandate of bringing minimally disruptive long-term sustainable solutions to their union and non-union staff of 1,100 employees in Canada. Upon reviewing their program, there were several issues. The most notable, and the one we will discuss was their high-cost specialty drugs program.

ABC Inc. had 12 plan members claiming a high-cost specialty drug, with a total of $550,000 in total claims. The issue here was not the occurrence of the claims or even the total dollar amount (when one considers the dependents of the plan, they are well below the average occurrence of 1.5% of Canadians). The issue was that ABC Inc., like many Canadian employers, was unaware that they could shift the cost and liability for these drugs to an alternative payer — effectively eliminating the claims costs and history, while maintaining coverage for the plan member.

In Canada, there are often 3 alternative payers available:
1. Provincial pharmacare plan
2. Drug manufacturer
3. Spousal benefits plan

The bureaucracy involved in successfully navigating these alternative payers can be complex and often results in delayed reimbursement, less than adequate coverage or outright declines for reimbursement. This coupled with the relatively recent phenomenon of high-cost specialty drugs, explains ABC Inc.'s inefficiency on the subject.

Thankfully, a solution exists, in the form of our third-party drug advocate partner. The drug advocate has a deep understanding of the bureaucracies of the various alternative payers, and has perfected plan member interaction and communication to ensure the process for coverage seamless.

Our third-party advocate went to work here and were successful in obtaining coverage for all 12 plan members through the alternative payers. At no point did a plan member go without a medication, there was no added out-of-pocket cost, and claims were eliminated from ABC Inc.

Here is how this solution satisfies Cost Effectiveness, Fiduciary Responsibility, and Employee Appreciation Understanding.

Cost Effectiveness
In year 1:
- $120,000 savings from claims under $10,000 stop-loss
- $80,000 savings from stop-loss charge
- **Total savings**: $200,000

Year 2 and onwards:
- A proven workable process is in place, shifting the responsibility and cost for high-cost specialty drugs to alternative payers
- **Total expected savings:** 20% of total drug claim spend and stop loss charges

The important things to note about this solution are that it's not a one-time savings or a simple marketing discretion. It is a gift that keeps on giving.

Fiduciary responsibility
An increasingly common solution in Canada is implementing a drug maximum, typically $10,000 per plan member. As the fiduciary ABC Inc. has a professional and ethical responsibility to take care of their

Canadian employees and their dependents. Implementing a $10,000 drug max with no advocate system, especially with 12 plan members already claiming over $10,000, would fail to fulfill their fiduciary responsibility. It would leave these plan members without coverage and without the tools necessary to obtain the medication they need through an alternative method.

Thankfully, ABC Inc. recognized the importance of fulfilling their fiduciary responsibility and opted for a complete and innovative solution—**effectively fulfilling their fiduciary responsibility**.

Employee Appreciation & Understanding

Without employee appreciation and understanding your Canadian benefits program, is a lost expense instead of a successful investment.

ABC Inc. was no different, but shifting high costs specialty drug costs and responsibility to an alternative source wasn't exactly an added benefit for employees, and if they weren't careful, employees would see it as a move to fatten the wallets of their foreign head office. This kind of thing, as would be the case in the United States, doesn't sit well for many Canadian employees.

So, we worked alongside ABC Inc. and our drug advocate partner to develop a strategy that would:

1. Make certain employees understood the purpose of the solution was to keep their strong benefits coverage affordable now and into the future.
2. Ensure all plan members received the medication they needed without interruption

Just some of the things we did to achieve this:

- Held an education session, that included the negative side effects other companies have faced from not implementing this type of solution
    - Other benefits being reduced
    - Lower annual salary increases
    - $10,000 drug maximums, which led some plan member exposure
- Gave all employees a confidential helpline to ask questions and voice concerns
- Our drug advocate reviewed each plan member's cases and found appropriate coverage methods before going live with the solution
- Leveraged their customized phone app, to ensure easy access to helpful information and assistance
- Implemented the solution with a 90-day grace period for high-cost specialty drug claimants to adjust to the new system.

Not only did we achieve our objective above, but we saw a marked improvement in employee surveys of their appreciation and understanding of the benefits program.

Conclusion

In Canada, this was a truly innovative solution that broke through the status quo and changed ABC Inc.'s benefits game. It helped employees and boosted their bottom line. This solution, along with several other minimally disruptive solutions helped ABC Inc. be cost effective with a total savings of $330,000, fulfilled their fiduciary responsibility and heightened employee appreciation understanding. We helped to unite the well being of their company with their employees by making them money, saving them money, and mitigating risk in ways they never knew possible.

Cross Border Benefits is an advising firm that specializes in group health benefits and group retirement for Canadian subsidiaries of all sizes and backgrounds. We can work directly with you or provide a unified approach with your US adviser.

To learn more about this case study and how it could apply to you, contact us at advisor@crossborderbenefits.ca

If you provide professional services to cross border companies be sure to visit https:// www.crossborderbenefits.ca/crossborderconsortium/ to see how you can provide greater value to your cross border clients.

Ron Hansell

President
Cross Border Benefits
Ontario, Canada

As founder and President of Cross Border
Benefits, Ron Hansell is passionate about uniting
the well-being of companies and their employees.
After 36 years in the business, he has developed
an understanding of how American companies
like to operate and has the ability to mirror this into a company's Canadian
subsidiary.

Over his years of experience, Ron developed the Golden Rules for Cross
Border Benefits:

- No Surprises
- Understand and identify your Problems, Frustration and Needs.
- Always provide ways to make you money, save you money, and miti-
gate risk in ways you did not know before

www.crossborderbenefits.ca
advisor@crossborderbenefits.ca

CHAPTER 25

THE MEDICAL ID CARD
The Riskiest Credit Card in America

Andy Neary

I t comes as no surprise that credit card debt is a problem in America today. According to NerdWallet, the average U.S. household carries over $16,000 in credit card debt. Using plastic to satisfy the need for instant gratification has almost become an addiction for some consumers.

Having the financial ability to purchase goods and services has become an afterthought, because the credit card gives us the ability to have what we want, and when we want it, because cold hard cash is not exchanged at the time of purchase. Now add in the exorbitantly high-interest rate tied to a credit card, and it's no wonder how an individual quickly racks up thousands of dollars in debt. Can you imagine what the spending crisis in America would look like if the following credit card was offered to consumers?

Imagine you are a bank, and you offer your customers a credit card that has no limit. Imagine that this credit card also comes with the promise that you (the bank) will pay all interest. Imagine that this credit card allows your customers to run up expenses with the comfort of knowing they never have to pay off the balance.

In addition, this credit card is going to be offered to customers who have little knowledge of where to go to use the card. To make matters worse, customers will be using the card to make purchases without a clue as to the actual quality or cost of the goods and services they will be buying. Now, if your bank was irrational enough to promote this credit card offer, it would have to come with serious stipulations.

First, you would spend enormous amounts of time and energy educating your customers on how to use the card. This education process would not just occur at the time the card was purchased either. You would make sure to set up year-long education and communication campaigns designed to ensure that customers are using their credit cards appropriately.

Second, you would put in effective controls to help your customers use their credit cards efficiently. You would limit purchases only to those vendors and retailers providing high-quality goods and services at a low price point. This is known as value. You know that if you allow your customers to use the credit card wherever they choose, your bank will quickly run out of cash. Yes, there are vendors and retailers out there offering perceived "discounts," but you are smarter than that, and you know these discounts are covering up inflated sales prices. You are also too smart to let your credit card customers shop at low-quality vendors and retailers because you know the goods purchased here often break or do not work, requiring customers to make return visits for more purchases. At the end of the day, it's about supply-side management.

Third, you would teach your customers *how* to purchase the goods and services they need. You would set up deals with specific vendors and retailers giving your customers the opportunity to buy goods and services without having to use their credit card at all. In fact, your credit card may even have a "cash back" rewards program when goods and services are acquired from these specific vendors and retailers. Yes, you read that correctly; a no-limit credit card with a "cash back" rewards program. How is that for customer friendliness? Now, you are not alone if you think this scenario is ludicrous. There is not a bank in America that would be naïve enough to offer such a credit card. Even without the presence of this fictional financial nightmare, credit card debt concerns continue to make headlines across the American landscape. Every year, debt levels rise as the addictive buying behavior of American consumers continues to worsen. However, in another newsworthy industry, the uncontrolled use of a similar credit card goes unaddressed, year in and year out.

Like the credit card crisis, it comes as no surprise that our country faces another problem; a healthcare problem. The rising cost of healthcare is the biggest financial threat our country faces, and our attempts to mitigate this threat have been ineffective, at best. Unexpected medical bills are the number one cause for the rise in personal bankruptcies in the United States. These same unexpected medical bills have torn into the personal savings accounts of most American households. For the past twenty years, eighty percent of the wage increases employers have doled out to the workforce have gone to pay for health insurance, a direct beneficiary of rising healthcare costs. Should employers be concerned about this? You better believe it! For most employers, the cost of health insurance is the second, maybe the third highest expense on the Profit & Loss (P&L) statement, and there is not another expense on the P&L rising faster than the financial burden of health insurance. So, how have we allowed the U.S. healthcare system to have such a huge impact on health insurance costs?

Several factors are to blame but none bigger than the construction of the typical health insurance plan. Simply put, employers have been building health plans backwards. First, employers (through the advice of the benefits broker) pick a large, national insurance carrier to provide the health insurance coverage. This insurance carrier often wins the bid by offering the lowest premium. Next, the employer vets the provider network to ensure all employees and dependents have access to a wide selection of doctors and hospitals. The final construction of the health plan occurs when the employer picks the deductibles, co-pays, and out of pocket limits from a list of plans offered by the insurance carrier.

Now, as health insurance costs continue to rise, employers begin shifting the burden. Deductibles are increased, employer premium contributions are reduced, and one insurance carrier is replaced by another. This dance is the health insurance equivalent of re-arranging the deck chairs on the Titanic. Year after year, employers look to short-term fixes instead of addressing the biggest problem inside the health insurance plan. The problem is not the plan design, the level of employer premium contribution, or the insurance carrier. The biggest problem inside the health insurance plan is the experience employees and dependents are having with the healthcare system. I do not care if a health insurance plan has a $500 deductible or a $5,000 deductible; today's healthcare experience is unacceptable. However, here's the problem. What company management sees as a medical ID card, employees view as an unlimited company credit card. As a result, the medical ID card has become the riskiest credit card in America.

The medical ID card represents an unlimited company credit card and, for most employers, there are no effective controls for how, when, and where the ID card is used. As long as employees stay in-network, they can go wherever they want, and they can spend whatever they want, and it is inside the provider network where uncontrolled spending can wreak havoc on a health insurance plan.

With medical ID card in hand, employees are buying healthcare services for which the quality and price are not disclosed. With one swipe of the medical ID card, an MRI can be purchased for $3,000. However, that same MRI can be purchased for $500 if the employee simply buys the service from another provider at a different location. With one swipe of the medical ID card, an employee can choose to undergo back surgery, which could easily run north of $50,000, when a second opinion could have revealed that surgery was not necessary. With the swipe of this same medical ID card, an employee can purchase a prescription drug at the pharmacy with an annual cost of $30,000 or more. However, this same prescription drug could be purchased for pennies on the dollar if bought through a different source.

The cost of healthcare is rising at an unsustainable pace, and providing employees access to an unlimited company credit card is only making matters worse. The health insurance rule makers (government, hospital systems, pharmaceutical companies, and insurance carriers) have designed a game that has a very predictable ending. By creating an opaque buying experience for consumers, the rule makers win, and employers lose. So, what can an employer do about it?

First, to have any chance of controlling healthcare spending, an employer must choose to self-fund the health insurance plan. Inside a self-funded health plan, upwards of 90% of plan costs are directly or indirectly tied to the healthcare purchases employees are making. The total cost for all healthcare purchases in a given year comes down to the following formula; *the number of units of care x the cost per unit of care*. If an employer can effectively reduce both factors in this formula, it stands a chance at reducing the cost of health insurance.

That said, eliminating the claims that occur inside the health plan should not be the focus, as employees should access the healthcare system when they have to. However, the focus should be on putting effective controls in place, helping employees slash the cost of the healthcare purchases they are making with the medical ID card. Employers cannot rely on the provider network discounts alone.

Network "discounts" are very deceiving. The size of the discount may look very appealing; however, if the discount is tied to a highly-inflated price, both employer and employee are coming out on the short end of the stick. Think of it this way. I can try selling you my iPhone for $2,000, and I can even try luring you in with a 50% discount but, at the end of the day, I am still ripping you off. Network discounts are no different. Employers have to implement effective controls to reduce the cost of the healthcare services purchased inside the health plan. By simply shifting how employees buy the healthcare services they need, employers are helping them buy goods and services at significantly reduced prices without sacrificing quality, but there is still more work to do.

Second, tools and resources must be put in place to help employees make effective healthcare decisions. Employers should strike deals with high-quality providers ensuring that employees have low-cost or no-cost access for the healthcare needs that may arise. Like the fictional bank above, employers should also provide employees with "cash back" incentives when the right healthcare purchasing decisions are made.

Today, most health plans have the employees navigating a large provider network alone where the number of misdiagnosis, duplicated services, and unnecessary procedures are rising at an alarming rate. Employees need help and want help. They must be provided with the right tools and resources so that navigating a broad provider network becomes efficient and easy. When employees are given the ability to purchase high-quality healthcare services at a low cost, the health insurance plan provides for a positive healthcare experience and reduced financial strain on the company's checkbook.

Now, in order for the medical ID card to be used appropriately, employees must receive the necessary education to facilitate a positive buying experience. Education must be a year-long venture focused on helping the consumer make wise healthcare decisions. Today, most of the education takes place during the annual Open Enrollment meeting and, unfortunately, employees forget most of everything told to them during the educational session. Healthcare is not something consumers prepare for. No one thinks about it until healthcare happens to them and if education is not provided to employees on a continual basis, they will forget about the tools and resources they have, and will go about making uncontrolled purchases with the unlimited company credit card. Education is the glue that holds a successful health insurance plan together.

When an employer can reduce the cost of the healthcare services purchased inside the health plan, it can reduce the cost of providing health insurance. It is that simple but, remember; employees are in possession of the riskiest credit card in America. Without effective controls and education, the use of the medical ID card can quickly get out of control. When quality and price are not easily accessible, it is imperative the right tools and resources are accessible. Buying healthcare services affordability and confidently is an experience employees will never forget. It will no longer be the rule makers, but employers and employees, who profit from this experience.

Andy Neary

National Adviser
Captivated Health
Boulder, CO

Andy Neary is a healthcare strategist with Captivated Health. He has more than 15 years of experience in helping employers affect the rising cost of healthcare through innovative strategies. He works with his clients to move them from the benefits status quo with innovative and creative strategies that provide savings for employers and a rich benefit plan array for employees.

He recently was named to the "Boulder 40 Under 40" list, recognizing his professional and charitable contributions to that Colorado community. He is a former professional pitcher with the Milwaukee Brewers.

As a former professional athlete, Neary understands the hard work and daily grind needed to perform at the highest level. He takes the same approach with his clients, guiding them through that daily grind to create truly elite benefit programs. It's the work done when no one is watching that generates success.

www.captivatedhealth.com
aneary@captivatedhealth.com
414-403-8383

CHAPTER 26

HOW MORE U.S. EMPLOYERS ARE MAXIMIZING HEALTHCARE DOLLARS

Nelson Griswold and Arthur Thomas Taft, Concentric DPC*

"Employers spend 51% of all U.S. healthcare dollars. As they gain greater control over healthcare costs, it will have a big impact on helping the U.S. healthcare system figure out how to generate healthier communities."
—Jeff Ellington, Concentric DPC

Nobody blames employers and employees for struggling under the current U.S. healthcare system. It's expensive, complex, and offers inconsistent levels of care quality. What it doesn't seem to do is reward primary care physicians for keeping people as healthy as they can be. The effect of having healthy employees and lower, predictable healthcare costs benefits everyone: individuals, physicians, employers, and communities. And, Direct Primary Care (DPC) provides a proven model for coordinating the tools and services to help physicians provide proactive healthcare that costs less, reward physicians for results, reduce administrative clutter, and restore the physician-patient relationship as primary *and* profitable.

What Are the Problems?

Studies indicate that:

- Healthcare fraud in the United States approaches 10% of the total amount spent on care.[1]
- "Current estimates for unnecessary expenditures on overuse range from 10 to 30 percent of total health care spending."[2]
- "A 2014 report from the Commonwealth Fund revealed continued trends that" showed the "US "ranked last overall among 11 industrialized countries on measures of health system quality, efficiency, access to care, equity and healthy lives."[3]

Few would debate that change is needed.

There is general understanding that these issues are at least in part the result of Physician/Hospital (collectively "Providers") incentives produced by the current healthcare payment system. It is referred to as "Fee-for-Service" (or FFS) because the more healthcare services

[1] "Healthcare Fraud: The $272 Billion Dollar Swindle;" The Economist, May 31st 2014
[2] "When less is more; Issues of overuse in Healthcare," Health Affairs, April 25th 2014
[3] "The Quality of US Healthcare Compared With the World;" AJMC.com; February 1st 2016

a provider delivers, the more money the provider makes regardless of the patient's actual health outcome or, in some case, the patient's actual health need(s).

A secondary cause often cited for the healthcare systems poor results is the "fragmentation" of the delivery system itself. As medical knowledge has expanded, the industry has seen an increase in both the number of specialties and the number of sub-specialties. Each group of providers have important knowledge sets but as an individual takes responsibility for specifics care topics they tend to assume that other providers will be treating the patient's' other healthcare issues. As a result, care coordination has become critical issues. Many look to the Primary Care providers (usually including "Family Practice,' "Pediatricians," Gerontologists," Internists," and "Ob/Gyn") to perform this function.

It is estimated that 30% of working adults do not have a relationship with a primary care physician. Even where a patient has a Primary Care relationship, individuals currently may elect to receive care from a variety of sources including Urgent Care centers and emergency rooms due to limited access to their provider outside of usual office hours. Primary Care providers also self-limit their service offerings based on a variety of Health Plan related factors including:

- Reimbursement rates and payment timing.
- Plan design including the administrative complexity created by the design.
- The number of patients the provider supports.
- No consequences for referring a patient on to another provider.

The result is that there are unclear roles in the marketplace with inconsistent expectations on the part of the patients and the providers.

Efforts to rethink current spending include:

- We assume we must have health coverage for all healthcare services, not just for a catastrophic event /illness. Overusing coverage drives up health plan costs. It also generates administrative clutter, and system fraud.
- The existing payment systems affects the quality of care by restricting how physicians adopt information technology tools to improve patient access and support patient education.
- There is no clear physician advocate role to help the patient stay healthy and navigate the healthcare system when they need care.

What Employers Can Do Now

Under a Direct Primary Care (DPC) model, Physicians receive a monthly rate per employee (a capitated rate) and are rewarded for maintaining their best possible health. An added bonus is that better systems and payment processes for primary care physicians adds an incentive for good physicians to remain in clinical practice and to inspire the next generation of physicians to enter the profession.

Benefits of Direct Primary Care

- Physicians and administrators gain greater control over time lost daily to insurance-related chores;
- Employees and their dependents benefit in overall health by taking and measuring a proactive approach to care.
- Employers reduce/control healthcare costs and reward physicians for helping employees keep healthy.

- The current generation of primary care physicians encourage the next generation to be physicians, too.

The current comprehensive healthcare system includes coverage for most basic healthcare services, not just catastrophic illness/events. This increases the cost of health care directly by including these services but also indirectly by increasing the cost of plan administration. Employers can pay less if traditional employee coverage was only for catastrophic illness/events. A Direct Primary Care (DPC) physician becomes an alternative way for the patient or the employer to support the non-catastrophic care needs of employees and their families. And, the tools/healthcare service available to support the physician teams the way they work now.

DPC physicians are responsible to be their patient advocate but the introduction of third-party coaching services, the expanded use of urgent care, and continued abuse of the emergency department has limited their ability to successfully fulfill this role. The DPC model provides patient access to this care via cloud-based accounting, advertising, telemedicine, and other remote practice management tools in support of 24/7 patient services. This change, plus the patient's commitment to the expanded physician relationship allows the DPC physician to re-establish their role in preventive care.

Price reductions are also to be expected. Specific DPC providers have reported overall cost of care reductions in the 15 to 17% range. This is not a projection based on a costing model. This kind of change needs to be visible in the organization's financial report. Short term expectations need to be tempered, but the planned source of savings are clear as shown here:

- Spending on third-party employee education and support programs can be reduced. The incentives often paid to encourage the employees and their dependents to use the program can also be phased out.

- Primary care incentives to reduce total cost encourage them to reduce specialist referrals and consider providing services where they are confident of success without changing their monthly fee.

- Recurring fixed monthly fees for defined services should lead to reduced administration fees on the part of the health plan administrator. That will likely require time and negotiation.

- Physician-led patient education and support as well as prevention support will reduce Emergency Room and Urgent Care visits.

- Many of the DPC Physicians are independent providers whose base fees are normally set lower than similar physicians owned by an Integrated Health Delivery System. Health plans normally allow a 10-15% difference in rates for the same service to the larger organization because they have a stronger bargain position. DPC helps to keep providers independent and indirectly leads to lower costs.

Employers should not expect immediate savings but should watch them develop over time as employee adoption with Direct Primary Care tools and service increase over time.

Visionary Brokers Are Committed to Healthcare Industry Change

Change will impact every portion of the health benefit planning process including brokerage and consulting services. Employers will need experienced third-party resources to help them through the transition. It is clear that the Broker–Consulting revenue model will change.

A visionary broker will realize that the current status quo is not meeting his or her clients' needs and expectation with regard to the quality and cost of the care delivered. With over 20 years of third-party patient education and support programs with provider oversight offerings like case management, the evidence is in that the status quo does not meet the employers or even the nation needs to lower health spending and reduce cost. Visionary brokers will recognize that DPC simplifies a very complex payment process, gets the Primary Care and other providers focused back on clinical care and the patient employees' needs, and offers a pathway for continued positive change.

It is important to find a broker–consultant who is willing and able to renegotiate their payment model and have the expertise to develop the healthcare delivery system the US needs.

A Call to Action

Concentric DPC: Systematically Getting Each Stakeholder
Knowing Their Role & Acting Upon It

To subscribe to Concentric DPC news updates
please send your name and email address to:

info@concentricdpc.com

Concentric DPC is a Physician Services Organization that supports physicians converting to the DPC model and offers a network of DPC providers to employers.

Employers	Physicians	Patients	Hospital Systems	Insurance Companies
DPC made part of plan design CEOs and CFOs buy into new model for employees and engage legislators	Fee-for-Service technology coordinated with DPC transition Engage with advisers able to guide transition and become health resource stewards	Adopt DPC concept. Engage with DPC and realize benefits. Build enthusiasm and promote concept to others	Use DPC for employee plan Assess strategic role for facility and capital deployment Address capacity changes	Develop high-value ancillary products around DPC model

ALL: Provide Telemedicine & other advanced technology to support DPC delivery

The sequence shown in the chart is a call to action. It recognizes that Employers are the most likely to lead change. What many employers may not recognize is that the Physicians also want change. The efforts by the Health Plans and others to help employers have actually disenfranchised the providers they are trying to manage. Physicians have clinical knowledge and want to use it. The administrative controls are largely adding costs without improving quality as it is taking time away from the patient. Now is the time to define what is expected of a Primary Care Provider, establish a fair and attractive rate for the service, and hold them accountable for the quality of those services. This first step is a beginning. Bundled payments models are the application of the same principle to specialty care. Both are standard management processes that are well known to employers but have not been applied effectively to healthcare. Now is the time as Direct Primary Care is emerging and it carries with it an opportunity for system wide changes.

Are Employers Doing the Right Things to Improve Their Healthcare Costs?

In an effort to improve their healthcare issues suggested by the current healthcare payment system, employers have made the system inefficient and ineffective. They tried to second guess the provider decisions with review services such as "prior authorization" and "case management." Employers also invested in patient education and support services to help their employees be better individual healthcare consumers. Employers are even taking responsibility for specific provider roles by offering annual health risk screenings with biometric lab tests that look more and more like annual physicals with many considering including behavioral health screening tools as a potential fix for this area of quality weakness in the normal delivery system. Employers are introducing employee incentives to increase their use of these services.

The results of these employer efforts are questionable. Actual reductions in health care spending or improvements in care quality due to specific interventions are hard to measure.

The overall trends, though, have been unchanged for multiple decades. In addition, while these offerings may assist individual employees / patients, they may be making the problems in the healthcare system worse. A typical provider will have over 20 health plan relationships. Within a single health plan relationship, the provider may be seeing hundreds of patients who are covered by unique employers. Many self-insured employers each have their own health benefit design often using a different third-party vendors to support the various fixes selected by the employer's' health benefit team and their broker/consultants. A provider, supporting a few thousand patient, may well be confronted with hundreds of different benefit packages. The result: the providers instruct their patients to simply listen to them as a way to cut down on the noise rather than to leverage the employer's' investment to increase their productivity and improve the quality of their care.

*The authors would like to thank A Jefferson Ellington, III for contributions and Janice K. Mandel, Strategic Communications, Concentric DPC for her contribution of editorial style. More at http://janicemandel.com

Arthur Thomas Taft

Chief Operation Officer
Concentric DPC
Burlington, NC

Arthur Thomas Taft joins Concentric DPC as an extension of his role at MedWorks Consulting, LLC, where he was Founder and Managing Director for over 15 years. At MedWorks, Art identified and completed assignments for multiple Fortune 500 companies and others in a wide variety of healthcare areas including but not limited to Employee Benefits, Pharmaceutical, Commercialization, and Technology.

Prior to forming MedWorks, Art held senior positions at SmithKine Beecham, Merrill Lynch, and AT&T with areas of responsibility that included Technology, Operational, and Sales/Marketing roles. He has also ghost written several articles on Chronic Disease Management that have been published in peer reviewed journals. And worked as an instructor at Xavier University (Business Statistics) and New York University (Telecommunications).

Art holds a Bachelor of Science and a Masters of Engineering in Operations Research and Industrial Engineering from Cornell University as well as an MBA in Marketing/Management from New York University.

www.concentrichealthsystems.com
ataft@medworksusa.com
336-294-9733

CHAPTER 27

THE ULTIMATE TRANSPARENCY TOOL

Stefanie Pigeon

(This chapter is dedicated to the clients I refer to as my early adopters and who have a tremendous amount of trust in our work. I thank them for their perseverance and willingness to follow us into the next frontier.)

Since 2007, the average medical trend increase annually has been 8.22%, causing employers of all sizes to look for cost containment strategies. Many companies have experimented with a variety of network styles to manipulate the overall cost of their health insurance. Prior to the existence of networks, it was common place to have an indemnity style plan which priced health procedures using a usual and customary formula for the geographic region. This often led to consumers paying the balance of the bill between what the carrier was willing to pay, and what the facility billed.

In 1973, Congress passed the Health Maintenance Organization Act which spearheaded the growth of HMO's. The intention was to reduce the cost of healthcare, while improving the quality of care through a gatekeeper system. Providers agreed via contract to set charges for procedures. To this day, many employers still use an HMO to address these needs. Preferred Provider Organizations followed HMOs as a way to offer discounted rates for a specific network of doctors while allowing consumers to pay additional dollars to seek out of network doctors. The evolution continued with the development of Exclusive Provider Organizations which do not allow for coverage outside of a given network, except in an emergency situation, and EPOs rarely require a referral. All of these forms of managed care worked to create some form of cost control. The most recent frontier of cost containment strategy is known as Referenced Based Pricing. In the truest sense, it eliminates the need for traditional provider networks and preset pricing contracts.

It is commonplace for employers, with the guidance of their benefits consultant, to contract with vendors who have developed a structured process for determining the reference based price. One of the most commonly used references is Medicare. In our upcoming case study, the plan uses a reference base of up to 150% of what Medicare will pay for a procedure. You may certainly structure a plan to pay less, such as 120% of Medicare; however, you are setting your employees up for a greater possibility of balance billing, the lower you go. Balance billing, in this situation, is when the provider or facility does not agree with the reference based price and proceeds to charge your employee the difference between the reference amount and the total physician or facility bill.

A reference based priced (RBP) plan that is willing to pay up to 150% of what Medicare is willing to pay causes approximately 2% of claims to fall into a balance bill situation, whereas a plan that caps their payout at 120% of Medicare equivalent payments is likely to have up to 10% of claims falling into balance bill situations. You should confirm that your plan has a vendor to provide legal defense against providers who balance bill and serves as a protective measure to keep the insured out of collections. Do not enter into an agreement involving referenced based pricing without the legal support to protect your employees from balance billing!

Ninety-five percent of the time payments are accepted at the original price or at a final negotiated price that is still well below the traditional HMO, PPO or EPO negotiated payment. Almost all cases are won with the use of the vendor's legal advocate. Few if any providers/ hospitals are interested in opening up their entire payment structure to the public and therefore come to an agreement with the help of the legal advocate. (The 95% figure comes from Steve Purkapile, vice president for underwriting at HUB International Insurance Services in Denver. *SHRM Online.*)

What difficulties to be aware of?

Education is key to both the employer, but more importantly, for the employee base. Be as transparent as possible with employees so that they understand why referenced based pricing is being used. They need to be a part of the solution, not a potentially disgruntled bystander when something happens with their claims that they don't understand. Employees must be made aware that they may receive a balance bill. Giving them assurance that they have an advocate that will negotiate on their behalf and protect their credit is critical. They must know how to access the advocate and when to engage the advocacy team. Remind them that they will learn more about medical billing than they ever wanted to know, but that they will have a chance to experience true transparency and take an active role in their health care decisions. Additionally, this is a strategy to contain costs and pass on savings.

Work with a vendor that negotiates fees with providers up front, not after the fact. Fees should be negotiated at the pre-certification level. It will not be uncommon to receive a balance bill when someone has to go to the emergency room unexpectedly, or has an accident and is rushed to the hospital. These will be negotiated after entrance to the facility. Again, make your employee base aware of this, and provide examples of how to handle the billing and how to engage the patient advocacy team.

The real value

In this hypothetical example below, you see immediately the real dollar value for both the insured and the employer's plan. Financially, this poses to be a win/win!

Sample Procedure	Traditional PPO Plan	RBP Plan
Starting Cost	$60,000 Hospital Bill	$12,000 (what Medicare might pay)
Plan Payment	$36,000 PPO negotiated reimbursement rate	$18,000 (150% of what Medicare might pay)
Deductible and Coinsurance	$1,000 + 20%	$1,000 + 20%
Insured Pays	$7,000 **Max Out of Pocket	$4,400
Employer Plan Responsibility (Plan payment—Insured payment)	$29,000	$13,600

Additional value includes the opportunity to provide a medical plan without borders. Meaning there are no defined networks of hospitals or doctors. In a sense, it levels the playing field with claims. It does not allow price gouging from one procedure to another to make up for the loss of revenue.

Ultimately, it sets a fair price at a reduced cost which passes on saving to both your employees and your company plan. Implementing such a plan requires a minimum of at least 10 participants, and that requirement may vary depending on your location. This is a relatively new approach as it came to life in the Fortune 500 companies who were fiercely trying to get a grip on their medical claims spend.

Reinsurance carriers are likely to be supportive of your effort to contain costs using the RBP model, and may pass on discounts to your plan for use of this strategy. Additionally, network access fees will no longer be necessary. For those of you that are considering migrating from fully insured plans directly to RBP models, you will have little to no understanding of these comments. However, as you start to compare plans outside of the fully insured market place, you will see the fee structures unravel and have more transparency in regards to the cost of the plan and administration fees.

Broker Transparency

Ask your benefits consultant about their experience with RBP. Ask them about the marketplace in your area and find out how receptive hospitals and doctors have been to the RBP process. Each and every region of our country has a different situation; in some areas, the hospitals have almost created monopolies and are terribly difficult to work with, while in other areas, there is still competition.

Through my personal experience as a benefits consultant, I have found that some providers will try to avoid coordination with the plan and may go so far as to tell your employee that they do not have coverage. The best way to alleviate this situation is to have informed employees, who are comfortable coaching the providers on their plans. More importantly, your plan vendor needs to have a strong legal advocacy group that is willing and able to push the providers to come to an agreeable resolution.

Remember in all of this activity is an employee that can become completely overwhelmed and burdened by the massive amounts of paperwork and confusion. Make sure your benefits consultant partner has an effective educational action plan for rolling out this style of coverage. It is also helpful if your consultant has a solid service team to assist employees when needed. Remember we only retain about 10% of what is shared in educational sessions, so do not assume that your employees will be ready to roll into the new contract year with 100% confidence. It is critical to have a process for continual repetitive education coordinated by your benefits consultant partner and your HR team with the opportunity for in-person education.

Ask your benefits consultant partner about the difference between a full RBP model and one that works with a physician's only network. It has been our experience that people have a tremendous amount of emotional attachment to their doctors, and for that reason, we have opted to provide an RBP model that incorporates a network for the outpatients' doctor visits, while leaving all facility charges to be negotiated through the RBP model, where the greatest discrepancy in pricing exists.

Where is the proof this works?

Not only are for-profit employers considering and implementing referenced based pricing plans, but states like Montana and California are finding the value in RBP. Montana refers to RBP as Transparent Pricing and implemented a plan in July of 2016. The estimated savings to Montana taxpayer by 2018, for a total participant load of approximately 33,000, is projected to be in the range of $25 million.

In Montana, under the former model of payment, hospitals and facilities could charge the state's health plan dramatically different amounts for the same service. For example, a hospital in Montana could charge $25,000 for equivalent knee replacement surgery, while another charged more than $100,000. The new form of reimbursing hospitals changes that model. Allegiance is contracting with facilities for more comparable costs by anchoring pricing to a national point of reference, Medicare, then paying hospitals a multiple above that. This will make medical costs more predictable, consistent and comparable among facilities. (Reference: Montana.gov website article—Friday, July 8, 2016)

Case study of an Employer averaging 46 participants

This table contains six years of total plan costs and various containments strategies.

Note the ** refers to the strategies used in the various years.

2011 $2,500/$5,000 deductible no co-pays EPO–$274,724**
        EPO network

2012 $2,500/$5,000 deductible no co-pays EPO–$287,087

2013 $5,000/$10,000 deductible no copays EPO–$260,360**
         increase deductible

2014 $5,000/$10,000 deductible no copays EPO–$283,148

2015 $5,000/$10,000 deductible no copays EPO–$289,935

2016 $5,000/$10,000 deductible with co-pays RBP–$287,796**
        improved plan reduced cost with RBP

Implementing cost containment strategies such as network adjustments, increased deductibles and referenced based pricing allowed this plan to stay at a relatively similar gross cost for five years running.

It is imperative for the employer to plan as far into the future as possible, projecting costs and strategizing over a number of years. The historical trends give great insight into the future cost. In 2007, the medical trend was 11.9%, whereas 2018 is projected to be 6.5% with an average of 8.22% over the last 11 years. This case study demonstrates that Reference Based Pricing may ultimately be a part of your cost containment strategy moving forward. (Reference — PwC Health Research Institute — medical trend)

Our process

Our firm's process is detailed as follows:

1. Confirm employer understanding and agreement to move forward

2. Onsite education in conjunction with electronic benefit enrollment containing strong educational material

3. Email blasts to employers

4. Suggestive approaches to reduce plan costs shared with you, the employer, through the course of the year—encourage and aid in implementation of effective wellness programs, telemedicine and Employee Assistance Programs that have a positive impact on the outcome of the health plan

5. Offer of mid-year onsite reviews in more casual and approachable atmosphere

6. Remind—Repeat—Remind—Repeat!! We are all busy and moving quickly today; therefore, it is imperative that we give our employees more than one opportunity to retain such an enormous amount of information.

Evaluate the RBP opportunity with these questions

- What experience does your partner consultant group have with RBP?
- What is the reference based price? Example - what measure (percentage of Medicare)?
- How often are employees balance billed?
- What can be put in place to protect employees from balance bills?
- What is the provider receptivity in the region?

- Is there safe harbor network for doctor's visits? If so, what percentage of providers in the area are participating?

Make sure your consultant partner group has an open door policy. Things will come up, and you may need extra help.

Interestingly, in 2014, about 10% of U.S. employers had adopted reference-based pricing; 68% plan to do so in the near future, according to a recent survey by the Society for Human Resource Management. (Reference—*Business Insurance*—Referenced based health care reimbursements require careful application, 10.7.2014)

Best of luck entering the next frontier!!

Stefanie Pigeon

President
Affiliated Associates
Essex, VT

Since Stefanie's start in the industry in 1995, her primary focus has been meeting client's needs and growing with her clients. Her mission is to use creative solutions to meet the ever-demanding issues that employers and employees are facing.

Growing an agency in a rural state like Vermont with limited insurance carrier options has forced her to utilize the most innovative strategies for groups of all sizes. One of her proudest moments was being recognized in a local business magazine and giving her staff the chance to share their story.

Stefanie has established four pillars to her agency that are illustrated through her logo: Communication, Education, Technology and Service, demonstrated by the service dogs on her card. Education is deemed as critical, not only for Stefanie's clients, but for her staff to stay current. She would tell you "don't let the tail wag the dog in the world of planning." For those of you who do not remember the old adage, Stefanie would smile at you and suggest that her firm is "Your best friend in insurance."

www. affiliatedassoc.com
stefanie@affiliatedassoc.com
802-861-2900

CHAPTER 28

VOLUNTARY DISRUPTION

Eric Silverman

As an employer, you spend a tremendous amount of time and effort formulating a cost containment strategy with your health broker to figure out ways to mitigate your yearly healthcare spend. After all, if you are like most employers, health insurance is one of your top three largest line items in your budget every year, thus the time and energy you spend on this necessary evil is more than justified.

Riddle me this… are all of your additional employee benefit offerings, whether employer or employee funded, strategically placed in concert with what you and your health broker have spent countless hours putting together, or are your additional employee benefit offerings thrown together with no rhyme or reason, in a way that resembles trying to fit a square peg into a round hole?

Throughout my 18 years in business, I have worked as a "brokers broker," strategically helping brokers all over the country to ensure their employer clients have a uniform and cohesive total employee benefits package available to their employees. The shortcomings of these packages typically lie within the benefits that are traditionally employee funded, or better known as "voluntary."

What I know for certain is that the "voluntary" employee funded benefits market is ripe for disruption and there are two crucial areas that employers must address and demand of their benefits broker.

1. The severe lack of transparency in the "voluntary benefits" industry—from the all too common and wasteful "product dump" that leads to the inevitable "commission grab," to the broker and adviser compensation model.

2. The elimination of this "product dump" and how to replace any unnecessary product offerings with more robust benefits at lower price points, while strategically matching and mirroring your long-term health insurance design.

I have always subscribed to the reality that failure breeds success, and where my business started to become the most successful is when I began having serious, and often times uncomfortable conversations, with my broker partners and our employer clients.

In full transparency and disclosure, I am going to walk you, step-by-step, through the systems and complete methodology I share with each of my potential and existing broker partners countrywide. This process is what I hope your health broker will share with you one day and there are no secrets, nor any reasons to leave anything out. If your current health broker is not candidly sharing everything with you as laid out in this chapter, then I urge you to consider moving your business to a broker who will break through the status quo on your behalf.

So, sit back, relax, and allow me to pull back the curtain on the industry formally known as "voluntary."

Disrupting The "Voluntary" Market

To "disrupt," according to dictionary.com, is a verb used to express "disorder or turmoil," while to cause "disruption," is a noun that in business, means to bring "radical change in an industry [or] business strategy."

"Disruptor"—the term most often used to describe healthcare industry thought leaders like David Contorno of Lake Norman Benefits in Charlotte, NC, Mick Rodgers of The Axial Company in Boston, MA, and Andy Neary of Captivated Health in Denver, CO. These healthcare rock-stars, among many others, have developed and adopted some of the most cutting-edge ideas and strategies to help transform how their employer clients view and fund health insurance, in ways that I have yet to see anyone write about when it comes to "voluntary benefits," or as Nelson Griswold and I refer to them as—"enhanced benefits."

Disruption Begins With Effective Word Choice

As an intern, green as can be, I found out the hard way that words are very powerful things that have intense meaning.

I had just begun working with my first employer client and I could not wait to educate each employee. While presenting, I proceeded to, innocently enough, refer to the majority of the employees as "tow truck drivers." Uh-oh—all of a sudden, I heard strong rumblings amongst the masses. Not realizing my detrimental mistake, most of the employees were quick to correct me; they are "auto recovery specialists" and just because they drive a tow truck that does not make them "tow truck drivers." Yikes—my ignorance and failure to realize the perceived differences nearly cost me my new employer client. I certainly meant no disrespect and I apologized profusely, but my lack of knowledge with respect to their profession made me see the potential irreparable damage that incorrect word choice can have in business.

Flash forward to my early experiences trying to partner with traditional "status quo" health brokers in the early 2000's. Nearly every health broker I met with did not care about what I now call "enhanced benefits," but are still commonly referred to these days as "voluntary." Most said there was no value in these types of products and that all their clients needed was a comprehensive healthcare program.

After many meetings with multiple health brokers, I noticed that everyone kept referring to enhanced benefit products as "ancillary."

According to Webster's online dictionary:
An·cil·lar·y (adjective)—Providing something additional
to a main part or function. Supplementary.

In the early 2000's, while in its truest form, the word "ancillary" may have been a semi-reasonable term for the times, however, it is most certainly not the proper terminology to use now. With the ACA making the current state of healthcare such a train wreck, most health brokers who used to tell me enhanced benefits had no value and were unnecessary "ancillary" add-ons, are now starting to jump feet first into the enhanced benefits space. Initially, because they wanted to make up for their dwindling health insurance commissions, but also because they were losing business to enhanced benefit sales reps who had been cutting them out.

With that in mind, I have had countless health brokers tell me that they are struggling with getting their employer clients on board with enhanced benefits for various reasons. They explain that even if they are able to install them, their challenge is that the employee participation levels are so low that it makes them question why they bothered placing enhanced benefit products in the first place.

The two questions I ask these struggling health brokers are:

1. What terminology and verbiage do they use when describing these benefits to their employer clients?
2. How do they advise their employer clients to implement their newly proposed enhanced benefits?

The candid answers that I continue to receive are that they refer to everything as "ancillary" or "voluntary" and that they enroll them using solely an online platform and/or call center.

Remember when I said, "words are very powerful things that have intense meaning?" What message is your broker sending you as their employer client, about the new employee funded benefits they are proposing, when they are constantly referring to them in a negative connotation using words such as "ancillary" or "voluntary?"

If your broker's only methodology to educate and enroll your employees is through an online platform or a call center, then are they truly expecting overwhelming employee participation and dare I mention, profitability for their agency? Let's face it, your broker is a for-profit entity and while you may not care, per se, if they are not profitable, they are not going to be able to remain in business any more than you would if your company was not profitable. If your broker goes out of business, then what good are they to you long-term?

The message they are sending you insinuates that the enhanced benefit products they are recommending are "unimportant (and) non-essential." Subsequently, the way in which they are primarily advising employers to educate and enroll these unimportant and non-essential benefits further exacerbates your initial employer, and your employee's, perceived message.

Bottom line: Your health broker must change their vocabulary to earn your business and they must adjust their primary enrollment methodology to earn more revenue for their agency. Perception equals reality, so when your broker finally replaces "ancillary" with "enhanced" and frames "voluntary" in a more "mandatory" setting, your company's benefits package will be second to none, and your broker's business will grow quicker so that they can remain profitable in order to be by your side for many years to come.

The Great Disruptor

How do you disrupt a side of the employee benefits industry that is not likely to have commissions disappear anytime soon, and where rising costs are not adding extreme pressure to a company's bottom line or an employee's paycheck? Sure, your broker could charge you, as their employer client, a consulting fee to lessen employee cost and offset their reliance on commissions, but then they are asking you to help fund the implementation, education, and enrollment of benefits that are purposely designed to be employee funded with no outlay of employer funds.

What about technology as a disruptor? Benefit administration systems and enrollment platforms have become so advanced and sophisticated that we now have multilingual avatars that can educate employees on the value and need for enhanced benefits through quick and simple white board videos in an interactive and (artificially) intelligent format. Each year, technology continues to develop and impress, and is certainly a disruptive force that challenges the status quo, making this type of technology a positive disruption to our market.

Nevertheless, I would argue that the most influential disrupter to our industry must be the willingness of the broker community at large, to adjust, adapt, and embrace the ever-changing enhanced benefits market. Let's face it, whenever a market changes, there will always be innovators who drive the change, early and late adopters who follow those innovators and help steer the change, and those who dig their heels in and turn a blind eye to the change.

I have found that most health insurance brokers fall into one of four categories with respect to how they approach enhanced employee funded benefits for their employer clients. Which category does your broker fall into?

1. Your broker generally ignores enhanced benefits unless you, as their employer client, inquires or asks about "voluntary benefits." Most employer clients do not proactively ask about these types of benefits, so it is typically prompted by one of your brokers potential competitors or a large carrier sales rep knocking on your door and giving you a great idea. This is more of a reactive stance on the part of your broker, that comes with low risk and minimal revenue growth to your broker.

2. Your broker outsources to a single insurance carrier and allows that carrier and their enrollers to handle everything. While this is a more proactive stance, it does come with higher risk

due to a large quantity of carrier reps who are often perceived by employers as not being very professional or experienced. In addition to not being very good for you as their employer client, this approach typically delivers minimal revenue to your broker, due to confusing and non-transparent carrier compensation structures that may also result in lower revenue shares. In addition, this approach is not carrier neutral and agnostic, which most times, prevents customizing the plans to your employees' needs and is not in the overall best interest of your employees. For the most part, the products are usually placed with little to no regard to the current benefits already installed due to minimal, if any, collaboration between your broker and the carrier rep. Of the brokers who try to be pro-active with their recommendations and installation of these benefits, this approach has still widely been considered the standard over the years and is the exact area of the "voluntary" industry that is ripe for the most dramatic disruption.

3.   Your broker hires an in-house Vice President of "voluntary" or an equivalent. Very proactive, with high risk and mid-to-high long-term revenue potential. Their ROI is dependent upon hiring the right person, and the time it takes to ramp-up. Typically, your broker will spend $100k+ on a base salary, plus they will share commissions, bonuses, and absorb all the other costs of doing business. Their upside is that your broker gets to keep 100% of the revenue and available compensation in-house. The downside comes with high fixed costs and overhead, as well as the need to retain enrollment firms that may charge upwards of 80% to 90% of your broker's total compensation, which can be a recipe for disaster. This approach is the most

challenging to execute and make profitable in a reasonable amount of time—leaving a large propensity to failure and your broker reverting back to categories one or two.

4. Your broker partners with a carrier agnostic benefits boutique with decades of proven experience in the enhanced benefits industry. This partner typically has staff with carrier and retail experience, so they know how to position the products and work on your brokers behalf, while representing your primary best interests, as an employer. This methodology is also essential and more efficient for both your broker and yourself, since your brokers' partnering firm will typically have a large national footprint with in-house distribution and an enrollment arm. This approach is extremely proactive, comes with medium risk and minimal to no overhead, while providing very high, short and long-term revenue potential. The risk level is mitigated for your broker as their partnership and trust evolves, while complete carrier compensation transparency is paramount—a true disruptor within this space. Your broker's partnering firm must also hold top carrier contracts with volume based carrier underwriting concessions that extend to you as their employer client, so that you can bolt on to the best available products and services to make available to your employees.

As you think about what category your broker may fall in, keep in mind that your broker should be adopting one of the more proactive approaches listed above, notably numbers 3 or 4 or a hybrid of them both, so that you can be shielded from one of the many thousands of cold-calling carrier reps who solicit and bother you every day. After all, you have hired and trusted your broker to advise and help you with your healthcare decisions—isn't it time they embrace the enhanced benefits industry and help guide you properly by eliminating benefit redundancy and wasteful employee overspend, while at the same time capitalizing on a new revenue stream that will allow your broker to remain in business and help navigate and guide you through the complexities of healthcare for many years to come?

Bottom line: While I realize that your broker's primary conversations with you will emphasize employer paid benefits and cost containment strategies—do not let your broker lose sight of how implementing a proactive approach to enhanced benefits can be very well perceived as rounding out your complete benefits package. With that in mind, I encourage you to push your broker to be more strategic and systematic, by proactively bringing enhanced employee funded benefits to the forefront of your healthcare conversations. A reactive approach by your broker is what allows random cold-calling carrier reps or other broker competitors to introduce themselves to you, and I suspect the last thing you are interested in is starting over and building a relationship with a new random stranger. Quite candidly, I always tell my broker partners to never forget that as one of their employer clients, they are your trusted consultant and adviser who you vet, hire, and compensate to give you well rounded, unbiased, and complete advice on all things benefits related—including enhanced employee funded benefits.

Selecting the Most Effective Enhanced Benefits Partner

As your broker begins to have proactive conversations with you to ensure you have the proper enhanced benefits being offered to your employees that complement their recommended overall healthcare strategy, it is important that your broker understands all of the available products and services that are available within the marketplace. Your broker's emphasis must remain steadfast, that they are looking to eliminate benefit redundancy, and any wasteful employee overspend that may have occurred during an initial "product-dump" that led to an inevitable "commission grab" by whomever first installed any enhanced products and services you currently have that have been put into place with little to no regard of your total healthcare plan.

Designing a Next Generation Benefits Package

For many years, most health insurance brokers have recommended and installed Short and/or Long-Term Disability, Life/AD&D, Dental, and Vision alongside health insurance. After all, these are usually considered part of the "core" group products that are often heavily subsidized or even fully funded by you, as the employer. I actually refer to these types of products as "traditional," whereby my definition of "core" greatly differs from that of a typical health insurance broker. That is not to say these traditional group products are not important—in fact, these benefits, along with a strong health plan, provide the base foundation to your company's total package.

The key is to take your "traditional" package and proactively transform it into a next generation offering that is second to none. To do so includes your broker strategically designing and recommending any of the following benefits and to ensure they are installed in harmony to fit within your overall healthcare strategy.

"Core" enhanced benefits typically consist of Accident, Hospitalization, and Critical Illness. As vital as these "core" benefits are in the enhanced benefits space; what about some uncommonly thought of benefit offerings?

Product Disruption

Has your broker designed a robust maternity package for your employees that far exceed an ordinary Short-Term Disability plan? What about helping to mitigate your yearly worker's compensation (WC) increases (whether your health broker handles your property and casualty or not) by proactively suggesting a company funded or partially funded Off-the-Job Accident product to help lessen any "Monday morning" WC claims you may be experiencing? When is the last time your broker recommended an employer funded GAP plan? Pairing an employer paid GAP plan with a high deductible health insurance plan can save you a significant amount of capital. Furthermore, offering your employees a voluntary buy-up option can minimize the out of pocket deductible for health insurance. Has your broker explained to you that there is actually a Term-Life product that goes past age 100, has paid up death benefits starting in year 10, and has Long-Term Care (LTC) built in that can pay up to three times the death benefit for LTC coverage?

These are just a handful of questions and ideas that a strong enhanced benefits partner should be having with your broker in order to begin an effective conversation with you to better serve your most valuable asset, your employees. All of these ideas provide creative new ways to increase employee loyalty at minimal to no cost and further improve your ability to attract and retain the best employees. Will each scenario mentioned be a perfect fit for every employer? Of course not, but that does not negate the fact that these questions, and ones like them, should be addressed and thought through with purpose and intent.

Value-Added Services and Non-Insurance Disruption

Would you and your employees see value in any of the following value-added services and non-insurance products on the market? Single point consolidated billing that is reconciled by a Third Party Administrator (TPA) so that all of your employee funded enhanced benefits can be placed on one single bill, a benefit administration and enrollment system, zero-cost Section 125 plan document preparation, flexible spending accounts, a zero cost discount prescription drug card and an identity theft and fraud protection program for each employee, telemedicine services, or even a single benefits "app" for you and your employees to access yours and their entire healthcare package on-demand, including a 24/7 concierge and healthcare advocate.

These are just some of the many services and non-insurance products that your broker should have access and ability to provide you and your employees. Does your broker offer all of these services and non-insurance products in-house? If not, have they aligned with a strong enhanced benefits partner who can bring all of these, and more, to your employees? If your broker is not proactively having these conversations with you, I assure that it is not a matter of "if" you will learn about these cutting-edge offerings, but more a matter of "when" and who proactively begins the conversation with you, and sadly enough for your current broker, earns your Broker of Record.

Bottom line: If your broker is not bringing these value-added services and non-insurance products to you, know that you are not alone. I would no sooner attempt to discuss health insurance and self-funding with any of my clients, then your health insurance broker should be attempting (on their own) to discuss enhanced benefits, since each industry is a unique specialty. Just as it took your health broker many years to become the health insurance expert that they tout themselves as today, understand that it also took me many years to become the enhanced benefits expert I am nationally recognized as. The fact is, it would not be feasible for your health broker to personally learn the enhanced benefits space at a level that would be beneficial to you in a timely fashion. Thus, why the brightest and forward thinking health brokers partner with a proven enhanced benefits boutique who can enable them to hit the ground running, maximize the opportunities within their existing client base, all while helping you as their employer client succeed in this specialized area of benefits.

Final Thoughts

As initially discussed, the most commonly used broker word choice, "voluntary" and "ancillary," insinuate "unimportant" and "non-essential." Is your broker using appropriate vocabulary to properly convey the right message to you and your employees? Do you currently offer any enhanced employee funded benefits, and if so, were they strategically placed to fit in accordance to your healthcare plan so that there is no wasteful employee overspend? If not, shouldn't they be? When is the last time, if ever, you have put your enhanced employee funded benefits package out to bid and had it aggressively shopped by a carrier agnostic benefits partner? You shop your health insurance benefits every year to find the best benefits and most affordable rates—why wouldn't you do the same for the benefits that your employee's fund? Not only is it the right thing to do, it is the fair thing to do. After all, your health broker should be looking out for you and your business, in the same way that you are always looking out for your employees.

Remember, whether your health broker chooses to outsource their enhanced benefits to one specific carrier, bring it all in-house, or partner with a carrier agnostic firm—just make sure that your health broker chooses to be proactive. Simply making the decision as to which approach they are going to adopt on your behalf is their most challenging part of the equation — once their decision is made, their strategy and installation should be effortless for the both of you.

* Variations of this chapter originally appeared in Employee Benefit Adviser and BenefitsPRO magazines.

Eric Silverman

Principal and Owner
Silverman Benefits Group
Towson, MD

Eric Silverman is Principal and Owner of the Silverman Benefits Group (SBG), a nationally recognized, disruptive, carrier-agonistic enhanced benefits boutique with in-house distribution and benefit communication & enrollment services. They partner with leading employee benefits firms across the U.S. to design and implement Enhanced (formerly voluntary) Benefits programs for small to large companies.

Over his career, Eric has recruited, trained, and developed more than 2,000 commission sales agents, interns, and broker partners over the last 18 years, and collectively, they have helped impact many thousands of employers and employees all across the country.

Silverman was awarded the prestigious "Voluntary Benefit Adviser of the Year" by *Employee Benefit Adviser (EBA)* magazine and has been nominated and elected to the Workplace Benefits Association Advisory Board. Honored as a "Rising Star in Advising" by *EBA* magazine, he was voted as one of the "Top 30 Benefit Pros to Follow" on Twitter, speaks regularly as an "Enhanced Benefits" expert at national industry conferences, and is a regularly featured monthly commentator on the online magazines of *Employee Benefit Adviser* and *BenefitsPRO*.

www.silvermanbenefits.com
esilverman@silvermanbenefits.com
443-676-0340
Twitter: @SilvermanSBG
Business Facebook: www.facebook.com/SilvermanBenefits.

CHAPTER 29

HSA STRATEGIES THAT WORK

Karin M. Rettger

After Health Savings Accounts (HSAs) were created in 2003, I became one of their biggest fans. I was sure they would become the 401(k)s of the new millennium. It took a while, but HSAs have finally come of age. The growth in HSAs exploded from $1.7 Billion in assets in 2003 to $37 Billion in 2017.*

Regardless of this impressive growth, I still find many employers reluctant to fully embrace HSAs. I also continue to find a great deal of misunderstanding about HSAs and how to incorporate them for maximum results.

HSAs help employers accomplish two important goals: 1) successfully begin to reduce the healthcare cost trend and 2) fund an additional source of retirement income for employees. How do you successfully transition from high-cost benefits plans to those eligible for HSAs? In this chapter, I am going to provide you with five strategies that work.

Why an HSA Should be on Your Radar

One of the biggest eye-opening statistics are these two numbers:

A. $250,000
B. $201,300

A. $250,000 is the amount a couple is estimated to need to cover their healthcare expenses in retirement—roughly $125,000 per person.** When I first heard this number, I thought it was exaggerated, but it's not. Let's think about these costs. There are Medicare Part B premiums, a Supplemental Health Policy and Medicare Part D (prescription) premiums. In addition, expect costs for routine vision exams, eyeglasses, hearing aids, dental and long-term care expenses—*NONE* of which are covered by Medicare.

B.   The second number—$201,300***—is the average balance a person has saved for retirement today. *HOUSTON—WE HAVE A PROBLEM!* The savings most people have accumulated will not be enough to cover their daily living expenses and their estimated healthcare costs. These two simple numbers should convince employers that an effective retirement plan for yourself and your employees needs to consider healthcare costs.

It's important to stop thinking about an HSA as a high-deductible health plan (HDHP) and focus on it being a long-term savings account for retirement.

* Source: 2016 Devenir HSA Research Report
** Source: Fidelity Investments
*** Source: Federal Reserve

The real issue is that if employees do not have adequate savings to retire, they will continue to work. There are many implications associated with an older workforce, including workplace modification, increased Disability and Workman's Compensation costs and increased medical premiums. According to 401kSpecialist.com Magazine (Issue 2, 2017), Prudential conducted research that determined an "incremental cost of over $50,000 for an individual whose retirement is delayed. This represents the cost difference between the retiring employee and a newly hired employee."

For an employer with 3,000 employees, they estimate the annual cost of a one year delay in retirement age to cost about $2 to $3 million. The Prudential survey estimated the annual cost to employers of employees who cannot afford to retire, is costing corporations about 1 to 1.5% of workforce costs. This creates undeniable consequences to corporations by decreasing their ability to survive in a highly competitive market with tightly controlled budgets. I further discuss these implications and solutions in the chapter, *"Retirement Readiness,"* in my book, *DOING MORE WITH LESS: 21st Century Benefit Strategies to Reduce Costs, Maximize Human Capital & Drive More Dollars to the Bottom Line.*

Let's start with the ABC's of HSAs

It's very simple until we make it complicated! I have been a Financial Adviser and Benefits Consultant for over 30 years. Whenever I am asked to explain a 401(k), I simply say:

- A 401(k) is a type of savings account—you stash away money from your paycheck, receive tax benefits on the money you save, and often get a matching contribution from your employer. You use a savings account at the local bank to pay for items you need today. You use your 401(k) savings account for the money you will need in the future and to help replace part of your income when you retire.

- In a 401(k) savings account, you can even choose how to invest the money, so it will hopefully yield a better return.

- Withdrawals/Distributions from a 401(k) are taxed at your current income tax rate. There's a tax penalty if you take a premature distribution.

- Is everyone eligible to have a 401(k)? No, you need to be eligible to participate in an employer-sponsored plan.

When I am asked to explain an HSA, I can explain it almost exactly the same way.

- An HSA is a type of savings account—you stash away money from your paycheck, receive tax benefits on the money you save, and often get a matching contribution from your employer. You use a savings account at the local bank to pay for items you need today. You use an HSA savings account for the money you will need in the future and to help pay for healthcare expenses not covered by your insurance (for example, copays and deductibles).

- In an HSA savings account, you can even choose how to invest the money so that it will hopefully yield a better return.
- Withdrawals and Distributions from an HSA are completely tax-free as long as the distribution is used to pay for qualified medical expenses. There's a tax penalty that will apply if you take a non-qualified withdrawal before age 65.
  - o This is the <u>triple tax benefit</u> commonly used to explain HSAs.
  - o Because of these tax benefits, a $5,000 HSA contribution costs most employees only $3,250.
- Is everyone eligible to have an HSA? No, you need to be participating in a qualified high deductible health plan (HDHP).

HSAs and the High Deductible Health Plan (HDHP)

To participate in an HSA, you have to be enrolled in a qualified high deductible health plan. Whoever wanted to encourage HSAs by using the term "high-deductible" created a nightmare. A high-deductible health plan is a point of contention and confusion for many employers, making them reluctant to participate in an HSA. The wording "high-deductible" can cause unease, making it difficult to communicate the plan's effectiveness. However, if the term "high-deductible" health plan is replaced with "low-cost" health plan, you emphasize the benefits of participating.

How do you implement HSAs in a positive manner? Here are five strategies that work.

Five HSA Strategies that Work

1) Create a five-year benefit strategy.

2) Create a three-to-five-year plan to eliminate low deductible plans from your health plan menu.

3) Develop a contribution strategy around the cost of your health plans to encourage employees to choose the "low-cost" option(s).

4) Begin a matching contribution or an employer contribution to fund the HSA as part of your three-to-five-year plan.

5) Educate your employees about the low-cost options, maximizing the HSA and your three-to-five-year plan.

Step One: Create a Five Year Benefit Strategy

Today's top benefit advisers are encouraging their clients to prepare a five-year benefit planning strategy. This engages the client's CEO, CFO and Chief Human Resource or Benefits Officer to work together to develop the long-term strategy. In other words, the C-Suite is aligned with Human Resources.

Without a long-term benefit strategy, you will remain in a defensive rather than an offensive position concerning benefit issues. A benefit plan aligned with the "C Suite" creates an offensive strategy and long-term vision, putting you in the driver seat to better control your benefit costs. To be on offense, you need a plan. Your benefit adviser or consultant can help you create and manage that plan.

Step Two: Eliminate Low Deductible Plans over a Three-to-Five-Year Period

This should be a part of your five-year strategy. If you want to take as much control as possible to reduce the long-term cost trend of health-care in your budget, you need to begin to eliminate the high cost/low deductible options. You cannot continue to "soft peddle" this by offering your employees a menu of choices with continued access to plans that do not engage employees in cost sharing.

Many employers want to offer their employees a choice of health plans ranging from lower deductible PPOs with copays, copay-driven HMOs and high deductible PPOs with or without copays. The biggest long-term issue with the copay-driven plans, is that the claimants (employees and their dependents) are not connected to the cost of care. If it only costs them $20 to see a doctor, they don't care what the actual cost to the plan is. As a result, the trend on these plans continues to rise beyond consumer-driven high deductible plans.

You can begin to eliminate the low deductible plans through a combination of contribution strategies and employer contributions to encourage movement to the lower cost plans. If you plan to eliminate the low deductible plans over a period of three to five years and you communicate this intention, it will make a smoother transition and more positive result. I will discuss more about this later in the chapter.

Step Three: Develop a Contribution Strategy Around the Cost of Your Health Plans to Encourage Employees to Choose the "Low Cost" Option(s).

You will need a contribution strategy to drive enrollment toward the low-cost options. In other words, you want to set the "pricing" for your healthcare menu to make your low-cost, higher deductible plans an attractive choice for employees. Here is a sample strategy that many clients use.

- Set your employer contribution of 80%—85% (this is the national average, but use the cost share you typically use) around the lowest premium cost option. This may be the highest deductible option.
- Have employees "buy up" to the other options

Example:

- Plan Option A is a $3,000 deductible plan with a cost of $600 per month for Single Coverage. The employer contribution is 80% (or $480 per month). The cost per pay for the employee is $120 per month or $55.38 per pay (using 26 pay periods per year).
- Plan Option B is a $1,000 deductible PPO with a cost of $720 per month for Single Coverage. You would apply the same $480 monthly employer subsidy (based on Plan Option A) and shift the remainder of the cost to the employee. In this example, the employee would pay $240 per month or $110.76 per pay for this option.
  - o If this is too aggressive for you, implement it over a three-year period. An example might be to have the employee contribution for Plan Option B set at $170 per month in the first year; $200 per month in the second year; and the full cost difference in year three.
  - o Also consider what you might do with matching contributions to positively encourage people to enroll in Plan Option A (a carrot approach).

o   I also recommend that your communications encourage employees selecting Option A to contribute to the HSA with part of their premium savings.

Don't be too passive on the pricing! If you set the contribution strategy at 20% for the employee for each tier, it might not be enough of a cost difference to drive a result.

Example:

If Plan Option A is $55.38 a pay and Option B is only $66.46 per pay, the cost difference alone will not be enough to encourage people to enroll in Option A.

Step 4: Begin a Matching Contribution or an Employer Contribution to Fund the HSA

By offering low-cost options with higher deductibles, the out-of-pocket costs for employees who incur claims can be potentially unaffordable. The advantage of low deductible plans with copays is it shelters the claimant from unexpected large out-of-pocket costs. As you move away from offering low deductible plans, you can continue to "shelter" employees from those unexpected costs.

You can accomplish this by providing employer contributions to the HSA and empowering employees to take more responsibility for their healthcare decisions. This is where true healthcare consumerism comes into play. Because the balance in the HSA account is owned by the employee, any savings accrues to their benefit.

There are various methods of determining the budget for the HSA contributions. Some employers set it based on the amount of premium savings they derive by offering the HDHP. Some employers may want to think beyond the premium savings to additionally fund an HSA as a supplemental retirement plan. As I stated in my introduction to this chapter, the annual cost to employers of employee's who cannot afford to retire is costing corporations about 1 to 1.5% of workforce costs (Source: 401kSpecialist.com Issue 2 2017). With this in mind, it makes sense to incorporate into your budget, a long-term strategy to reduce the cost of retirement delays.

As a side note, I want to talk a bit about some other strategies sometimes used instead of the HSA.

- For example, HRAs (Health Reimbursement Accounts) can shelter employees, but because they don't own the balance (like a savings account), it does not accomplish the same result. The HRA does not empower employees.

- FSAs (Flexible Savings Accounts) provide tax-free dollars to pay for out-of-pocket expenses, but because of its limited rollover capability, it does not provide a growth savings account. If employees have to spend the majority of the funds they set aside in the plan year (due to "use it or lose it" rules), that effectively eliminates any savings potential.

The HSA is the only true option that will empower employees and drive consumerism.

You have almost limitless options as to how to design an employer contribution to an HSA. According to the Plan Sponsor Council of America's (PSCA) 2017 HSA Survey, the most common method of providing employer contributions to an HSA is by coverage level. The following is an example of a contribution based on coverage level.

Example:

In the first year, provide an employer contribution to the HSA equal to part or all of the premium cost difference between the High Deductible Plan and the Low Deductible Plan. Using our previous example:

- Option A: Total Premium Cost $600 per month
- Option B: Total Premium Cost $720 per month
- If you fund the difference, you might contribute:
  - $100/month or $1,200 for single
  - $200/month or $2,400 for single plus one
  - $300/month or $3,600 for single plus two or more

I suggest you start with "front loading" this contribution so that the money is in the account at the beginning of the year. According to the PSCA survey mentioned earlier, front loading is the most common method currently being used. The second most common is a pay-period contribution.

*****Devenir Research 2016 HSA Research Report*

- If you follow the above funding example and you have a $3,000 deductible plan and if the employee is contributing a similar amount to what the employer is contributing, they will have deposited a large part of the deductible into the

HSA. Over two to five years, they should be able to have funded enough to cover a high claim cost year.

Remember that the employer contribution reduces the maximum that the employee can contribute. In the second year, you can modify the contribution, if needed. While you have the flexibility to change the contribution strategy at any time, I would not suggest you make a change mid-year as it could reduce employee confidence in the plan.

Step 5: Educate Your Employees about the Low-Cost Options, Maximizing the HSA and Your Three- to-Five-Year Plan

According to Kaiser Family Foundation/HRET Survey of Employer Sponsored Health Benefits 2016, the average deductible is now $1,478. As a result, your employees are becoming accustomed to higher deductibles. Today, you have resources to educate employees about these plans and how they work. You can also provide tools to help them find quality lower-priced providers and treatment options. Some of the tools we have been using with large success are Telephonic Medicine, Provider Finder based on quality and price metrics and Concierge Services to assist employees to navigate, resolve problems, negotiate and solve issues without calling Human Resources.

The triple tax benefits of HSAs need to be stressed in all communications. If an employee can contribute $5,000 to the HSA, most employees will save approximately 35% (federal, state and FICA); which means that $5,000 only costs them $3,250. That already provides them with a tax savings of $1,750, to use towards claims. These special tax advantages seem to be missing from most communications, but it is a HUGE benefit! Compounding this amount year after year to a tax-free distribution is the key reason employees will participate. This is like having a pre-tax 401(k) that NEVER gets taxed in the future. Your highly-paid employees should be all over this!

Because the tax benefits can be confusing to the average person, I would suggest a combination of media, which should include:

1) Group Education Meetings or Webinars
2) White Board Animation
3) Written Communication Materials (flyers, brochures, etc.)
4) Videos
5) Call Center or 1/1 coaching with an adviser

If you never had an HSA option, I would begin educating employees a few months prior to enrollment so that they'll have a better understanding during open enrollment.

HSAs as a Retirement Savings Tool

At the beginning of this chapter, I provided some startling statistics around the lack of savings in 401(k)s, as well as the lack of awareness about savings needed for healthcare expenses. In order to provide an effective retirement plan for yourself and your employees, you need to consider healthcare costs. Stop thinking about the HSA being a high deductible health plan and focus on the HSA being a long-term savings account for retirement.

In the past, employers have focused their sole attention on a Pension or 401(k) Plan to fund retirement income for employees. Too often, an HSA is overlooked as another retirement income source. **The bottom line is that an HSA looks and acts like a pre-tax Roth 401(k) on steroids.** Employees can enjoy the benefits of pre-tax contributions (with FICA savings as an option) with tax-free growth and tax-free distributions! If we could get all this in our 401(k)s, more people would be contributing the maximum allowable.

What if you have no medical expenses in retirement? Count your blessings! If you end up not using your HSA for medical expenses, it will be taxed at retirement (age 65+) the same as a 401(k).

In addition, HSAs are currently considered individual accounts under IRS regulations and not under DOL regulations. This means HSAs are less costly to administer because there are no separate ERISA requirements. While 401(k) plans have been the subject of increased fiduciary concerns and numerous lawsuits, HSAs are considered individual accounts under the IRS rules. Employers currently have limited fiduciary oversight of the funds used in an HSA. It is generally advised, however, that employers provide employees with a choice of HSAs in which to invest so as not to restrict choice.

HSAs are easy to set up. To offer an HSA, an employer simply needs to make a payroll slot available and remit the contributions to an HSA provider. Most employers choose a vendor to receive the contributions, but allow the employee the option to transfer the balance to an HSA of their choice.

HSA investment fees may be higher than your 401(k) because the balances in HSAs are typically a lot less (at the present time). As balances grow in these plans, participants can transfer their balances to another HSA of their choosing. It is not restricted like a 401(k). This allows the participant the ability to search for fees based on their account size. I believe that as HSAs grow, the fees will become closer to 401(k)s.

Summary

At the beginning of this chapter, I identified the impressive growth in HSAs. The use of HSA's will help employers accomplish two important goals: 1) successfully begin to reduce the healthcare cost trend and 2) fund an additional source of retirement income for employees. An HSA really is a pre-tax Roth 401(k). Throughout this chapter, I discussed Five Strategies that Work—all geared to successfully get results with HSAs.

Regardless of your motivation to offer HSAs over the long term, this valuable account will help employees become better healthcare consumers, while building additional dollars to use during their retirement.

Karin M. Rettger

President
Principal Resource Group
Glen Ellyn, IL

Karin Marrs Rettger, MBA, AIF is President and founder of PRG. She has over 35 years of experience advising clients on employee benefit, investment advisory services, retirement planning, and wealth management. Having worked with well over 100 employer clients representing tens of thousands of people, Karin has gained a rich insight that allows her and her team to provide proactive solutions that create meaningful impact.

An established industry thought leader and recognized non-profit retirement plan expert, Karin has been a featured speaker on 403(b) Plans and Health Savings Accounts (HSA). She is co-author of the books, *DOING MORE WITH LESS—21st Century Strategies to Reduce Costs, Maximize Human Capital, & Drive More Results to the Bottom Line* and *401(k) Plans.*

Her expertise and achievements have been recognized by the industry multiple times. *Employee Benefit Adviser* magazine identified Karin as one of the *Most Influential Women in Benefits Advising.* The National Association of Plan Advisors named her to their list of *America's Top Women* and the Plan Sponsor Council of America appointed her to their board of directors. *Employee Benefit News* magazine named Karin one of the *Top 30 People to Watch in Employee Benefits* for 2017.

www.prgresource.com
krettger@prgresource.com
630-858-5430

CHAPTER 30

REFINANCING YOUR GROUP HEALTH PLAN

How to Improve Benefits and Pay Less

Mark Krogulski

Let's begin with some...

Sobering Statistics

To many, the idea that you can improve the health insurance benefits you provide to your employees while at the same time lowering the overall cost of the plan is inconsistent. I understand your skepticism.

The information you are getting from insurance carriers and insurance brokers is that costs are going to continue to rise. You are also hearing that solutions generally gravitate toward cutting back on benefits and passing along more of the rate increase to employees in the form of higher payroll deductions. But that's not the only solution, and it's not one that I would ever advocate.

The data supporting the many reasons that health insurance is expensive is widely available. I won't repeat what you've read, heard or already know. You are also aware that multiple surveys confirm that health benefits are the most sought after employee benefit, so they really matter to you and your employees.

In many states, the individual market is in shambles. Insurance carriers are withdrawing from the Affordable Care Act (ACA) marketplace due to high underwriting losses. The insurance carriers that remain are offering plans with higher deductibles; $3,500 to $5,000 per person. In addition to higher out of pocket expenses, the networks are getting smaller and more restrictive. Other plans no longer reimburse for out of network services. That means more individuals are looking to their employer to provide a valuable health insurance option, and also pay a significant portion of the cost.

This graph illustrates the unfortunate reality that as health care costs for active employees has spiked; the investment by employers in retirement plans has dipped. Employers are struggling to balance employee expectations with budget reality.

I'm not telling you something you don't already know. What I will tell you is there are solutions that you are not hearing from insurance carriers or the status quo insurance brokers or consultants.

Figure 2. Share of cost between active health and retirement plans, weighted by employer size, 2001 – 2015

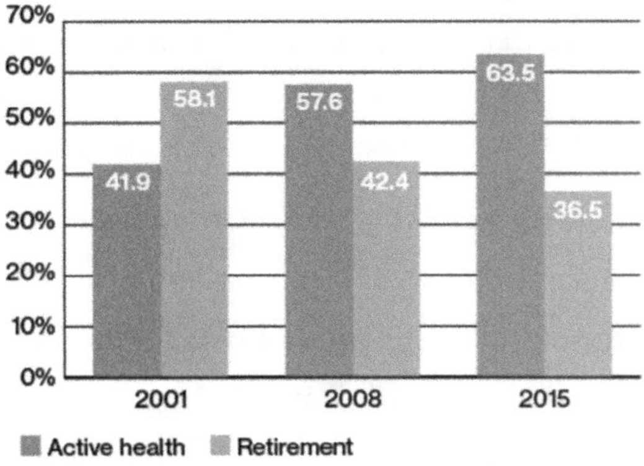

Source: Willis Towers Watson Benefits Data Source

The Cruelty of Compounding

Since 1998, The Henry J. Kaiser Family Foundation has performed an annual survey of employer group health insurance plans. According to the latest report, showing data for 2016, the annual average premium for employer sponsored family coverage is $18,142. Of that amount, the employee pays an average of $5,277. That means, on average, the typical employer spends almost $12,000 to provide health insurance for every employee who elects to cover a spouse and children. In the past five years, the cost of family coverage has increased 20%. Since 1998, the first year of the survey, the average annual premium for family coverage has increased a staggering 191%.

Even if the average cost of family coverage at your firm is less than the Kaiser average, you are probably experiencing higher increases than the survey states. I often talk to employers getting a 20% increase in just one year, let alone a total increase of 20% over the past 5 years. I know too many employers who've seen their average family cost nearly double in the past five years.

Compound interest is great for your 401(k) plan. Investment advisers universally agree that you should leave the interest you earn on your deposits in your retirement account. With regular deposits and the benefit of compounding, your retirement plan assets grow significantly.

When your insurance rates increase every year, the current increase is on top of all of the previous increases. Over time, the rule of compound interest adds to the overall cost of your group health insurance plan. You are experiencing the cruelty of compounding.

For example, if your insurance rates increase only 10% a year, a realistic and relatively conservative number, in 5 years your total cost of insurance increases over 60%, not 50%. Here's how the math works if your total gross cost of insurance in the first year is $1,000,000 and the annual increase is 10%:

Year 1 Increase in Total Cost of Health Insurance: $1,100,000
Year 2 Increase in Total Cost of Health Insurance: $1,120,000
Year 3 Increase in Total Cost of Health Insurance: $1,331,000
Year 4 Increase in Total Cost of Health Insurance: $1,464,000
Year 5 Increase in Total Cost of Health Insurance: $1,611,000

Unless you are engaging in strategies to lower the cost of your group health insurance plan, compounding is not your friend.

The Health Insurance Monitor

A robust toolset—and skills to use it.
Our Health & Welfare solutions are driven by data and insights. Proprietary analytics, benchmarking and measurement processes bring real-world data into focus, so that you can make

strategic decisions about your benefits plan, your future, and the needs of your employees.

You have access to our substantial toolset of analytics that includes planners, data modelers, workforce evaluation systems and more. You'll get the insights you need to build not just a great employee benefits and compensation plan, but also a great workforce that's engaged, motivated and invested in your organization's success.

What you just read came from the website of a publicly traded insurance broker. Analytics, benchmarking and measurement are all important tools providing a rear view mirror look at your benefit plan costs. If you look through any big insurance broker or consultant's website, or read their promotional materials, you will find marketing material similar to the above. **But there is something missing.**

Nowhere in all of the glossy materials, the graphics and inspiring text, will you find a focus on lowering the cost of your group health insurance plan on a year over year basis. And isn't that the most important item to you?

All publicly traded insurance brokers or consultants are capable of producing thick reports for you full of color charts, graphs, and data. The reports will be full of information on communicating with employees, technology options, and compliance requirements. Of course, you will probably only read the executive summary and a few other pages. The rest of the items are typically boilerplate material anyway. While the topics of communication, plan design, compliance and related topics are all important requirements of operating your group health insurance plan, they are merely some of the basic requirements you should be paying your broker or consultant to provide.

Your number #1 issue for your group health insurance plan is:

<u>Reducing Your Costs.</u> Benchmarking can be a constructive tool, but it's often used to let you know that you are pretty much like every other employer or maybe that your rate increase is slightly lower than the average.

Don't hire a "Health Insurance Monitor" who is very good at pointing out that you have a problem, but not capable of implementing a strategy to lower the overall cost of your group health insurance plan. Work with an adviser who has the resources and ability to show you how to pay less.

Misaligned Objectives and Paying For Performance

Ok, so let's talk about money. In social or family situations, it can be an awkward or sensitive topic. In business, it's a discussion you have with all of your suppliers, except maybe your insurance broker or consultant.

Historically, insurance brokers have been paid a commission, a percentage of the premium paid to the insurance carrier, for placing coverage with the carrier. This is different from the typical way in which an insurance consultant has been compensated by charging a fixed fee. Today, the line between a broker and a consultant is blurring, as is the way they generate revenue.

Insurance consultants are now selling products through private exchanges and accepting commission payments from insurance carriers. Insurance brokers continue to be compensated heavily by insurance commissions and fees paid by vendors, administrators and pharmacy benefit managers. Some brokers are also charging employers a fee to make up for reduced insurance carrier commissions.

One of the most significant items that closely bind brokers and consultants to insurance carriers is the payment of bonuses and overrides. It is at this intersection that alignment begins to veer from putting the employer's needs first.

Insurance carriers have a multitude of bonus plans that incent production and override arrangements that reward persistency. These payments are substantial and add significant EBITDA for publicly traded insurance brokers and consultants.

A new compensation model emerging is one where an employer pays for performance. Under this model, your adviser is compensated through a percentage of the savings produced for you. For example, if you implement a strategy that reduces the investment in your benefit plan by $200,000 a year, your adviser might be paid 20% of the savings, and you retain 80%. This model properly aligns the employer's goals with those of your adviser. If you aren't saving, your adviser is not getting paid.

Publicly traded insurance brokers and consultants need to drive revenue growth just like your company. Their revenue growth has to come from increased earning on their existing clients, acquiring new clients or buying other firms. Make sure you understand how and how much your insurance broker or consultant is being paid by you. The right alignment is necessary to drive EBITDA for your company and not for your insurance broker or consultant's company.

RETHINK: It's a Bad Investment Perfecting the Inefficient Procurement Practices of Group Health Insurance

The goal shouldn't be to make unnecessary, redundant systems and practices more efficient; it should be to eliminate the unnecessary and redundant systems and practices that are causing the problems.

— Tevi D. Troy, Chief Executive Officer,
American Health Policy Institute

It wasn't too long ago that it was common for insurance brokers or consultants to get 10, 15, or maybe even more proposals from different insurance carriers to underwrite your group health insurance plan. Right now, that number in many markets is more like 3 to 5 insurance carriers. Primarily through consolidation and the inability to compete with the market dominant plans, most employers are left choosing from one of the BUCA (Blue Cross, United Healthcare, Cigna or Aetna) carriers. Some markets are fortunate to have one or two independent or provider sponsored options. In markets that are dominated by one of the BUCA carriers, and it's typically the Blue Cross plan, the quotes are usually not lower than your current carrier's rates, assuming you are looking at similar benefit levels and networks. With the exception of a few geographic markets, the era of carriers competing for new clients ended years ago.

Your insurance broker or consultant still relies on spreadsheets because that is their primary cost management strategy. You will see a multitude of plan designs showing you ways to reduce your costs. The networks will be different and will use names like Premier, Select, High Performance, Choice and similar names. The plans will have descriptive names like HSA, HRA, HDHP, High Option, Low Option, and Consumer Driven to name a few.

It is important to understand that the plans on the spreadsheet were designed by insurance carriers to generate revenue for the insurance carrier. The plans do not reduce what you paid the previous year unless you make drastic cuts to benefits or the network.

The spreadsheet could have 20 different options for you to consider. It will be confusing, and that's on purpose. The incumbent carrier retains the advantage as you try to find an alternative plan. You've been through this drill before, and it usually ends with you selecting a plan with reduced benefits from the current carrier, or you make the difficult decision to endure the disruption of changing to a new carrier. Those are the only two results you will get from trying to perfect the spreadsheet game.

The lowest price on the spreadsheet does not equal the lowest cost option you have. It merely shows the options you have available in the *retail* market. Lower costs are available if you look at options available in the *wholesale* market. Perfecting the product peddling spreadsheet is not going to improve your group health insurance cost structure or improve the benefits you provide to employees.

So, if your broker's primary cost control strategy is to shop the market, don't expect any game changing solutions.

RESTRUCTURE: The Difference Between Health Insurance, Health Care, and Health Benefits

It's common to hear the terms health insurance, health care and health benefits used to refer to your group insurance plan. Politicians often use those terms to confuse the national health debate. But the terms have different meanings, and it's important to clarify them in the context of Group Health Plan Refinancing.

Health Insurance pays for medical, surgical, hospital and prescription drug expenses incurred by the insured. For the employer and employee, this provides catastrophic risk protection from an unexpected costly medical diagnosis.

Health Care is the field concerned with the maintenance or restoration of the health of the body or mind. These are the doctors, hospitals and related health professionals we see for care.

Health Benefits describes the cost of health care services that are not paid by health insurance. This is the deductible, copayments and out of pocket costs that are the responsibility of the insured.

These distinctions, especially the difference between health insurance and health benefits, are important to the basic understanding of Group Health Plan Refinancing. When you purchase a retail health insurance plan from an insurance carrier, insurance and benefits are combined. When you Refinance your group health insurance plan, you separate the purchase of health insurance from the determination of health benefits.

With Group Health Plan Refinancing, you have control over setting the health benefit levels. That means you decide the amount of the deductible, the coinsurance percentage, the out of pocket maximum, the physician copayments, pharmacy copayments and other benefit limits. You are not limited to just choosing what the insurance carrier has designed and sells. Again, those plans are designed by the insurance carrier to make a profit for the carrier; not save money for you.

By separating the health insurance purchase from the health benefits, you have many more insurance carriers willing to provide a quotation. This simple step of moving from **retail buying** to **wholesale buying** is the first step in creating savings for you.

REFINANCE: Supply Chain Management for Health Care

Most employers are only being show strategies that impact the top of the iceberg; the health benefit levels. It's below the surface that really requires your attention. At that level you can deploy strategies that can really impact the cost of your group health insurance plan. You need to focus on the supply chain in healthcare to drive savings and improve EBITDA.

For retail, manufacturing, healthcare, transportation, oil and gas and other companies, the topic of supply chain management is integral to driving EBITDA to the bottom line. These employers invest heavily in managing the cost of suppliers and the process of getting their product to market.

Let's look at supply chain management by comparing it to something all employers have; an expense manual describing the type of employee business expenses that are reimbursable by the employer. These policies cover simple expenses such as the purchase of office supplies and consumable goods, reimbursement of meals, cell phone usage, and detailed coverage of travel and entertainment expenses and the use corporate credit cards. Most employers spend a lot of time developing and monitoring their business expense rules. Often employers provide a corporate credit card to employees to be used to make reimbursable business purchases.

While detailed and strict rules are written and given to employees regarding use of a corporate credit card, no rules exist for the use of the corporate credit card employers give to all employees covered under the group health insurance plan. This credit card enables employees a virtual unlimited credit line to purchase health care services. If you buy a fully insured group health insurance plan, the insurance carrier has a lot of control over how your employees use your health care credit card. But for employers that self-fund their group health insurance plan, where the money comes right from your bank account, there are typically very few rules.

To drive positive financial results, employers need to give greater attention to the corporate health insurance credit card. Applying sound supply chain management principles to the group health insurance plan is the best way to drive higher EBITDA. Most employers are just managing the tip of the iceberg. But it's what's below the surface where the greatest danger lies and also the greatest opportunity for savings.

Write an expense manual for the company credit card you give to employees that has an unlimited credit limit on it—your group health insurance ID Card.

Case Study: Better Benefits and Lower Costs

Several years ago, I was introduced to a small manufacturer who was getting an increase of over 30% from their insurance carrier. The introduction occurred just a couple of weeks before his plan renewed and the new rates would be effective. His adviser had shopped the market to see what other carriers were willing to offer. None of the quotes were lower than his increase.

The advice the client was getting was to reduce health benefits and increase the employee payroll deductions. During prior renewals, payroll deductions were purposefully kept low, as this was a priority for the owner. He didn't want payroll deductions to consume the entire raise the employees received. In order to reduce the premium rates, more attention was paid to reducing health benefits. Now, no more cuts could be made as the plan already had a high deductible, a high out of pocket limit and all expenses were first subject to the deductible; copays had already been eliminated.

After we completed a quick review of the plan, we refinanced the plan using an alternate carrier willing to offer a high deductible insurance plan that generated considerable premium savings. We then added a new health benefit plan, shown below, that improved the coverage for the employees. Given the combined savings for the plan, the payroll deductions remained the same and haven't increased in three years.

Prior to the decision to implement the plan, I asked the owner and the CFO how much product they would have to sell to earn the equivalent amount in EBITDA that resulted from Refinancing the plan. They replied that they didn't have the capacity to produce the amount of product to sell to generate that level of profit; they would have to hire more employees and add a second shift. We were able to generate EBITDA for him by refinancing his group health insurance plan.

	Old Plan In-Network	New Plan In-Network
Deductible and Coinsurance		
Individual	$2,000	$2,000
Family	$4,000	$4,000
Family Deductible	Aggregating	Embedded
Coinsurance	80%	80%
Maximum Out-of-Pocket		
Individual	$6,350	$5,000
Family	$12,700	$10,000
Office Visits		
Primary	20% after deductible	$40 copay
Specialist	20% after deductible	$60 copay
Emergency / Urgent Care		
Emergency Room	20% after deductible	$300 copay
Urgent Care Facility	20% after deductible	$60 copay
Hospital Services		
Inpatient	20% after deductible	$500 Copay then 20% after deductible
Prescription Drugs		
Generic	20% after deductible	$10 copay
Formulary Brand	20% after deductible	$40 copay
Non-Formulary Brand	20% after deductible	$70 copay
Specialty	20% after deductible	25% max of $300

Three years later, the per employee per year costs are still below his pre-renewal rate level with the former insurance carrier.

Myths and Facts

When I'm asked what I do, I answer "I refinance group health plans for employers." It's an unusual statement, and almost everyone wants to know more. I get a lot of questions and some suspicions. So here are some answers to questions you may have.

Myth: If this worked, my broker would have shown it to me.

Fact: Perhaps, but I can't say for sure. I do know that a publicly traded insurance broker or consultant is typically paid a commission based on a percentage of your premium. Lower premium rates for you means less commission for them. Stock analysts do not reward companies whose revenue is falling.

Myth: Big brokers and consultants have access to the best ideas and best practices.

Fact: This book illustrates that some of the best ideas and creative strategies come from small, innovative insurance professionals. These ideas are the "next" practices.

Myth: This isn't legal.

Fact: The core concepts of health plan refinancing are rooted in several tax laws dating back to the 1950's. These laws have been around for a long time. The Affordable Care Act has introduced some new concepts we use. Everything we do complies with applicable tax law.

Myth: Insurance carriers design plans to save employers money on their group health insurance plans.

Fact: Publicly traded insurance carriers design plans to generate revenue for themselves. If their revenue were to decline, stock analysts would punish their share price.

Myth: I'm not a risk taker.

Fact: Of course you are. If you are a CEO or CFO, you have responsibility for the profit and loss of your firm. You don't have to take a lot of risk to drive savings in your group health insurance plan. You can start from a conservative risk position and move toward more detailed strategies as your comfort level increases.

It's time to start thinking about group health insurance plans in a new way beyond just looking at the status quo.

Refinancing your group health plan is a good place to begin.

Mark Krogulski

President
E3 Strategy
Raleigh, NC

Mark Krogulski is and adviser to CEOs and CFOs on group health plan refinancing and supply chain management. With over 28 years of benefits & insurance expertise, he is a true resource to his clients for employee benefit programs. He is the founder of The HFA Plan, a unique health insurance program for employers to manage employee benefit costs.

Mark served as Managing Partner at The HFA Plan in Chicago since 2011 until launching E3 Strategy, a boutique business consulting firm, in 2017. Prior to that, Mark was a senior consultant in the health and welfare practice at Towers, Perrin and Willis. He studied management at St. Mary's University in Minnesota.

mark@thehfaplan.com
312-646-9366

CHAPTER 31

UTILIZING TECHNOLOGY TO ENHANCE YOUR BENEFITS DEPARTMENT

Derek Rine

What if you could offer an additional benefit to your employees that would enhance their lives, increase organizational efficiency and cause employees to perceive your organization as a forward-thinking company?

The employee benefits industry has been lagging behind others in technology for years. Only the largest companies invested in the technology to streamline their processes, and that came at a high price. Too high of a price for small and mid-size companies to make the same investment. Today, companies of all sizes have access to technology systems at a minimal cost.

The challenge is the implementation and learning curve for both the HR Department and the employees. "There's no way our employees are capable of logging on to an online portal to make benefits elections or fill out electronic applications! Half of them don't even have a smartphone." I received this objection from a large manufacturing client who realized that no matter how effective our technology solutions were, his organization would not be the right fit for these solutions. I didn't put up a fight, but I reminded him that in 5-10 years, his workforce will shift as more millennials are employed, and they will expect him to offer this technology or his organization will be viewed as "behind the times." Age and income are the primary objections I receive for why a company will not move forward with new technology solutions. Over half of Baby Boomers now have a smartphone, and the percentage is much higher for the Millennial generation, so what's the holdup? I think the fear of the unknown and the ease with maintaining the status quo is a huge problem.

The implementation of forward thinking strategies starts at the C-level, not the HR Department. The CFO or CEO is the one who realizes the need to stay up with the times, and then makes the executive decision to move forward with the technology solutions as the burden is then passed onto the HR Department for implementation. It's amazing how grateful the HR Department is, once they realize that we just cut the amount of time they spend on benefits in half. Here's how one of my clients responded in 2017 after a month of utilizing one of our systems: "Derek, thank you so much for convincing us to move forward with your technology solution. The reporting capabilities alone were worth it for us!"

There are two technology solutions that every organization with

30 or more employees should offer by 2020:

1.   A Mobile Benefits App
2.   A Benefit Administration System

The sad reality is that only a small percentage of advisers are even offering these services. I estimate that less than 25% of advisers offer a benefit administration ("ben admin") system and less than 10% of brokers offer a mobile benefits app. Fortunately, many payroll companies are offering a ben admin solution, but that comes at a cost. It's not only important to employ progressive technology strategies, but it's equally important to employ a progressive consultant who offers them.

As you've been reading this book, you have likely already recognized the need and benefits of implementing a ben admin system, so I am going to focus more on the need to utilize a benefits app, an often ignored, yet incredibly powerful tool for your employees and your health plan.

"Do you have a cell phone app yet that handles everything when it comes to our benefits?" This question was posed by the CEO of a 5,000 employee operation. When my colleague in the insurance industry told me that he didn't have one for this client, I just about fell out of my chair. I said "Well you better figure that out fast, or else you can kiss this client goodbye." This happened in 2017 by the way.

Earlier this year, I was strategically introduced to the CFO of an organization with about 3,500 employees and 1,000 on the benefits plan. He was employing one of the largest broker firms in the country and contemplating moving to a more progressive regional firm that was also much larger than our agency. When I asked him what app he was currently using to streamline the benefits component of his organization, he responded, "We haven't been presented with this technology yet." We later won the case almost solely by having this conversation. How can a company this size with a national broker lack such basic technology? Especially when we're talking about an employer's second or third largest expense to their organization after payroll. What makes the app even more necessary is the lack of knowledge employees have when it comes to utilizing their benefits plan.

What's more important in your life than your health and the health of your family? I bet the list is pretty short. Health insurance is one of the most important investments you can make, not only for your physical well-being, but the financial protection when your physical well-being is jeopardized. When is the last time you had an MRI or a surgery? Were you surprised to see that those services cost thousands of dollars? Did you bother to shop around to make sure that the facilities and doctors you used were not overcharging for those services?

The sad reality is that most consumers do not use the same consumerism mindset with their healthcare as they do other areas of their life. I'm not talking about life-threatening conditions, which require world-renowned specialists, but basic healthcare items such as diagnostic testing and minor procedures. When it's time to shop for a new car, do you automatically go to the dealership that your doctor recommends and buy the most expensive model that he suggests even if it's out of your budget? When you do your grocery shopping, do you have your doctor write a prescription for the supplies he thinks your family should pick up that week? Rather than pack your child a turkey sandwich, the doctor recommends that your son Billy eat filet mignon every day, but who are you to question it? You're just following instructions of course, which you feel are absolutely necessary because that's all you've ever done.

I would estimate that 95% of your employees approach their healthcare this way and who can blame them? After all, they are not medical or insurance experts. They rely heavily on the advice of their physicians and to a large extent, they should. I'm not saying that they shouldn't follow their doctor's professional advice. I'm just arguing that they need some guidance and education on how to become smarter consumers of healthcare in areas that are well within their control.

That's precisely where the app comes into play. Now, you as the employer, can provide your employees with the tools necessary to become smarter consumers of the healthcare, while increasing employee morale, reducing absenteeism and creating the perception that your organization offers a first-class benefits plan. Does that sound a little dramatic? It's not. Your prospective employees will take slightly less pay and seek employment opportunities at your local competitor if offered a more comprehensive benefits package. In today's world, we see this all of the time because healthcare is more expensive and the landscape is more difficult to navigate than ever before.

An all-encompassing benefits app should offer the following:
1.   Concierge service
2.   Telemedicine
3.   ID Card Storage
4.   Benefits Plan Design information
5.   Prescription Advocacy services

I'll briefly elaborate on each category.

#1 — Concierge Service

The concierge service is the most important component of any benefits app. This service provider will have access to all of your benefits plan information, while experienced subject matter experts are available to assist your employees 24-hours a day, 7 days a week. Unlike an insurance company with normal business hours, employees can speak with professionals any time. These professionals will not only provide advice on insurance matters, but also guide your employees to low-cost facilities, help them source prescriptions at extreme discounts, assist with claims and even negotiate with providers on their behalf.

The concierge service proactively impacts your bottom-line, while holding your employees' hand through the process. The concierge service is also valuable for linking other aspects of the benefits app together. Although the app allows employees to utilize telemedicine, view benefits plan design info, shop in-network providers and engage in prescription advocacy services on their own, the concierge service will provide most of these services on your employee's behalf.

Talk about changing the culture of your organization. Imagine an employer with medical, dental, vision, disability, critical illness, accident and life insurance spread out amongst 4 different carriers. Do you think it's easy enough for the employees to navigate 8 different benefits and 4 carriers? Wouldn't it be convenient if the employees could call just one number and receive education and assistance for all benefits? That's exactly what the concierge service is designed to do. Your employees don't have to become smarter consumers of healthcare overnight when they have a service that can do it for them.

Your job as the employer is to make sure your employees are engaging in this service. This requires consistent communication and incentives. Imagine if your HR Department could cut the time they spend answering employee questions in half? By encouraging your employees to call the concierge service for all benefits-related questions, this may become a reality.

#2 — Telemedicine

It's 2:00 a.m. and you wake up with the same ear infection that plagues you twice a year. You have a very important day ahead of you and can't afford to drive to the doctor and wait 30 minutes in the waiting room, while missing an hour or so of work. Well, you are in luck. With the telemedicine feature on your benefits app, you can Skype with a doctor right then and there. The doctor is even capable of writing a prescription, which is transmitted to your local pharmacy, so you don't have to miss a second of work. The even nicer part is that the doctor visit costs you absolutely nothing! You can Skype with a physician for free anytime you deem necessary. It's commonly estimated that over 70% of all doctor visits can be handled via telemedicine.

Each time an employee uses telemedicine, your organization saves money. If the doctor charges $120 per visit and your employee has a $20 copay, who pays the remaining balance on that doctor visit? Your organization does. If you are fully-insured, the $100 difference is applied to your loss ratio, which translates into higher premiums at renewal time. If you are self-insured, you pay the balance directly. Imagine an employer with 1,000 employees and 5,000 doctor visits annually. If half of those doctor visits are handled via telemedicine, your organization saves $250,000. Although the savings is nice, the benefit that you are now offering your employees is tremendous. Never before have they utilized a service like this and you, the employer, are the one who took proactive measures to provide it. This service will increase their morale, reduce absenteeism and impact your bottom-line simultaneously.

#3 — ID Card Storage

It's been a rough day, and you're at the hospital, but forgot your purse. You have no proof of insurance, and you live 30 minutes away. No reason to panic. You calmly pull out your cell phone (hopefully that wasn't in your purse too) and select the "ID Card" tab on your benefits app. "What's your email address?" you ask Stacey in the Billing Department. With the click of a button, you email Stacey a copy of the medical ID cards stored on your phone. This is yet another convenient feature which may come in handy at the right moment.

#4 — Benefits Plan Design Information

"What's my deductible again?" I wonder how many times a year your HR Department is asked this question because an employee either lost their plan documents or SBC. Fortunately, they will have the capability of pulling up their plan design right on the app. This is not limited to just the medical plan. The plan designs for the dental, vision and other ancillary products will be available as well. Employees can see their deductible, coinsurance, maximum-out-of-pocket, doctor copays, prescription copays, etc. Just another feature that will reduce the amount of time your HR Department must allocate to assisting employees.

#5 — Prescription Advocacy Services

Did you know that 20% of the prescriptions used on your plan could be driving 75% or more of your total pharmacy costs? Of those 20%, at least half of the high-test prescriptions can likely be sourced outside of the health plan for extreme discounts. You may not have been aware that there are many alternative sourcing solutions available that are financially beneficial for your employees and your company, while existing outside of your corporate plan.

For example, pharmaceutical manufacturers are required to do a certain amount of charitable giving each year. This allows your employees to enroll in manufacturers' assistance programs, which generates a substantial savings to your organization. Let's use the example of an employee on Humira, which costs around $5,000 per month. Your employee pays $100 under the specialty tier co-pay, and then you pay the remainder under the health plan. There are programs available that will enable your employee to obtain Humira for $30 per month outside of the health plan, while eliminating the $4,900 expense to your organization.

In many situations, these pharmacy advocacy services will even source prescriptions from tier one countries like Canada at 50-60% discounts if a manufacturer's program is not an option. If the prescription cannot be obtained through either of these services, I often advise my clients to check GoodRx.com. There is typically a link right on the benefits app. This site offers pharmaceutical coupons at no cost, which often eliminates a significant portion of the prescription expense at the pharmacy. If you could reduce your pharmacy spend by 30-40% in two years simply by turning on the app, wouldn't you be crazy not to?

#6 — Provider Transparency Services

Earlier, I alluded to the lack of due diligence a typical consumer of healthcare uses when receiving service from a healthcare institution. The provider transparency tool on the app is designed to not only identify in-network providers, but to evaluate reasonable and customary pricing for items like diagnostic testing and basic procedures. Some apps even have a rating system, so employees can see which providers are overcharging for services and which are right in line with their pricing. At the very least, employees should have an idea of what they should be charged on the front end. If a provider then tries to significantly upcharge for a service, the employee can contact the concierge service to negotiate on their behalf. Services such as MRIs can vary by as much as 300%-500%, so it's important to encourage your employees to keep tabs on the pricing.

I hope by now you recognize that a benefits app is an extremely valuable tool for your company that will enhance the perception of your organization, increase organizational efficiency, reduce absenteeism, increase employee morale and change the overall benefits culture of your company. Providing your employees with an app will not make this type of impact overnight. It requires consistent communication, educational videos, and other incentives initially. These materials are available through virtually every service provider that offers an app, so it's a matter of selecting the one that best meets your company's needs.

I understand that it may seem like a huge undertaking to plunge into the technology arena when it comes to managing your corporate benefits, but please keep in mind that if you don't move forward with offering these services, your competition will. Apps of this sort are not outrageously expensive, so you don't have to be concerned about a significant investment. The pricing typically ranges from $5–$10 per employee per month and the savings we have discussed will pay for the app 10 times over. A progressive organization like yours is always looking for ways to enhance the employee experience and set themselves apart from other employers. This is an opportunity to do just that.

Derek Rine

Vice President & Benefits Practice Leader
David Rine Insurance
Fairlawn, OH

Derek Rine heads up the employee benefits practice at David Rine Insurance. As a Group Benefits Consultant, he does a lot more than just identifying and meeting the insurance needs of his clients. While protecting personal, business, financial and human assets is a top priority, he also assists businesses in bringing more value to their companies in many other respects. David Rine Insurance exists in part of make life easier for HR professionals through advanced software and other technology.

Derek has spent the last several years evaluating the healthcare climate to identify new strategies and resources to better protect the long-term interests of their clients. These innovations include alternative funding strategies for employer health plans; elite concierge services to gain transparency with providers and guide clients' employees to high quality but low cost facilities in order to improve their loss ratio and ultimately lower their premiums; and proprietary pharmacy programs, which are able to source prescriptions for 50 cents on the dollar in many cases.

Derek recently was profiled in *Employee Benefit Adviser* magazine for his innovative strategies to enhance the benefits plan while driving EBITDA to the client's bottom line.

www.davidrineinsurance.com
derek@davidrineinsurance.com
330-375-1909

CHAPTER 32

EMPLOYEE CONTRIBUTIONS STRATEGIES

Lambert Hsu

E mployers have been continually challenged by the increasing cost of providing health coverage for their employees. Research from the Kaiser Foundation shows that the cost of providing coverage has increased over the past decade by more than 58 percent.

Facing this cost dilemma, employers are faced with absorbing the entire increase, reducing benefits, sharing premium costs with employees, or a combination of these approaches. Most employers realistically have not been able to absorb the full cost of increases year over year, so have opted to share the cost with employees. This chapter will focus on comparing the most common approaches.

Percentage Contribution

This is the most common approach, whereas, the employer contributes a "percentage" of the premium, and the employee pays the balance. For example, the employer may agree to pay 80% of the premium, leaving the employee's contribution at 20%:

Example - $500/mo Employee premium
- $400/mo paid by Employer (80%)
- $100/mo paid by Employee (20%)

Most employers contribute different percentage amounts towards employee vs. dependent premiums, with their contributions towards the employee premium being higher. For example, the employer may contribute 80% towards the employee premium, and 50% towards the dependent cost portion of the premium.

Example - $2,000/mo Family premium ($500/mo Employee + $1,500/mo Dependent cost)
- $400/mo of Employee (80%) + $750/mo of Dependent (50%) cost paid by employer = $1,150/mo *paid by Employer*
- $100/mo of Employee (20%) + $750/mo of Dependent (50%) cost paid by employee = $850/mo *paid by Employee*

Note that increases in future premiums will automatically increase the amount of the employee's contribution.

Flat Dollar Contribution

Another common approach is to define a "flat dollar" cost that the employee would pay for their coverage.

Example - $500/mo Employee & $2,000/mo Family premium
- $120/mo for Employee only coverage
- $500/mo for Family coverage

This approach is easier to calculate; however, the employees' "flat dollar" contribution would need to be adjusted annually with future increases in premium to maintain the cost-share ratio.

Defined Contribution

This approach limits the employer's contribution or "allowance" to a fixed dollar amount (which can vary by coverage tier). Some defined contribution plans allow unused amounts to be applicable towards others employee benefits, such as dental or vision coverage.

Example - $750/mo "allowance" from Employer
- Medical Options: $500 employee only, $2,000 family
- Dental Options: $60 employee only, $200 family
- Vision Options: $15 employee only, $50 family

Employee may choose to enroll in the following:
- $500/mo - Employee only Medical (spouse has coverage through their employer)
- $300/mo - Family Dental
- $50/mo - Family Vision

- $850/mo - TOTAL PREMIUM
- Less $750/mo - *Employer's defined contribution allowance*
- $100/mo - *Balance paid by Employee*

Salary Based Contribution

A less common approach is to vary the contribution amount by employee salary. The idea is to ensure that the lower income will have "affordable coverage" as required by the Affordable Care Act and also subscribes to the philosophy that higher income employees can afford to pay more for their coverage.

With this approach, salary or income tiers are set up and assigned to employees, which will define the contribution amount make to elect coverage.

Example
- Income under $30K - $50/mo
- $30K to $74,999 - $100/mo
- $75K to $149,999 - $150/mo
- $150K+ - $200/mo

Buy Up Strategies

When approaching overall cost management strategies, besides adjustments to contribution methods and amounts, the employer can deploy a "buy up" strategy. This would involve offering at least two plan options: a "base" (lower cost) plan and a "buy up" (higher cost) plan.

As alternative renewal options can offer significant premium savings by increasing deductibles and copays or restrict provider networks, they may significantly impact your employees with higher out-of-pocket expenses and restrict access to their providers.

The employer can adopt the new "lower cost" plan as a "base" plan, and still continue to offer a richer plan option as a "buy up." In such scenario, the employer would tie their contribution to the "base" plan premium, and employees electing to "buy up" would be responsible for paying the difference between the "base" and "buy up" plan costs.

Example

- $400/mo for high deductible "base" plan, $550/mo for richer "buy up" plan
- $320/mo paid by Employer (80% of "base" plan)
- $80/mo paid by Employee for "base" plan (20% of "base" plan)
- $230/mo paid by Employee for "buy up" plan (20% of "base" plan + $150 premium difference)

Additional variations of the "buy up" (or dual option) contribution strategy include percentage contributions towards the "base" and "buy up" premiums. For the above example, applying the 80% contribution to both the "base" and "buy up" plans would result in a more affordable "buy up" option for the employee:

Example

- $400/mo for high deductible "base" plan, $550/mo for richer "buy up" plan
- $320/mo paid by Employer for "base" plan (80% of "base" plan)

- $440/mo paid by Employer for "buy up" plan (80% of "buy up" plan)
- $80/mo paid by Employee for "base" plan (20% of "base" plan)
- $110/mo paid by Employee for "buy up" plan (20% of "buy up" plan)

Contribution Benchmarks

Average employer contributions vary significantly by industry, geography, and state of the economy. Professional "white collar" industries, such as high tech, engineering, law firms, etc., traditionally have higher employer contributions (and income). They usually contribute 80% to 100% of the employee and 25% to 50% of dependent premiums.

"Blue collar" industries such as manufacturing and construction often have lower employer contributions ranging from 50% to 80% of employee premiums and no contributions towards dependent premiums.

Since HR surveys continue to confirm the importance of affordable benefits to job seekers evaluating job opportunities, companies need to consider their plan offerings, contribution amounts, and methodologies to remain competitive in their industry, and the local job market to effectively recruit and retain your workforce.

Pretaxing

As premium increases are cost shifted to employees, their payroll deductions for medical, dental and vision coverage can be "pretaxed" through a Section 125 Premium Only Plan (POP) or Flexible Spending Account (FSA).

By "pre-taxing," the IRS allows premium contributions to be excludable from taxable income, reducing employee's net cost by lowering their FICA (Medicare and Social Security), as well as Federal and State income taxes.

The resulting tax savings can be 20% to 60%, depending on their individual state and federal income tax brackets.

Regulatory Considerations - Aca & Affordability

The Affordable Care Act created a "shared responsibility" regulatory mandate that large employers (with 50 or more employees) must offer "affordable" coverage, or pay excise taxes for not meeting this ACA requirement.

To be compliant, large employers must offer full-time eligible employees "affordable" coverage, most commonly tested by ensuring that the employee's premium contribution for single coverage is less than 9.5% (adjusted annually) of their income.

For employers offering multiple health plan options, the affordability test can apply to the lowest cost "base" plan available to the employee, as long as it meets ACA's minimum coverage (Bronze level or 60% actuarial value) criteria.

Clearly an employer has multiple options in establishing the formula and the amount of employee premium contributions. While this decision can be confusing, a knowledgeable employee benefits adviser can be tremendously helpful in making a decision that maximizes the value of the benefits to the employee while meeting the financial goals of the employer.

Lambert Hsu, RHU

President
Benefit Pro Insurance Services
San Diego, CA

Lambert Hsu founded Benefit Pro in 2001, successfully building the organization into a thriving and well-respected, cutting-edge "NextGeneration" benefits agency. He has consulted with legislators in both Washington D.C. and Sacramento, sharing his significant expertise of the employer and individual health insurance marketplace.

Lambert has frequently shared his benefits expertise as guest speaker for numerous organizations, including: San Diego Society of Human Resource Management, California Employers Association, San Diego Employers Association, San Diego Employers Advisory Council, Asian Business Association, Business Healthcare Connection, Cal Asian Pacific Chamber of Commerce, Association of Legal Administrators, San Diego Association of Health Underwriters, San Diego Insurance Women, Financial Executives Networking Group and Sharp Health Plan.

He has served on Boards for numerous organizations including the Cal Asian Pacific Chamber of Commerce, Alliance Healthcare Foundation, Asian Business Association San Diego, YWCA of San Diego County, San Diego Regional Chamber of Commerce Healthcare Committee, San Diego Foundation for Medical Care Agent Advisory Council and San Diego Incubator Corporation. He has earned the distinction of the prestigious "Golden Eagle Leading Producer's Round Table Lifetime Award" from the National Association of Health Underwriters.

www.benefitpro.com
lambert@benefitpro.com
619-294-7800

YOUR NEXT STEPS...

"What's next?"

Not being able to answer this simple, two-word question is precisely why so many smart and motivated leaders are never able to reach their next level of success. This book, however, is filled with a wide variety of practical and proven answers to that very question. Because the contributors to this project are all practitioners of what they preach, you can rest assured the strategies, methods, models, and approaches you've read about here are working for other companies and likely can work for you, too.

Of course, there's a lot of information to digest in over 400 pages, so this section will give you direction and guidance on what to do right now. After all, as you know, even priceless knowledge unused is worthless. So here is the question we will help you answer in the next few pages:

What specific steps should I take when I close this book to ensure my company simply won't continue to practice an unsustainable status quo?

Naturally, the outcomes and results you derive from the following process will be unique to you and your organization. There is no one-size-fits-all strategy that works equally well for every situation. Therefore, please understand that you won't be able to implement this process to break through and move beyond the status quo overnight, but you can (and MUST) implement it over time…*if* you are to see the same kind of positive results and successes that have been reported throughout these pages from all over the country.

Let's begin…

Next Step 1 – Commit to Better Outcomes

It's highly doubtful that you would read this far without a healthy level of commitment to pursuing better outcomes than the status quo currently is providing your organization and its employees. Nevertheless, this is the first key: Refusing to accept the situation as is, but rather seeing what it *could* be.

Your commitment to better outcomes means you (and your leadership team) will do your part to ensure both the organization and its employees have more valuable and profitable results. This is not just about saving dollars; it's about saving livelihoods and, often, about saving lives. A strategically designed benefits program that is integrated into the overall business planning of the company can produce worthwhile results for all involved—and in today's world, there's simply no excuse for anything less. It begins with the commitment from leadership to no longer settle for the status quo.

Next Step 2 – Determine How "Status Quo" You Are

Once you decide the status quo is no longer for you, you must determine just how "status quo" your organization is. Ultimately, this determination should be based on the outcomes (negative or positive) your organization consistently experiences.

Of course, if your company doesn't experience increasing health insurance renewals, maintains a healthy and productive employee workforce, is able to provide a robust total rewards package, and can control its own destiny related to those areas, then you've already left the status quo behind. However, if you're like the vast majority of other businesses, those are not your realities and the negative aspects of the status quo are pervasive.

Any worthwhile strategic benefits adviser such as the contributors to this book will be able to help you identify where the status quo is holding your organization back. That brings us to Step 3, which is a critical one that most leaders will ignore to their own detriment.

Next Step 3 – Select a Worthy Benefits Adviser

The benefits adviser you engage is inarguably the most vital component in successfully breaking through the status quo and achieving better results for your organization and your employees. This is such an important issue that several chapters in this book speak directly to properly vetting and selecting an effective NextGeneration Benefits Adviser.

This selection process begins with an objective and thoughtful review of your current broker. While this section is not the place to rehash much of what has already been shared earlier in this book, it is worth repeating that the time for working with a "transactional broker" is past; instead, you should engage a consultative "strategic adviser." The difference is easily seen in four glaring differences…

- Brokers sell you products. Advisers educate you about strategy.
- Brokers brag about their capabilities. Advisers share their clients' successes.
- Brokers talk only benefits. Advisers provide a broader

strategic and integrated outlook.

• Brokers are commissioned by insurance companies for the products they sell. Advisers are compensated directly by you for the value they bring.

The list above easily could go on for pages, but these four key distinctions are good guidelines for you to follow to do a quick assessment.

Before leaving this step, here are two other important notes.

• **RFPs rarely identify the best adviser.** If you believe that insight, on-point and proven expertise, context of the client experience, and trustworthiness can be determined from pages of sterile, status quo questions and checklists of capabilities you may or may not really need, then by all means keep using your antiquated RFP process. Otherwise, have a face-to-face meeting, ask questions, be open minded to innovation, listen, and then make a thoughtful decision.

• **Bigger is not inherently better.** Organizations often (yet wrongfully) believe that as they grow, they must engage larger, national brands. This premise is based on an age-old and pervasive fallacy that "bigger is always better" and it just isn't true—especially when it comes to identifying a truly strategic, innovative, non-status quo advisory firm. In fact, in most cases, it is exactly the larger firms that depend on—and benefit from—the status quo. Do not fall into the trap of believing that more people, more offices, and more revenue inherently means more value—often, it is precisely the opposite.

Next Step 4 – Identify Solutions that Resonate with Your Organization

There are literally dozens of different methods, strategies, and tools your organization could use to produce substantially better results—many of them are described throughout this book. That said, don't become so overwhelmed by all of them that you decide to adopt none of them. Unfortunately, this happens all the time. As humans, when we are faced with too many options and choices, we tend not to change anything for fear we may make the wrong decision. However, in this case, not taking a new action, not making changes, continuing to maintain the status quo… is what you should fear most.

Instead of deferring new ideas and strategies to "next year," simply identify the ones that resonate with your organization the most right now and act on those. As the saying goes, you should strive for "progress, not perfection." You do not have to change or do everything all at once, but you do need to do *something*. So, review the innovative strategies and approaches you now have available, and begin with the ones that resonate with your company the most.

Next Step 5 – Take Meaningful & Consistent Action

Ultimately, there is no substitute for work. Action must be taken and it must be meaningful. Most organizations make minor, tiny changes within the scope of the status quo. They are effectively rearranging the deck chairs on the Titanic. Once you simply acknowledge that the old way, the "normal" way, the traditional way is unsustainable, then you'll understand the imperative of taking meaningful (instead of menial) action consistently.

The good news is you don't have to do this alone; in fact, you really should not even try. Your strategic adviser should be there alongside you, guiding you, helping you make decisions, and even facilitating much of the work with and for you. (This is yet another reason why choosing the right strategic partner is so critical.)

Remember, consistent positive action will yield consistent positive results. Let that truth be a motto for the changes and innovations you implement to produce worthwhile outcomes.

Next Step 6 – Keep Learning About (And Leveraging) New Solutions

As with all worthy endeavors, this one will not end. Strategically planning, developing, and managing your benefits program and its related issues will never (and should never) be "set it and forget it." Like it or not, to achieve the best results for your organization and your employees, this must always be a "work in progress."

Therefore, it is necessary for you to continue learning and leveraging new strategies and solutions. Your strategic benefit adviser should provide a steady flow of new strategies, concepts, and methods to help you achieve the best outcomes possible, but you must be open to them and willing to consistently embrace new ideas. More than merely being willing to consider new approaches, seek them out yourself, look for innovative solutions to problems that may not even exist yet, be proactive and preemptive with your outlook and planning.

The opportunity to affect real, positive change in your organization has never been greater or more demanded. Empowered now by the expertise, ideas, and strategies throughout this book, you now have the responsibility to take action that will produce positive and meaningful results for your organization and its employees. The authors you've learned from, these NextGeneration Benefits Advisers, are available to support your efforts and provide the expertise and strategic guidance you want and need.

On the behalf of all the authors, we wish you the best of success in breaking through your own status quo!

About AIL Press

AIL Press is the publishing division of the Association for Insurance Leadership—an organization committed to elevating the employee benefits industry by helping advisers become more effective and valuable to their clients. Through publications like this book as well as other programming, AIL Press strives to bring new, meaningful insights to the marketplace.

Learn more at: **www.AIL-Assn.org**